GARBAGE AND THE GODDESS

the last miracles and final
spiritual instructions of
bubba free john

compiled and edited by
sandy bonder and terry patten

in collaboration with
bubba free john

the dawn horse press
·lower lake, california·

The Dawn Horse Press
P.O. Box 677
Lower Lake, California 95457

First Edition

Portions of comments by Bubba Free John in Chapter 4, "God-Possession: The Third Miracle," and the talk entitled "The Three Dharmas" in Chapter 11, "The First Great Guru Day," have been published previously in *The Dawn Horse* magazine and *The East-West Journal*.

International Standard Book Number 0-913922-10-2

Library of Congress Catalog Card Number: 74-19796

Printed in the United States of America

ACKNOWLEDGMENTS

The Invocation (*Narayana Sooktam*) quoted in Chapter 9, "The Divine Person," was edited, revised, and its technical terms translated by Bubba Free John from an English translation of the Sanskrit original which appeared in *The Mountain Path*, Volume 9, number 2, April, 1972, published by Sri Ramanasramam, Tiruvannamalai, South India. *Narayana Sooktam* forms a part of the *Maha Narayana Upanishad*, Sections 1, 13, and 23.

Illustrations by Lydia Blas. Photographs by Nick Elias, Joe Kahn, Steve Karlin, Bruce Lindberg, Hal Okun, Jerry Sheinfeld, and Francois Villon. Cover and book design by Pat Morley and Joan Kelley.

Contents

Preface

THE LAST MIRACLES AND FINAL SPIRITUAL INSTRUCTIONS OF BUBBA FREE JOHN

In March, 1974, Bubba Free John began to perform his "last" miracles. They were to continue for nearly four months, until July 7. Traditionally, miracles are signs in the world and in the experiential life of those who witness and value them of the specific Perfection and Power brought to the human plane by some Divine Agent. They are sought for this reason, and, if they are found and also verified as authentic, this is considered a kind of "proof" of Divinity, and grounds for elation, mysterious awe, and belief. The miracles of Bubba Free John, however, are extensions of his humor. They are merely instruments for his instruction of devotees. They are part of his theatrical strategy to draw men out of the whole game of search and fulfillment via the ways of experience, into a radically intelligent, free, and unreasonably happy life.

The early months of 1974 were a unique and special period in the history of Bubba Free John's Ashram[1] Community. The entire Event was his conscious and uproarious creation. It began suddenly, unexpectedly, even though he announced late in 1973 that great events would soon begin which would culminate in early July. Inner and outer miracles have always been manifested in

---

[1] Please consult the Glossary at the end of the book for clarification of unfamiliar technical and non-English language terms.

vii

Bubba's Presence since he began his direct work with devotees in 1972. But this was an especially intensified, dramatic, and full time of his spiritual Revelation, and it was marked by celebrations of all kinds, from week-long parties to mystical apparitions, from miraculous manipulations of the weather to outrageous sermons on the fruitlessness of every kind of attainment. This period also marked the final establishment of Bubba's Perfect Function of Guru in God. July 7 was the date he indicated for the completion of his communication of the Dharma, the radical path of Understanding. From that time he relaxed the Siddhi or Power whereby he displayed the Teaching to devotees, and he came to rest in the Perfect Power and Presence that is the Heart, the Nature or Self of all, and its Conscious-Light, the Condition of all beings, things, and worlds.

Thus, July 7 also marks the real beginning of the responsible activity of his Community of devotees, The Dawn Horse Communion. From that time, the Community has been active, principally, to communicate the radical import of Bubba's Revelation and Teaching and to invite all who are interested to participate in the life of Grace that is regenerated in his Company.

During these months Bubba blessed many of his devotees with sudden and dramatic experiences of the One Reality, the very Divine. Some of them were brought through extraordinary mystical experiences and graced with intuitive enjoyment of Bubba's own Perfect Realization. Many enjoyed at least temporary service as vehicles for his Presence and Divine Siddhi, or spiritual Power. Through certain of these devotees, selected apparently at random, he manifested the Divine to his entire Community of devotees, provoking genuine spiritual experiences in many of them. Bubba also manifested, as signs of this process, more outward miracles, such as furious storms and winds that appeared out of nowhere, a brilliant corona that stood around the sun for a full day, and a series of seemingly interminable celebrations that overwhelmed and ultimately undermined the "good time" needs and visions of every one who participated in them. To serve their spiritual awakening, he continually disrupted the conventional life of every member of his Ashram, by making havoc of daily routines and common social arrangements. And, regardless of the "spiritual" or "ordinary" quality of any moment, his laughter was omnipresent: "It is all garbage. Throw it away. Only God is the Condition of consciousness and life."

When it was all over, Bubba returned the life of the community to relative normalcy and demanded that all his devotees live on the basis of what had been shown to them: There are no separated individuals, there is only One Reality, eternal God, the Nature and Condition of all beings and worlds. In the weeks that have passed since July 7, this demand has taught Bubba's devotees a lesson in true understanding, and it has worked to free the community from its daily dependence upon the Guru's personal, supportive influence.

As he promised, Bubba has returned to his true and perfect Function, which is to be a "mere" Presence in the lives of his devotees. He told us often that he intended to become a madman and simply roll around his Ashram "eating owl sandwiches." What he meant was that he would be yielding his outward responsibilities for the Community to the Community itself, while he retired from "Bubba Theatre" to the Functions of the Heart. As a result of Bubba's relaxation of his more active role in the creation of the day to day drama of life in his Ashram, his devotees have had to become responsible for his Gift of freedom and fullness, and more and more of them have begun to live Bubba's "radical intuition of God" and to serve as living vehicles for his Teaching and his Presence in the world.

This same period saw the continued and intensified revelation of Bubba's "final" Teachings. These Teachings are not final in the sense that Bubba has left us or ceased to speak. But they are final by virtue of their fullness as a description of the way of Divine Grace, and of true Understanding, the intelligence beyond all dilemma and seeking, wherein our eternal and prior Nature and Condition is known to be the Divine. Bubba teaches the same Truth indicated by the great spiritual and religious teachers of history, such as Jesus, Gautama, Krishna, and, more recently, Ramana Maharshi, Shirdi Sai Baba, Ramakrishna, and Bhagavan Nityananda. Bubba represents the fulfillment of the work of the transcendent line of "Siddhas," the completed ones who have served mankind in Truth. He represents the radical, complete, and most specific living expression of the Nature and Condition of God, man, and the world, and of the graceful Divine Process, wherein that Nature and Condition is always already enjoyed as one's own. Bubba has said of himself: "The Form of the Lord is manifested fully in me." For those who have come to him, his Teaching is simple: "I am the Heart. Always live with me. Always meditate on me."

Bubba Free John is a genuine Siddha, one of those rare beings who arise in random times and places, already free, perfectly conscious of Reality on all levels. He has appeared in a world which lives only the problematic struggle for individual survival and fulfillment. Among human individuals, every one of whom is always trying to feel free or to be free of the usual search in dilemma, Bubba is already free, already perfectly happy. He doesn't live as a separate one with an individual and mysterious destiny. He knows who he truly is and lives as That. Bubba is perfect Reality, prior to all limitations, prior even to appearance in any form.

"Bubba" means "brother" and implies closeness. He is here for devotees, to offer them a relationship whose content is the Divine. That is Satsang, or Divine Communion. His work is not that of the traditional holy man, who gathers a following and teaches men techniques or strategies for improving themselves or finding God. Bubba's work in the world is the radical communication of his very Nature, eternal God, and the establishment of a Community of devotees, free men and women who live in the conscious, present Condition of the Divine.

Bubba appeared at birth, in 1939, on Long Island, New York, conscious as the unobstructed Presence of God. Soon afterward, he assumed conventional psycho-physical limitations, and began to dramatize his apparent life in the way the usual person does, imagining himself to be a separate individual in need of real happiness. His name was Franklin Jones. He lived the adventure of a human and spiritual seeker. But in the progress of his experiences, radical understanding of his apparent condition continually undermined all his "own" achievements and results, finally revealing his individual life as utterly non-existent in the eternal Form or Process that is Real-God. His life's adventure took the form of a series of revelations of non-separation, culminating in September, 1970, at the Vedanta Society Temple in Hollywood, California. At that time all obstructions to the manifestation of his Perfect Nature were understood and dissolved, and he simply remained intuitively alive as the Unqualified Divine, which is also the Nature and Condition of all beings and worlds.

"Free John," drawn from the name "Franklin Jones," describes the character of Bubba's life in this world. "Franklin" means "a liberated man," free of all binding contracts, non-separate, and perfect. Yet Bubba has an ordinary body, and he uses conventional human language and the common possibilities of human behavior to communicate Truth. He is a paradox. He can be recognized only intuitively. Only those who have become sensitive to their own suffering can sense what Bubba is and find his qualities and demands acceptable as the Principle of real life. He is not some separate super-individual, but their own real Self, asserting Itself in their minds and lives.

"Jones" is a Welsh version of the name "John," which means "God is gracious." All men, and all aspects and parts of the cosmos, communicate their state to the rest of manifest existence. Because of the conventional and traditional habits of life and realization long established in this world, the principle of separation, limitation, and consequent seeking is constantly communicated and reinforced among men, and throughout the universes. Therefore, Bubba communicates his Nature and Condition also, and he offers all men a relationship already full of God. He lives the miraculous grace of Real-God to those who will turn to him. Those who make that relationship the principle of their lives participate in the Divine Process by Grace. That very relationship, Satsang, is itself real life and freedom, prior to any search in dilemma toward the countless conceived goals of mankind.

Garbage and the Goddess consists primarily of talks given by Bubba Free John during the period extending from March to August, 1974. They are interspersed with descriptions of miraculous events and personal accounts of the profound experiences of many members of Bubba's Community. It provides an overview of his work, which is, fundamentally, to create true devotees in God.[2]

I am incarnating as the Community of my Devotees. Those who live in constant Communion

---

[2]The Teachings of Bubba Free John, as they are given in this book, may be read without any previous familiarity with his work. However, the reader would do well to read his two earlier books, *The Knee of Listening* and *The Method of the Siddhas* (both published by The Dawn Horse Press), for a clear understanding of the principal and technical aspects of his general instruction.

with me are the living manifestations of my Presence and Power. I send them into the world and make myself known through them. This is the secret of my spiritual work. My Devotees are the way to me.

The creation of a community, and, ultimately, of a world of genuinely free men and women is the primary purpose and effect of Bubba Free John's personal work on this earth. He would see a world of men in which life in Truth is not merely the humorous enjoyment of a few remarkable individuals, but the common, uncomplicated virtue of all men. This book is offered in the certainty that it can be so. The great Community of unreasonably happy men is the real and truly humorous miracle that Bubba would instigate through the influence of his devotees.

Persimmon   Sandy Bonder
September 3, 1974   Terry Patten

Introduction

>>>>>>>>>>>>>>>>>>>>>>>>>>>>>>>>>

HUMOR IS THE BODILY CONFESSION
OF GOD

BUBBA: The other night some of us were sitting together and I jokingly said to our friend Vince: "Some time tonight, how about talking to us about God?" Then we had a little dinner, and I said, "Well, Vince, are you about ready to talk to us about God?" I let it go for awhile, and then I finally asked him definitely to start talking about God. And he had nothing to say. So I asked each person in the room to say something about God. And not only did nobody have anything to say, but everybody began to get very serious and quiet. I pointed out to them that last week, when we had a party, everyone laughed, had some wine, and all of that was considered an amusement. But now, when I asked them to talk about God, they got very serious. I began to speak to them about this:

"The fundamental embarrassment is the confession of God. It is to dwell in obvious ecstasy in the company of other beings, to be already free, to be fundamentally happy, to be conscious in God, and even to be outwardly expressive in that state, to speak of God, to think of God, to act in God, to be ecstatic. That is the taboo, not mere drunkenness and mortal confessions of pleasure and suffering, which mean nothing. To require it of a man to talk of God makes him feel embarrassed. He becomes ashamed. Because in order to talk about God, he must lose face. To be extraordinarily and unreasonably happy and to

live that way embarrasses him. To be full of love and only
talk that way, so foolishly, so naively, is socially unacceptable. We are supposed to be cool and hip and straight,
oriented toward our survival, worldly and wise. But to be
simply alive in God and happy, and to speak about it and
act that way and think that way, is absolutely unwanted
and not allowed. So we become seekers.

"It is all right to *seek* God. That is acceptable enough,
because it calms everybody down a little bit, it makes
them go out and get jobs and not kill their neighbors. So it
is all right to seek God. But to *realize* God while alive is the
absolute taboo. You might be allowed to sit quietly and
meditatively. Everybody likes all this Oriental meditation
because it is just a matter of being quiet and inward. You

are allowed to meditate on the Self, realize Nirvana and disappear. That is acceptable. But to start talking about God, to think God, to act God, to make the Divine the present Condition of the world, to live in that Siddhi or Power, to live that Light, to be full, that is unacceptable, that is not permitted. As soon as you do it you begin to become unusable. You can't be exploited any more and you can't be embarrassed anymore. You cease to be concerned for the taboos of men, and their rules, their seeking.

"A cultic object is allowed to be Divine in this world, a conventional Guru is allowed to be Divine, a God in a book is allowed to be Divine, all kinds of fetishes are allowed to be Divine, but *you* are not allowed to be Divine! You are allowed to worship cultic objects and assume them to be Divine, but you cannot become Divine. You are expected to seek, to control yourself and seek, and always look forward to the Second Coming or the crash through the sahasrar or something. But in this moment you are not permitted to be happy. It is taboo. It is taboo to be already happy. You must *seek* happiness.

"To seek to find God, to seek to be realized, why does that seem so obvious to you, so reasonable? Because you are *only* reasonable. You have ceased to be unreasonable. You have ceased to live in your fundamental and prior Condition, which is enjoyment, bliss, happiness, fullness in which everything is justified, in which all functional conditions are justified and eternally free.

"You also imagine that the Divine withdraws universally and actually as a result of human sin and other such mythological defects in the world. But the Divine has never withdrawn. The Divine has never withdrawn from the world or from a single living being. That has never happened, and it never will happen, because the Divine is the always present Source of the world, the always present Nature, Condition and Sustainer of the world, and the absolute Destiny of the world. The Divine is infinitely Present, perfectly, absolutely and eternally Present, and available. The Divine must be lived, not sought. The Divine is the Condition of the world, not the ultimate hope of the world. There is no hope whatsoever. If the Divine is not *presently* lived, there is no Second Coming, no Millenium, no Revelation, no Liberation, no Nirvana. But if men began to live the Truth, if men became capable of ecstasy in society with one another, not simply in the rituals of privacy, you would see a vast and immediate transformation of the world."

After I had said a few things like that, I again asked everybody to talk about God. I said, "I am going to suggest a title for a story. I will begin it, and then each of you continue the story in turn." We did that, we went around once or twice, and it became obvious to everybody how unimaginative and dry and really stupid it was. Nobody was saying anything with any energy. It was hardly even amusing. So I said, "Well, let's do it again, but this time you are to speak ecstatically. You are not to think about what you are going to say first, you are just to keep speaking." So we started going around like that, and each one would try to think and try to not think. It got to be a little looser. It came around to me again, and I made up a nonsense poem and I sang it a little bit. Then we went around a couple of more times. Finally, we got to Marie and really worked her over, and Marie really started to sing. Then nearly everyone in the room began one at a time to sing ecstatically, crazily, about God. We were all clapping and shouting, praising God. It was just nonsense singing, ecstatic singing, happy singing.

All that was just a way of communicating something of the humor of spiritual life. It is basically humorous and happy. Not uptight and straight, lean and serious, waiting to understand. Understanding is an instant process, a really intelligent process, a happy process, not one of meditating on your own limitations, but a process of instantly transcending them in Reality. There is, of course, a relatively disciplined phase of the life of understanding, but as it matures it becomes more and more full, more and more ecstatic.

I have reminded you several times that there is a phase of my spiritual work in which I want to communicate the Teaching, and the appropriate life conditions, and create the Community, but there will come a time when I am essentially going to be finished with that, and I am no longer going to be concerned to create any images whatsoever or to make any sense at all. There literally will come a time when I no longer care to make sense. At least I will no longer accept it as a continuous responsibility. And I am just going to enjoy myself. The land we have just purchased in northern California will give me a place to do that, a place where the Ashram as a whole can do that, where the Ashram Community can live and have the refuge for its own life.

Once the Teaching and the Community are fundamentally established, the "reasonable" aspect of my function will be fulfilled. Just so, your own spiritual lives must also be fulfilled, in the Ashram, the Community of all my devotees. You must realize the mature phase of this work and become simply and unreasonably happy in the body. Not only in your room, not only in silence, but even verbally and dramatically. The time will come when you will be converted from your cultic and cultural ways and become unusable again, and only happy, and at that time you will have to make your peace with the rest of the world in order to make your living, to make your appearance. But you will be without concerns and without any more dues to pay. You will no longer be embarrassed by the demand to speak about God. You won't much care to do anything else.

That game that we played the other night, telling a story and then singing about it, it was just that, a game, a way of instructing. It is not that to speak of God you must only babble incoherently. That game was only a way of bringing people to realize, through instruction, the quality of their relationship to speech, to action, and to their own minds. When that realization has taken place, all speech becomes already ecstatic. And in the man of understanding there is no non-ecstatic speech, no action that is not full of ecstasy, no moment, no condition, no thought that is not already merged in God.

Bubba Free John gave this talk in his Ashram in Los Angeles on December 27, 1973. It is a good illustration of the way he teaches his devotees outwardly, by giving them verbal instruction in the midst of an unexpected conversion of their social situation and exerting the force of his presence to loosen them up, to make them available to God. As such, the excerpt also provides a glimpse into the whole story to be told in this book.

Bubba had been working formally as Guru with disciples and devotees for approximately two years when he gave that talk. After the Guru-function awakened in him in the winter of 1970, he began working informally with his friends in that capacity, and they began to experience the effects of the Guru-Siddhi, or Divine Presence and Power. In the early spring of 1972 he opened an Ashram and bookstore in a Hollywood storefront. Between then and December, 1973, his Community, The Dawn Horse Communion, grew to include about sixty people. Late in December, Bubba relaxed the strict behavioral conditions that he had required of his devotees for almost a year, and he declared a series of wildly ecstatic parties, in order, as he said in the talk above, "to communicate the humor of spiritual life."

In January, 1974, the Communion made a down payment on "the land up north," a forty-three acre former hot springs resort in northern California. Bubba moved there in February. By March, most of the members of the Community, which by then had grown to include about one hundred fifty people, had moved to San Francisco, where they established a public center. The rest of them moved to the new property, which Bubba named "Persimmon." Shortly thereafter, Bubba began to deliver the Teachings and produce the miracles chronicled in this book.

THE LAST MIRACLES OF BUBBA FREE JOHN

1. THE SATURDAY NIGHT MASSACRE AND THE CULT OF PAIRS

At seven-thirty, on Saturday evening, March 23rd, everyone gathered in the lounge at Persimmon to watch a movie. Before it could begin, Bubba asked Neil Panico to repeat some of what he and Neil had been talking about in a long conversation earlier in the day. At thirty-eight years of age, Neil was older than most people in the Community, and he had been with Bubba almost since the beginning of the Ashram, two years before. He administered one of the principal businesses owned by the Ashram and carried a great deal of responsibility for the overall administration of The Dawn Horse Communion. In addition, Bubba spent more time with Neil than with most others, generally in a friendly, informal, "unteacherly" way. He appeared, for these reasons, to be one of Bubba's close disciples.

Neil spoke for several minutes. He told those present that Bubba had said they must become more responsible for their lives in Satsang. He said they should be talking about God all the time, not getting exclusively absorbed in daily affairs. Members of this Community, Bubba had told him, must become much more intense. When Neil finished, Bubba ridiculed him, calling his talk "mediocre," and said of him, much to the amusement of everyone present, that he was "one of the most cultic personalities I've ever known." Then, spontaneously, Bubba began to talk about the responsibilities of devotees in a different way, saying things no one present would ever forget.

3

The Saturday Night Massacre
(March 23, 1974)

BUBBA: There are two responsibilities that the spiritual
Community has, and I mean this spiritual Community,
because I don't know of any other. The responsibility you
all know about, since we have talked about it many times,
is to communicate the availability of Satsang, the availability of this work. That is the responsibility of the
Community in the world. It is not my function to go about
and give lectures and convince people there is only God. It
is the responsibility of the Community to do that, and in
living ways, not just by giving formal, public presentations, but in your relationships with people. Not in formal
conversations only, in which you try to turn people
around, but in the force of your presence with your
friends. But we have already discussed all of that. That is
the public responsibility of the Community.

The other responsibility, which has not been developed, and which I have just recently been talking to you
about, is an internal one, and that is the responsibility to
undermine the cult of this world in your relationships with
one another. You can't do it in the world, because that
would be too revolutionary, but you can do it within the
Ashram. We have found Persimmon, this place in relative
isolation, where we can live basically as we please. The
reason we gather here is not just to be entertained or to
hear spiritual lectures and acquire a lot of philosophy, but
to practice an entirely new way of life based on an entirely
different principle than that upon which the cult of this
world is based. The cult of this world is based on the
principle of Narcissus, of separated and separative existence, and the search for changes of state, for happiness.
But the Ashram is based on the principle of prior happiness, or Satsang. And the Community of the Ashram is an
entirely new possibility. It is the possibility of existing in a

Condition wherein God is Truth, wherein God is the very Condition, presently.

There is not now, nor has there ever been, nor will there ever be an individual being. There is no such thing. All of the cultic ways are strategic searches to satisfy individuals by providing them with various kinds of fulfillment, or inner harmony, or vision, or blissfulness, or salvation, or liberation, or whatever. But the truth is that there is no such one to be fulfilled; literally, there is no such one. Everything that arises in consciousness is something that you may observe. You can observe your experiences, you can observe the world, you can observe

your thoughts, strategies, and actions, you can observe the
sensation of "me"—all of that is something you can
observe. The one who observes that is your very Nature,
the absolute intensity of real existence, which is being
endlessly and universally modified, appearing as all forms
and states. The principle of spiritual Community is that
there is already no such person, no such separate one, no
such dilemma.

The cult of this world is based on the assumption that
there exists such a separate one, who needs to be realized
or fulfilled or made healthy or made happy or whatever. All
of that is a colossal lot of nonsense, because there is no such
one. There is already no such one. You do not have to run
through aeons of time for there to be no such one, to
destroy this phantom ego. There is already no such one.
He does not exist to be destroyed. He does not exist.

The communication of Satsang is the communication
of that very One, that Intensity, that Absolute existing
One, who is not individuated, but who is apparently
endlessly modified, appearing as all worlds, all forms, all
states, all beings. So within the spiritual Community, all
the cultic forms of contractual existence and strategic life
are already obsolete. It is not the duty of the spiritual
Community to go on forever with the temporary and
strategic assumption that all of these dilemmas are the
case until you overcome them. It is the duty of the
spiritual Community to live always and already as if there
were no such thing. This cannot be practiced in the world.
It can only be practiced in the spiritual Community itself.

Therefore, it is the fundamental responsibility of all
those who live in the Ashram to continually undo the
practice of the cult—the cult of Narcissus as it appears in
groups of twos and threes and manys, in groups of people
who for one reason or another are thrown together each
day, or for reasons of personality or karma associate with
one another by preference. The world is filled with the

forms of the priesthood of Narcissus, all of which reinforce the sensation of separate existence and the dilemma that the sense of separate existence requires.

Everyone comes into the Ashram filled with life-contracts they want to dramatize, but none of that is appropriate in the Ashram. Because people do not tend to live intimately, marriage is appropriate. But the instant you marry, you must discard it. Otherwise marriage is another cultic form, a sex-contract, in which you become medievally involved with personality forms, making yourself strategically unavailable to the rest of life, and again mutually create the sensation of separate existence, including "poor me" or "fantastic me." You all know what it is like sitting down at the table with one another and reciting the same old horseshit. The same conversation takes place between friends, repetitively, day after day after day. The same event takes place between married people day after day after day, because all of our so-called relationships are cultic associations that are created in order to guarantee the sensation of security, in order to guarantee to the ego, the separate one, the sense and drama of separate existence, wherein it cannot be interfered with by the random world.

Such a cultic existence has no fundamental value at all. It has value in the cult of this world, which thrives on this separate one, but it has no value from the point of view of Truth. Not only hasn't it any value, it is an absolutely negative influence in the life of persons. It is obvious, if you observe people in the Ashram, that they are all belonging to various forms of this priesthood. They all dramatize one or another form of the cult, with their married partners, with their friends, with the groups with whom they have had common experience.

It is the responsibility of the Community to continually undo that process, to undermine "marriages," to undermine "groups," and to undermine the strategic power of personality in this limited sense. Not that, in the conventional way, something like the love relationship between friends, or the love relationship and energy that is generated among those who have common experience, not that any of that is not conventionally appropriate, but all of its usual implications are false.

A marriage is not a sex-contract. Marriage is an acknowledged relationship. Sexuality is a phenomenon of nature. It exists universally and has no individual form. It is a process prior to personality. So those who are married do not properly enter into a sex-contract. Wherever that exists, we have the cult. Wherever there are the usual mutual friends, there is the cult. It is a contract of communications, of assumed limitations that are recited hour after hour, again and again, in which images and symbols and forms of experience are continually recited and repeated in order to guarantee to the mind the sensation of individuality, of separateness and immunity.

All of this works against Satsang. Satsang is not just the formal occasion when I sit with you all, when you enter into meditative kinds of experience or listen to the Teaching. Satsang is the manifest Siddhi of the Divine. The Guru is not identical to a person. The only reason an apparent human individual can function as Guru is because he has consciously ceased to be identical to a human individual in limitation. A profound sacrifice must occur in order for the function of Guru to exist in human form, and there is no longer any sense whatsoever in the human Guru of separate existence. None. I am all-pervading.

In order for this Satsang to manifest itself in Truth it must be permitted to function under all conditions, not just under the conditions of these formal teaching occasions, or formal meditating occasions. And the only way the real manifestation of Satsang or Divine Communion can occur for you is if you responsibly break down the cultic form of your lives and eliminate the barriers of assumed separation. All of your functions must be available to all beings, not just to those with whom you have contracts. Notice how solemn and precious you get with friends, with lovers. You become unavailable, you become contracted, separate. You are not truly loving. You are entering into the cult again, into solemnity, into the loss of humor, or into comedy, but not humor, not Divine knowledge.

To be free is the ultimate discipline. Sadhana is not to go through this weary self-discipline, self-limitation, self-frustration, in which you are endlessly learning all kinds of bullshit lessons. The discipline is happiness. The discipline is freedom. To live in this free state under all conditions is sadhana. Sadhana is not the endless, apparent discipline of seeing always that you are living as a separate one: "Oh yes, oh yes, oh my goodness." That is not sadhana! Sadhana is life in the condition of Truth. So sadhana has nothing whatever to do with the cultic solemnities of traditional spirituality. Sadhana has to do with continuous happiness, continuous bliss, continuous freedom, continuous Satsang. To live Satsang under all conditions is the discipline of our work.

But you notice in your relationships with one another that you do not do any such thing, that you are not already free in your relationships, you are not already free within yourself, you are not already free one to one, you are not already free in groups. You are always drawing the perimeter, you are always sizing up the pond. Such is the mind and strategy of Narcissus. So you do not manifest this freedom. You are not exalted, you are not exhilarated by the endless phenomenon of the Divine. It is only when you have died to yourself that spiritual life occurs. It is only when you live in Satsang that spiritual life occurs. All these cults are phenomena of this world. They are extensions of the ego. Just as the typical, traditional, spiritual group is an extension of the ego, the scapegoat game, your individual lives and mutual relationships with others are forms of the same cultic phenomenon. They are extensions of the same activity that you always perform personally, inwardly.

It is the responsibility of the Community to undo that phenomenon mutually. Every one of you must examine your unavailability to other devotees, and liberate your functions from the strategy and humorlessness of Narcissus. If you are to do that, the Teaching must remain conversational in a natural way, day after day after day. You do not *tend* to live free. You *tend* to live the karmic principle of limitation. So the Teaching must be communicated and realized continually, in functional terms. In place of all the bullshit you recite to one another, all the humorlessness, all of the imagery of ordinary life, in place of all of that, ecstatic communication must begin. You will notice how exhilarated you become when on a daily basis you begin to deal humorously and radically with your own bullshit. Therefore, when you are drawing lines around yourselves at the table, or in your little hovels, it is even the responsibility of other devotees to deal humorously with you.

It is your common responsibility to deal with the sensations and conditions that are being manifested in this Community. Among devotees there are no marriages, there are no brothers, sisters, husbands, wives, mothers, fathers, cousins, karmic friends, there is none of that. All of that is obsolete. Such conditions will tend to maintain themselves automatically, but they are not true. You will discover that you are always trying to create the cult again. As soon as one little secure cultic relationship is abandoned, with husband, wife, friends, mothers, fathers, you try to create another one to replace it, because you always pursue the security, the immunity of Narcissus. And that tendency must be undone through the daily living of devotees with one another.

That is the responsibility that you must begin to assume. It is profoundly threatening, but spiritual life is threatening. Spiritual life is not leading toward your fulfillment in some great vision. Spiritual life is leading to the absolute undermining of your separate existence. Absolutely. That is what this work is all about. So it is the responsibility of the Community to manifest the Teaching in common, in relationship.

The Teaching must be communicated broadly. It must take place in the world, in relationships, among human beings, not just as an inwardness, a philosophy, a subjectivity, a visionary state, a sense of inward freedom. It must be enacted, and it has never been enacted. It always tends to stop at the subjective level, at the point of some modification of one's psycho-physical state, wherein you feel a little blissful, a little loose. It has never been manifested as a Community of free persons, who no longer live the principle of individuality in the common sense, who live in the Divine, and who are free to put up with the randomness of this world in which there is no apparent security, because they depend utterly on the Divine.

That is what faith is. It is the assumption of the Divine as the active Principle and Condition of your life rather than the little twenty watts, the field of ego in which you enclose yourself day to day. Then you begin in utter freedom, in the infinite intensity of God. On the basis of experience, the shock of birth, we all begin to assume limitation and form, and we reinforce that mutually through the cult that is passed on from generation to generation. In very short order, every person is assuming himself to be this little twenty watts, and is no longer consciously conducting the Divine Force, which is limitless. Every person tries strategically, from the point of view of this little twenty watts, to survive, to feel consoled, to feel unthreatened, all of which is absolutely impossible, because every single one of you is going to die.

You are not going to go to heaven from here. You are going to die: literally and absolutely. Not just a little bit. It is not just your body that is going to die. *You* are going to die, and that is the truth. All of these consoling philosophies try to make you assume that only your body is going to die, and somehow you, the same as you are now, are going to pop out and zap around in some wilderness of light. That is absolutely not going to happen. You are going to *die*.

So you must realize, during life, that real and prior Condition of existence which is always already transcending psycho-physical life, which is always already transcending the psyche, the mind, the person, the limited one. Then you will realize that happiness that is not concerned to be reincarnated or not. It does not make any difference how many thousands of times you have been reincarnated. You do not by tendency remember a damn one of them, other than this one. What is so consoling about reincarnation? You can just put it aside. It makes no difference whether it is a fact of this universe. You have nothing whatever to do with it, because you are utterly ripped off every time you pass out of life. The whole psyche that you have built up is ripped off. It dies, absolutely. It does not survive any longer than the body. And if you are smart you will realize that transcendent existence while alive. That is what spiritual life is all about, not all the soul and occult bullshit about survival. You do not survive. And that does not mean that you are annihilated, that death is death. It means that your existence is of a transcendent nature, not of a limited one. Nothing that is conditional survives. You live in God, and you are utterly of that Nature, and within the Divine Nature you appear periodically to move through changes, processes of various kinds, but you never lose the status of the Divine.

If you assume the status of any limitation whatsoever, you will suffer the death of that, and while alive you will feel as if you are dying, you will feel as if you are lost. The only point of view from which to live any life in any world is that of absolute Self-realization and God-knowledge. Everything else is ripped off, it does not survive. So the spiritual Community must always *live* as if that were so. Your tendency is not to live as if that were so, your tendency is to live the cultic life of seekers, in dilemma, pursuing the states of conceived happiness through various means. All of that is without real foundation, utterly and already false. It is the cultic doctrine of Narcissus, it is utterly fruitless and without foundation.

The Ashram is not just a collection of people who happen to be involved with the Guru individually, and who try to get along with one another in the usual way. The Ashram is the Community of devotees, who are not just aligned to the personal Guru, but who are aligned to the Guru in Truth, as He is, and who therefore are liberated to an entirely new form of existence. This is the great discipline, and it is frightening, threatening to the poor little mind, to Narcissus, because he will not tolerate such a radical transformation of life. You can spend the rest of your days struggling with all of that bullshit if you like, but it has nothing whatever to do with the Dharma, the Life of Truth.

I expect, as a discipline, that all devotees live Satsang, not just in formal meditation, when they are with me personally, but in every stroke of life, conducting the Divine Life with every breath, each enquiring of his own activity in every instant of consciousness, and living the Divine Condition in the form of every relationship. That is a profound discipline that requires you to get off your ass and yield all of your psychological strategies, all of your self-protection, all of your boredom, and be happy, ecstatic, free at last. It requires you to live with one another as if you were already free, not cultically involved with all kinds of secondary contracts with other limited beings, but absolutely free, free to share the force of life with all beings, and free to allow all of your intimates, all other devotees, to share that force of life with all other beings, in the form of every function in which you are all present to one another.

In order to do such, you must be free of all conventional social requirements in the Ashram. In the world, live outwardly as disciples, fulfill your social obligations in the conventional sense. But inwardly, and with one another, live as devotees, be free, and continually deal with one another in such a way that the cult becomes obsolete in every form in which it appears, in the form of every kind of relationship. Make yourself functionally available to all other devotees, without limitation, with profound intelligence, with profound intensity.

I could spell all of that out to you, but it seems perfectly obvious what I mean. I mean all of it.

This requires great humor, great discipline, great intelligence, great energy. It is a profoundly exhilarating process, a happy process, in which this separate one, this Narcissus, is continually undone, socially undone, personally undone. Only this way does an Ashram become an Ashram. Anything less than that is the cult of the usual bullshit, the search for subjective change.

Does anybody have any questions about that?

DEVOTEE: I would like to know the forms that the smashing of cults you see arising in the Ashram must take.

BUBBA: What do you think?

DEVOTEE: Well, I think just making a totally serious demand and telling somebody to drop it, while communicating love at the same time, and not being expected to explain. A person basically has the responsibility to enquire into the strategy of his own action right off. I think there shouldn't have to be a discussion involved.

BUBBA: Devotees cannot be an offense to one another. Only the usual man can offend his friends, but the devotee cannot be an offense to another devotee, even if he is wrong. Even if he is wrong, that is not an offense. He is just wrong, that is all, and that is humorous enough. You should be free to say anything you like to anyone here, and that should be a completely humorous affair! "Look, Smack, you're an asshole. I've been wanting to kiss your cheek, and I can't even shake your hand. I've been wondering how to love you, and you're full of shit. Forget this fucking rice and vegetable meal, let's arm wrestle."

DEVOTEE (laughing): This is totally revolutionary!

BUBBA: I have mentioned marriages in the Ashram again and again, because marriage is a particularly "serious" affair. It is a way for people to lock one another in with a sex-contract. As I said, exclusive sexuality has nothing to do with marriage itself. Not that people who are married are not sexually involved with one another, but the binding and exclusive sex-contract has nothing whatever to do with marriage. Marriage is simply an acknowledged relationship, in which, as far as sex goes, the individuals remain as free as the wind. They should be as free as they like to do whatever they like with the force of life, without denying that one they love in marriage, without threatening that relationship, because marriage is itself the acknowledgement that it cannot be threatened to begin with. That relationship already exists, and if it is acknowledged, what is the problem? So the sex-contract has nothing whatever to do with marriage, and should be kicked out the window.

DEVOTEE: So then, what is the point of all of us getting married?

BUBBA: You cannot be intimate with all mankind in the same room. Marriage is a conventional value, it is an acknowledged intimacy, it is a way of developing or practicing intimacy in the midst of the practical and otherwise karmic or hard-edged affair of money, food and sex from day to day. Since it exists as a convention, it can be used and realized in freedom, and so it is good. It is just that it should not involve this contract, this suffering, this mutual reinforcement of separate existence. It is the same with friends. You may have many friends, but at each moment your friendship is one to one with each of your friends. Having one friendship does not exclude all others, and you don't exclude your friends from being friendly with others. Well, the same should exist in the midst of all relationships, in the midst of all conventions.

In that same spirit of freedom, the Community of devotees should also feel free to create entirely new forms of social life, entirely new forms of household, entirely new forms of generating children. The Community, not exclusive pairs, produces children. Children are the responsibility of the entire Community. Your children are not the reflections of you in person. But in our isolated little households, which are the conventional symbol of our social life at the present time, it is assumed that you create children, they are your personal reflection, they perpetuate you in some way or other, they stand for you in some way or other. Whereas your children are, truly, a free manifestation in God. They are the product of the human community, not the product of individuals.

It is very possible, and already not uncommon, for married people to bring up a child that is produced through the agency of some other person or couple. Perhaps also one partner in a marriage can produce a child in some other household. Or perhaps there can be many people in a household. All these things are possibilities, but that does not mean they are also appropriate in every case. In every case children and households must be the product of a realized life. But all such unusual possibilities exist. And the Community of devotees should feel free to create a community life in which there are many forms of household, in which children, like all other devotees in the Ashram, are the product of the entire Community, and in which all present share the responsibility for the develop-

ment of each person in Satsang, rather than the development of each person in the isolated cult of two personalities. Only in such a Community can human individuals
arise already free, remain free, grow up free, and live free.
Otherwise they must struggle their entire lives to break
down all the character barriers that are created by that
limited beginning.

The spiritual Community should not reinforce or
initiate the phenomenon of separate existence in any form
whatsoever. It should not serve that cult in any form
whatsoever. Every devotee is wildly and priorly free in
God. There is no curse, there is no ultimate demand from
on high for a particular form of social life. The demand is
for love, to share, through the mechanism of the human
vehicle, the force of life which is every moment being
generated from the Divine. And how you organize your
life in the midst of such a Condition is entirely up to you.
There is no prior guilt, no praise, no blame. There is a
demand, and that is for the Divine Life itself. That is
entirely separate from all of the usual moralistic horseshit.

Unless there is this understanding and this continuous
communication that breaks down the cults, every time
you approach someone you are in mortal fear of violating
his contracts. So you are never certain whether that person
is going to kill you, or somebody he knows is going to kill
you. Because you are not certain of that, you do not share
the force of life, you do not love.

DEVOTEE: There is also a certain kind of righteousness.
People who have been with you for a long period of time
sometimes seem to feel they are more enlightened, or that
they are more free to love than others in this Community,
and I think that is bullshit.

BUBBA: Certainly. Exactly.

DEVOTEE: I for one would enjoy loving everyone. I've been in mortal fear of one person who has been with you for two years. I've only been with you for three months, and I've been afraid to express myself. I don't want to continue that any longer.

BUBBA: Good. But a lot of that is your own hallucination. There is no superior person by virtue of experience, because experience is not the process of spiritual life. Spiritual life is a Condition into which all devotees enter and in which all enjoy the same privilege and responsibility. So it is your responsibility to love and to be free and to break down the cult, whether you have been here for years or three and a half days. When you gather together to study the Teaching, or just to talk with one another, or casually to be with one another, that responsibility holds at all times. When somebody is leading a study group or some other group in the Ashram, he is not the "leader," he is not the authority, although you may tend to make him that, and so reinforce the demand or need within him to act like an authority, to be the source. The leader of a study group is just somebody who is moderating, who is simply managing the display of communication so everyone has the opportunity to get his communication across. That is fundamentally the only responsibility such a person has.

It is the responsibility of each one present to live in freedom with all the others, to be open and communicative, to deal with whatever is present, and to make all of the Narcissistic crap that comes across by tendency unnecessary. And you only make it unnecessary by living the humor of Satsang. You should be laughing like me, all the time free, happy. Also touch one another, love one another, deal with one another as intimately as you please, not like gangsters, rapists, and whores, but in that radical freedom that should be understood by all devotees. The freedom to approach one another directly should be understood, and there should be no fear of violating hidden contracts. There should be no such contracts, and if they are there, they are simply "hidden," they are simply subjective bullshit, and it is everyone's responsibility to deal with that personally and not to manifest it in secretive ways or in strategies in the Community.

One of the "secrets" of spiritual life is continually to violate your own contracts. If you do that with intelligence, with understanding, you will continually be free. To the degree you do not understand, to the degree you do not do that in freedom, you will suffer, but you will also give yourself conditions in which understanding may arise. If you continually violate the contracts that you most fear to have undone from without, you will serve the transformation of your own psycho-physical life. Whereas if you live in mediocre patterns, always fearing the violation of these contracts from without, they will never change, because, fundamentally, they do not get changed from without. You may be manipulated from without, threatened from without, but you will never transform the fundamental vehicle in which you pass through life unless you take responsibility for the cultic contracts that you are dramatizing from hour to hour.

You can serve one another by continually engaging in the conversation in which the violation of these contracts becomes possible, in which you continually set them aside, are purified of them, become humorous about them. The more you understand, the less you will feel the form of inner suffering that is necessarily created when your contracts are violated.

As soon as your intimates and your loved ones and your friends are intimate and loving and friendly with other beings, you tend to begin to suffer, you begin to contract, to withdraw compulsively. But if you understand in the midst of that reaction to the violation of your contracts, you make your contracts obsolete, and you will cease to suffer. Simply as a strategy, the mere violation of your contracts will only create suffering, psychological or personal suffering, but doing it in Satsang, with understanding, is a self-purifying responsibility.

I expect you to do that. I expect you not to repeat the mediocre round of this priesthood, but to vanish it in this Ashram. You should leave it at the gate of Persimmon. You should leave it, period, but if, as a discipline, you need just to leave it at the gate, do it that way for the time being. When you come to Persimmon, do not assume any contracts to be inviolate, do not assume any contracts to hold. Live freely at Persimmon, create the Community of devotees, make this coming together at Persimmon a creative occasion in which you manifest the Divine Community, rather than just some tawdry weekend in which you do a little work and hear some lectures and sit down in quiet meditation. Make it a creative occasion in which you make the cultic life utterly obsolete. Make it an exhilarating condition, allow the Divine to create your event. The Divine is always creating a perfect event. The Divine Power or Siddhi is infinite. As long as you live from the point of view of your twenty watts, you are always creating the karmic event, the limited event, non-fulfillment, the separate one. If you live by faith, in other words if you live always already in Satsang, Divine Communion, and allow the manifestation of your event, your life in any moment, to be the Divine occasion, perfection will always be manifested in the form of conditions appropriate to this moment in God.

That is the secret of non-karmic life, of living in God, who is not conditioned. Whereas living from the point of view of your karmas, your tendencies, always manifests more of the same, always carries with it the implication of that separate one, and that separate one is the core of your suffering. There is no such separate one. Literally there is no such separate one. Presently, there is no separate one. There is only an infinite modification of the Divine Reality, and that Divine Reality is modified as forms, with varying degrees of subtlety: solid things, watery things, fiery things, airy things, etheric things. And that Divine intensity is modified as forms of consciousness. Indeed, all modifications, all events or conditions are forms of Consciousness, which is the Nature of your consciousness.

So your very consciousness, your own consciousness, is the Divine Self. It is presently that Divine Self. It has no form whatsoever, no limitation. It is not a soul, it is not a psyche, it is not a person. It is infinite, formless, unqualified, unconditioned, absolute Consciousness. That is your Nature, that is the Nature of every being. It is also the Nature of the Guru, but the Guru knows it, the Guru lives as That. The Guru manifests the perfect possibility that exists in human beings. If you make a cultic figure out of the Guru and allow him alone to be enlightened, allow him alone to be free, to roll around and do what he likes, while you yourself live as some limited asshole, you have prevented the Teaching from fulfilling itself. Whereas the Guru does not call disciples and devotees to be cultically involved with him. He calls disciples and devotees to be free with him, to enjoy the humor of his Nature and Condition, which is the absolute and eternal Nature and Condition of all worlds and all beings.

It is your responsibility to live Satsang in this practical form. Until you do that, I can press the Divine Light into your brains for eternity, and it will do nothing. I do not care how many kundalini experiences you have, or how many changes of state you have. They are themselves still only modifications of the One Reality. So you yourself must live understanding, you yourself must become conscious, you yourself must become responsive and responsible for the Divine process in your life, in the mechanisms of your apparent individual life, and in the form of all relationships. Because that responsibility holds, the Community of devotees is possible, and it is a unique possibility. It has never been done, never. There has never been a true Community of devotees. There have been cultic communities, but never a free Community of devotees. It has never been done. It is the most violent, revolutionary thing you can do as a gathering of men, because it requires you absolutely to undo the cult of this world and all of the social contracts that are the theatre of your suffering, your Narcissistic drama.

Does anyone have any more questions about any of that?

DEVOTEE: I completely and clearly see what you mean, but it absolutely fucks my mind up, and makes me terrified, absolutely petrified. But I love you more than I love "me."

BUBBA: Individuals are terrified in the face of the Divine demand. But because the Divine is so elusive, so subtle, they can live as if there were no such One, they can live as if it were untrue. They can be atheistic, confused, neurotic, but when the Divine manifests as the Guru, he can no longer be refused, he cannot be put away, unless you do him in within yourself. The Guru enacts the threat of the Divine, which is an absolutely transforming and absorbing Force. In that case you no longer truly have the mechanisms by which to refuse the Guru, because he is present in the fundamental ones that you would not refuse for yourself. He is bodily present, he is humanly present, he is psychologically present, psychically present, his life-force is present. He is always undermining the principle of your separate life and the drama into which you are always evolving it. So the Guru is a dangerous person.

DEVOTEE: Are you saying that any exclusive relationship violates the conductivity of the life-force in the individual and the world?

BUBBA: Yes. Relationship is not exclusive. It is a happy, free affair. It is a form of enjoyment. It is the principle of enjoyment or delight. Exclusive relationship is a way of contracting on a social level, on every psycho-physical level. It makes two people, or three people, or fifty people, an individuated thing. But these are all forms of contraction dramatized on the social level. Relationship should be love, without contracts of any kind. Life should simply be direct, free, acknowledged relationship in God.

DEVOTEE: You also mentioned that this should be handled with intelligence, with humor. It shouldn't go to the point of mere self-indulgence. Have you spoken about that before?

BUBBA: Self-indulgence is only an alternative form of behavior, like self-discipline. Self-indulgence and self-discipline are both in themselves mediocre. Neither one of them is more "spiritual" than the other. Therefore, the life of the true spiritual Community is not one in which behavior is dictated in a formal way, in the form of exclusive discipline or self-indulgence. It is not one in which there are alternative kinds of contracts in which behavior is merely determined by rules different from those of common society. It is a Community of *devotees*, those who live the Divine Communion, in whom the principle and force of Divine Communion generates the qualities of their common life. So it requires great intelligence, great understanding, great energy. That is the discipline, the discipline of that happiness, that freedom, that fullness of Satsang. That will determine all of your behavior in a natural and appropriate way, without your concern about behavior itself. It will cause you to create forms of relationship in a new way, according to this new principle. Simply to generate behavior is another form of the same old thing. If you undo the cult at the level of your personal life, then you become free to generate relational life in a new way. Only then you will see what it truly and practically means in your own case.

DEVOTEE: Does that mean that on the deepest level there can be no withholding?

BUBBA: What are you doing when you are withholding? There is nothing peculiarly "psychological" about it. There is one food, and that is the Divine, and the Divine is absolutely subtle, perfectly transcendent. The first level on which we realize the modification of the Divine, the stuff of the Divine, is in the forms of consciousness. The superconscious organs through which we intuit the Divine food, the Divine Presence as Life, are in the upper part of the brain. In the midst of the brain are the forms of mental consciousness, less subtle than the superconscious. The psycho-physical origin of the life-force, the entrance point of the universal Shakti, is in the throat, and it is etheric, subtler than all of the natural forms, the vital forces. Grosser than that dimension of the life-force is the airy life in the midst of the body, in the heart, the region of the life-psyche. Grosser than that, just as the heart or living psyche is grosser than the mind, is the fiery elemental life of the navel. Below that is the watery life of the root of sex. And below that is the solid life of the physical body. But there is this one food, which is the Divine, above all of this transmuted or modified, which descends into this whole order of grosser and grosser manifestation.

The food that we share with one another, the true human food, is the life-force, whose entrance is felt in the throat. But we deny one another the life-force in the

absence of love. The withholding of love is only the
contracting of the life-force, the contracting of the availability of the life-force to other beings and to yourself. It
takes place high in the body, high in the subtler dimensions of our life, so that down into the living parts of us,
into the heart, into the navel, into the sex-life, into the
physical body, where there is no love as a result, the thing
that we ordinarily call life is absolutely solid, rigid,
without energy, without the relational process. So to love
is a principle that transcends the elemental parts of our
existence, the elemental forms of our functions. To love is
to share principal food, to share the Divine. The mind is
simply a modification of the conscious elemental, and it
does not move down into the life. Only in loving do you
permit the life-force, the life-energy, principal food, to
manifest on the functional human level. So you can think
all that you like, but until you love, you do not make the
life-force available, you do not feed others. The reason our
common life, our social life, is unsatisfactory is that there is
no communicated life-force. We are starving. We do not
love.

Loving is not just a psychological and personal affair.
It is not just good for psychological health and society.
Loving is absolutely essential for life itself, because it is
simply the functional manifestation of the universal
life-force, principal food. So the crippling of the capacity
of human beings to love one another directly, without
contracts, is also the crippling of the capacity of the race
of human beings to perpetuate itself. It may perpetuate
itself chemically, elementally, but it cannot perpetuate
itself in Truth, as real and conscious life, as humanity. The
common or cultic community perpetuates its lower life,
and it perpetuates its conventional conscious life, its
mentality, but it does not perpetuate its very life, the
life-force, within the conventional theatre of life. Only
through the manifestation of love does this principal food
appear in human terms.

There can't be any withholding, for any reason whatsoever, without violating the fundamental functional demand of human life. Love is not a petty affair. It is not just better if you love others. It is an absolute demand and responsibility to love and be free. Only thus do we make available in human terms the Divine process, and only thus is anything like the perfection or true realization of human existence possible. It depends on love. Then it can become elemental and alive. Then the bodies can be improved, and all the rest. But until love is established as the communicated theatre of our common life, there is no perfection, no evolution of humanity. It is mired in its lower life, and detained in its mental life.

The life-force is only released in love. So the only way in which it may be released is through understanding, the understanding of your own process, your own strategy, not through any mere yogic process, not through any perfection of your mental life, not through any physical culture, but only by unloosing your fundamental presence in the world. To love requires a great transformation. It requires first of all your realized acknowledgement of the Source of the life-force, which is above the life, above the super-conscious, above the body, the mind, the world, even the soul and spirit. It requires your absolute realization of the fundamental Nature of your condition, which is not this separate one. It is not the one who is mysteriously appearing in some world out in the midst of who knows where, but the very Self, Brahman, the intuited Real-God, the absolute Divinity. Without the realization of the Heart, the intuition of Real-God, and without the realization of the Divine Light, which transcends even superconscious life, vision, perception, or cognition, there is no true humanity, and no love.

So the real manifestation of love depends on the generation of spiritual life in Truth. Not just the attachment of individuals to some yogic or esoteric process wherein they, individually or subjectively, are trans-

formed to some visionary condition or other, but the
transformation of literal humanity, the functional and
relational condition of human beings. That is the require-
ment, that is realization. Not subjectivity, not personal
evolution in inward terms, but the Community is the sign
of the Divine process.

So the sign of the Divine Presence in this world is not
even Siddhas and Gurus. The sign of the Divine Presence
in this world is the Community of human beings who love
consciously, who are always already free in God. The Guru
adds nothing to this world, because God is always already
Present in this world. So the mere presence of the human
Guru has not added anything, fundamentally. He only
establishes a process in which people may realize their
Condition, but he has not added anything, ultimately, to
the world itself. Only the Community of devotees adds
something to the world. Only the Community of devotees
represents a change in the world, and makes something
new in the world by action.

Don't get the impression there is anything serious
about loving someone. It is fun. There is nothing serious
about it at all, as a matter of fact. Therefore, you will also
discover, in the spiritual Community of devotees who
truly live as such, there is an absence of irony, whereas the
usual man thrives on irony, on subtle negativity. All our
usual humor, so-called, is irony. Most of our conversation
is irony. We tend either to be ironic with one another, or
else to tell one another ironic stories about how ironic life
is. Or how ironic it all was: "How ironic it was that this
and that happened when I was twelve." So we generally
communicate irony, rather than love, and the analytical
hammering of one another, the righteous correcting of one
another, is a form of irony. Really, it is fundamentally
unnecessary. You should feel free to correct one another
where it is appropriate. But if it becomes a repetitive
liturgy, you yourself are bound to the principle of irony or
Narcissus, which is the refusal and withholding of love.

You should simply feel free to be happy, rather than always only to deal with the ritual report of your memory, and your ironic experiences, and the failure of it all, and the boredom of it. You should feel free to say anything. Sooner or later I say everything. I allow myself to feel free to do anything I like and say anything I like. You are always already free to do and say absolutely everything, with humor, with understanding. The freedom to do and say anything contains humor, and not irony.

The cult of Narcissus, the cult of this world, is all about the suppression of ecstasy, the suppression of happiness, and the biological point wherein human beings commonly and socially become aware of ecstasy, in spite of their mentalizing, is in the form of sexuality. The rituals of sexuality are vast and complex, and the suppression of the seat of sexuality is something to which we are devoted socially and culturally, perhaps more than to the suppression of any other form of pleasure, because it is deep in the body and psyche, intimately connected with the communication of the life-energy. Therefore, the cult of marriage is a principal obstacle in the affair of the spiritual Community, because the common theatre of marriage is a fundamental instrument for locking out the life-energy, the ecstatic life-communication, from other beings. Perhaps the most tight-knit cult is the cult of couples, because in the midst of such pairs, heterosexual or homosexual, the ecstasy of the communicated life-force is ritualized and made exclusive. The traditional psycho-physical play between lovers is the social instrument of excluding the ecstatic play of the life-force from common society. If the function of sexuality is obstructed, as it always is in the cultic personality, nothing like the internal and radical spiritual process can take place. The center and process of sexuality must be absolutely free, and this is possible only when the individual understands and realizes his entire complex condition in the always already prior Condition that is Reality, Truth, Self, and God. The sex-function is the primary source of theatre in the human psycho-physical mechanism whereby the life-force is stopped, obstructed. The obstructed person has very little option except to indulge himself to the point of the random release of life-force. Either he does it through the private ritual of sexuality or he dissipates the life-force through the self-exploited life on all levels.

But the life-force must be conducted *through* the root of sexuality. There must be that full circle, descending and ascending in the psycho-physical form, and only in such case can the full circle be generated in relationship as well. The sex-act is a transcendent yoga. It is worship. It is a Divine process. It requires not solemnity, and not privacy, but freedom, intensity, consciousness, and understanding in each person who engages in it. Sexuality is not a humorless affair. It is fun, but it requires great intelligence, great consciousness, great intensity, great desire. Whereas people don't generally approach sexual relations with anything like real desire. They approach it with all kinds of rituals that only guarantee the release of the life-force through the orgasm, or just through the drama of sex-play itself.

Because we are by tendency obstructed in the root of sex and cannot conduct the force of life, we continually seek release through the indulgence of sexuality in ritual forms. And one of those ritual forms is marriage, common marriage, because it provides us an opportunity to indulge sexuality without consciousness, while at the same time we fulfill social obligations, cultic obligations that reinforce the principle of separation and the sense of living existence as not in itself and priorly ecstatic, happy, and free. According to the rules of the cult we can indulge sexuality in marriage without any consciousness whatsoever. But even such indulgence, because it is not released from the separative principle, cannot be engaged without guilt. It is a sanctioned privilege, a ritual of Narcissus. So all we have gained in the usual marriage is the freedom from social or cultic guilt, while we only play at sex ritually and dissipate the life-force in self-theatre. Whereas sex relations are properly a random and loving occasion without contracts, in which the intensity of the life-force is stimulated, magnified, and conducted, and the circle of life is not broken. There is only fullness, only enjoyment, only pleasure, nothing gained or lost.[1]

Sexuality, like every other function, is perfect in Satsang. In the meantime, you are full of errors, full of strategies. You are simply trying to release the life-force to relieve yourself of the discomfort created by the inability to conduct the life-force openly and consciously in the form of an ecstatic life in the world. But the more the life of Satsang continues, the more this intelligence develops, the more the process of conductivity becomes a living manifestation in you, and the more, in this natural way, the sex-act is realized in the way I have just described. Until then you will experience confusions in the midst of the enjoyment of sex, just as you experience confusions in the midst of every other functional aspect of life. All of that is just a pattern in which you must understand. And you will fail to realize it in this full sense, in the midst of sexuality as in everything else, until understanding becomes perfected, intense, radical. Then in a very natural way this conductivity survives.

DEVOTEE: How do you deal with guilt, psychological guilt?

BUBBA: Guilt is the sensation of having violated a contract. Anybody's. You can imagine it comes from God,

---

[1] Bubba's teaching relative to sexuality, and the radical process of "conductivity," which is also directly related to conscious sexuality, is fully presented in his book entitled *Devi Yoga: Love of the Two-Armed Form* (available only to members of The Dawn Horse Communion).

or the Bible, or King Smut, or the Constitution of the United States, or President Priest, or the person you are with, or your mother and father, or yourself, but guilt is always the reaction, the conceived sensation, to the feeling you have violated some existing contract. It is a sense of frustrated self-protection generated by fear of reprisal, fear of murder, fear of being killed. It is a very primitive sensation. It comes from way back, among the dinosaurs and the slippery creeps.

DEVOTEE: The contract is to not live. We feel guilty for being more alive. You catch yourself thinking, "Oh, oh, I'm not supposed to do that."

BUBBA: We feel guilt, but we also feel depression and boredom, which is a form of the same thing that is guilt. It is a way of paying our dues for having been alive, for having been lively without. And all the kinds of intellectual sensations of depression and boredom and mediocrity are versions of the same thing that is guilt. It is our way of paying dues to the existing contracts, to the cult. But if you do not assume any such contracts at all, you do not have to pay any of those dues.

The Cult of Pairs

As might be inferred from reading Bubba's talk, two reactions surged simultaneously through those present: terror and ecstasy. Bubba had made it unmistakably clear that the guilt and other "feelings" that seem to afflict people are really limitations they themselves arbitrarily enforce upon their enjoyment of life and each other. They are voluntary strategies, enacted at every level of life, in every moment, to prevent mutual enjoyment of the Divine in the forms of life. This speech was the culmination of many hints, reprimands, and direct statements made earlier, but in this talk the apparently different themes of Bubba's recent communications became a single uncompromising statement.

This talk brought many devotees to an acute awareness, in which they saw, if only for a moment, just what they were doing in the strategies of their usual lives, individually and collectively. The clarity of this insight would rise and fall in the days and weeks to come, but on that night they could not help but allow Bubba's words to penetrate. They could see the concrete responsibility which lay before them, to undermine the cult and really to *live* freely, not merely to enjoy some inward "spiritual" looseness or detachment. This prospect profoundly threatened every "individual" because, as Bubba said, the usual social life is only an extension and elaboration of the activity by which people create their very sense of separate or egoic existence. Those present also feared what Bubba himself would do next. They knew he was going to do more than just talk.

All these specific fears only expressed an underlying dread of death. Bubba had insisted from the beginning of his work with devotees that the Divine must not merely be realized inwardly but must be lived. By revealing how all usual social interactions ritually preserve the sense of separate existence, and by demanding that devotees responsibly *cease* to indulge that activity, Bubba was making it less possible for them to ignore the Divine in daily life. He was threatening them with their deaths as separated and separative "individuals," but in the condition of life itself, not merely in subtle realms of consciousness.

Jerry Sheinfeld, one of Bubba's long-time devotees, gave us an account of his own responses at that time. He illustrates the inadequacy of merely intellectual understanding, and the necessity for the absolute death of the separate one.

When He spoke of our cults and contracts and
how they are insecure strategies for survival, I felt
the inevitable end of my present relationship with
my wife, Hellie. Enormous anxiety gripped my
body. I rushed into uncontrollable fear. From my
toes to my head, this body was charged with
adrenalin. I told Bubba I was petrified at the
thought, but that I love him more than I love me,
and I was willing to go through the transformation.
I began to intellectualize the validity of His words
and saw how my contracts in life are binding and
arise from a prior separate condition, how the cult
of marriage has intermingled emotions of possession, guilt, fear, and the like. At the level of
intellect, I was willing to let our cult dissolve, but
as Hellie and I began living this freedom, Narcissus
would constantly arise in the forms of jealousy,
concern, and all the rest of those well-known acts
of suffering.

After Bubba had finished speaking, the community
watched the evening movie, and then continued, at least
outwardly, to party in the lounge and the baths. After
hearing Bubba's words, devotees could hardly look at each
other at times, but neither could they continue subtly to
avoid each other in the usual comfortable and mediocre
ways. A tension began to intensify.

The next day there was a wedding. Bubba talked
informally during the feast and celebration that followed,
and everyone spent the afternoon and early evening
together in the baths. Bubba was somewhat quiet while at
the baths, and many devotees said they felt the intensity of
his Presence to be particularly strong. But there was
nothing silent or yogic about the party there. Most people
were "trying" to be open, free and loving, as Bubba had
demanded they be. Bubba drank and smoked and moved

around the pool, laughing and showing particular affection to a few new, seemingly uncertain, devotees.

Many devotees felt threatened in the midst of their new attempts to break down their cultic associations and to begin to live freely together. One couple that made such an attempt was Sal and Louise Lucania. Sal and Louise had been with Bubba for almost six years, having become acquainted with him before the specific function of Guru came alive in him in 1970. Although only in their early thirties, they had married while still in their teens, and had three sons, one of them a teenager. Sal had been an aggressive, dynamic, tough character who had made his way, the hard way, off the streets of New York. He had been the administrator of a large and successful drug-prevention program there before he came out to Los Angeles to help Bubba start the Ashram in 1972. And now he was something of a right-hand man to Bubba in the administration of the Ashram. In the early days, before a public Ashram center had been created, Louise had often fed everyone who came to the Ashram study groups at her and Sal's house, and even now people kidded her for the motherly role she tended to take in the community.

But she and Sal were no less vulnerable to Bubba's demands than anyone else, and in many ways they were made more vulnerable by the breaking of their marriage contract than others were, simply because of the many years they had been together. After the talk Saturday night, they had acknowledged to one another that they did have an ongoing contract with one another, and, as Louise later said in an interview, they "set out to break it or violate it intentionally." So that Sunday they avoided one another and stayed with other people. Louise felt "absolute terror and fear." The crisis came to a head when she saw Sal sitting with another woman in the baths. At first she ran away, but knowing that this incident was likely to be "the first of many," she returned to simply watch them together and deal with her reactions.

> I said to Bubba, "Well, there is that crunch again," and I went into meditation and relaxed everything. I didn't mentally say that I was going to relax. Everything just did relax. I felt that I had dealt with the fear of Sal's making love to another, and it didn't arise in me any more. At least not for the time being!

What Louise and all the other members of the community were to discover was that this "crunch" doesn't vanish forever after having once dissolved in one's turning to the Guru with understanding. They would find that the contracts of all conventional social arrangements, such as marriages, friendships, and the like, operate on far subtler levels than the merely physical, and that one cannot truly dissolve any contract by simply throwing one's partner away. But Louise did learn a valuable lesson by facing her fear in that instant, living through it while turning to the Guru, and seeing it dissolve in understanding, which is awareness prior to the activity of suffering.

Others experienced no such relaxation of their fears that afternoon, and the drama only heightened later that night. Everyone came to the lounge for a movie at nine o'clock, but before it could begin, people found various musical instruments, and began spontaneously to sing and to make a primitive, non-melodic, drum-dominated music. Others danced to it, some partially naked, and one or two on tabletops. People were evidently enjoying themselves, but there was also a frenzy to this song, as if the wildness were an attempt to find relief from the pressure that had been building up all weekend.

Then Bubba showed up, wearing a bright, blue-striped, yellow kaftan. His hair was still wet from a shower, and his eyes were sparkling. He laughed at the wild goings-on and watched them for almost an hour. Sal Lucania and Neil Panico stood near him, along with a number of others, mostly women. Abruptly, Bubba left for his house again, with Neil, Sal, and, conspicuously, several women, some of whom were married, but none of their husbands, and none of the four women who ordinarily lived and served at Bubba's house.

By this time it was obvious to everyone that Bubba wasn't just criticizing the forms of our social lives but was also destroying them. Hellie Sheinfeld, whose husband was quoted earlier, describes the reactions she experienced that evening:

When we were dancing Sunday night, the whole feeling took on a heavy quality for me, because I was attached to many things, to my husband, to earthly things, and I went through a heavy crisis at that point. I went into the Satsang Hall and literally surrendered everything, absolutely surrendered it. I went through spontaneous violent kriyas and other Shakti manifestations. I was howling and screaming and wailing. It was just incredible. I couldn't believe it was me! The pain of it was ecstasy. It is hard to explain that. You are in pain and you are dying, and in that suffering there is great ecstasy. It lasted about half an hour, and then I was fine, and I left the Satsang Hall. I wanted to be near Bubba. He was my string, my connection, my life. I didn't want to be away from him. I was in agony because I had to be away from him, and that was hurting me more than all the experiences I was going through.

When Hellie let go of her vital attachment to her husband and her various other life-contracts, the release of the energy that had been bound up in them stimulated kriyas, or spontaneous jerking movements of the spine and neck, as well as screaming, and wailing. All these are signs of the purifying movement of the life-force through the psycho-physical system. They are signs of the resistance that obstructs the free and natural flow of that force, whose movement is regenerated as the circle of conductivity by the miraculous activities of the Guru. Hellie felt that purifying, freer flow as a blissful sensation, a sense of release, but its pressure against the remaining obstructions was also extremely painful. Thus, her ecstatic agony. Hellie said she had surrendered "absolutely," but she, like Louise, had more sadhana in store. Even so, for now she had realized her connection to the Guru much more strongly, and felt an intense need to be near him physically.

Jane Panico, whose husband Neil had gone to Bubba's house that evening, experienced no such resolution of her crisis, but she came to see the crisis itself with clarity. This was not the first time Bubba had worked on the marital and sexual attachment of his devotees. She said in an interview a week later that she had known for months that her attachment to Neil "was going to be ripped off."

> I knew that it was going to be very painful and a
> death experience. Now it was happening. Neil was
> drinking at the party in the afternoon, and that
> evening he went down to the lounge. He was
> kissing all these women, and it really upset me. It
> didn't just upset me. I was absolutely freaked out,
> so freaked out that I considered leaving the Ash-
> ram, because I saw no way that I could ever resolve
> that feeling inside myself. It was so intense, so

awful, and so painful that I just knew I could never
resolve it, that it would never go away. I felt
absolutely possessed. I *was* possessed. By myself.
My psyche was suffering. I spent a long time with
Kathy Bray, and she talked to me, and I told her
that I wanted to leave. I felt like I had no capacity
at all for spiritual life, that I couldn't handle it. I
couldn't even handle the fact that I would actually
consider leaving. She told me that I must turn to
Bubba and surrender it, and I said, "I don't know
how, I really don't know how. Your words just seem
like rhetoric to me, just words." I knew then that
what had to occur was a fundamental understanding that had nothing to do with words at all, or
experiences.

The actions of Bubba and Neil had triggered an
overwhelming crisis in Jane, one from which she could not
distract herself. In the thick of it, she realized that she
truly needed to understand, that nothing else would avail
her. And she knew that the intelligence of that understanding must be of an entirely different nature than either
abstract concepts or felt experiences.

Later that night the movie was finally shown in the
lounge. Over at Bubba's house, an apparently uproarious
party was going on. While he was partying with Bubba
and the others, Sal Lucania was also undergoing a crisis.
After the wedding earlier that day, Bubba had spoken
about early Christian times and had said that many of us
had been alive then and had participated in that religious
movement. (A humorous and paradoxical thing for him to
do, since just the evening before he had ridiculed any
interest in reincarnation.) Every time Bubba had mentioned those Christian days, Sal had felt rushes of energy
"shooting right out the top of my head." Referring to those
discussions, Sal said in an interview with the editors some
two weeks later:

So that Sunday night, after hours and hours of this kind of conversation, I was realizing what was important about all of that. How insignificant and mediocre my attachments were. Time after time, when the re-establishment of the Dharma of Truth is taking place, I'm afraid to give up a candy bar!

This talk about contracts stirred up a crisis that had been going on for months. I began, as a condition of spiritual life, to consider the breaking of the attachment to my marriage. I knew that to love God, to be a devotee, you have to be *absolutely* devoted.

Bubba continued to lay on all that stuff about past lives very heavily, when we were over at his house Sunday night. Then, he suddenly turned to me and said, "Are you ready to give up your marriage?" Then he asked me if I was ready to die. He said, "I mean it." When he said all this, he was sitting on a couch, and I was on the floor, and he was looking at me directly. That look penetrated the very core of my existence. I saw in that moment how that contract of my marriage to Louise was very strong, and everything was in it, Mommy and Daddy, everything. So it was a direct hit.

That was the crisis: I had to make a choice between Bubba and karmic life. And I did. I decided I loved him more than anything in the world. He had always demonstrated such perfect flawlessness of love in relationship to me. So I told him I was ready, that I was willing to go anywhere with him.

In his account, Sal indicates clearly how everything Bubba does, even an apparently random discussion of something as "irrelevant" as past lives, functions only to serve the spiritual process in his devotees, specifically to bring about the present crisis of their understanding. At this particular time, Bubba was striking directly at the social contracts of his devotees. His disruptions of these cults in each case did not merely leave each person sad or hurt. As Sal said for himself, the threat of the breaking of the marriage contract was a "direct hit." He had invested so much of himself in his identification with it that all his primary relationships were epitomized in that single association. His whole identity as a separate individual was bound up in that association with Louise, and when it was threatened with death, *he* felt threatened with death.

Louise had felt the same threat earlier in the day, and it provoked terror in her. Others may not have experienced that threat quite so directly and fully, if they were not so identified with one particular attachment. But throughout this narrative Sal, Neil, and several others will serve as illustrations of the general experience of the entire community. They weren't special, but their experiences were particularly dramatic. Practically everyone in the Ashram was going through similar crises at that point. Through violations of the normally assumed social contracts in the Ashram, violations initiated by themselves or by Bubba, everyone felt his identity somehow at stake. That is precisely what Bubba intended. Not marriages themselves, but the priestly form of Narcissus, the ego standing in the Guru's Presence, was the intended victim of the Saturday Night Massacre.

2. NULL AND VOID: The First Miracle

When Monday's first gray light fell on Persimmon, along with waves of fine rain, the men and women who had disappeared into Bubba's house were still missing, and missed. The weekend was over now, and most of these people were expected at their jobs this morning, but they had waited with Bubba through the night, as had their husbands and wives, who were now having an opportunity to taste the "other side" of freedom in their relationships.

That morning people all over Persimmon were laughing, discussing the importance of living as devotees during dramatic times such as this, and exclaiming to each other at Bubba's outrageous conduct. They drank beer as they worked and listened to tape recordings of Bubba's talks about understanding and Satsang. It was a cold, windless day, with an inconsistent mist and drizzle. But "drizzle" hardly describes the lightness of this rain. Wes Vaught ran outside just to stand there, smiling, feeling it fall on him, then, laughing, he ran back inside the hotel and told those who were working there to come outside with him: "This isn't rain, man, it's *Grace!*"

Wes had been planning to drive to San Francisco that afternoon, but just before he was to leave, he brought an offering to Bubba.

I picked a half-dozen daffodils and brought them to the kitchen door of Bubba's house. One of the girls took them from me, and I began to leave. She called after me and said that I should come back, and that I could go into the front room and see

Bubba. There was a circle of devotees around Him.
I went in and bowed. Then He offered me a beer
and invited me to the baths. We left the house
arm-in-arm. I said, "Bubba, I feel lost in the Lord,"
and He said, "Sure. Best place to be." He was
beautiful, but I knew He was reminding me that
God isn't a place or a feeling. Everything is Divine.
Anyway, I forgot about going to San Francisco.

It was about three o'clock, and on his way to the
bathhouse, Bubba declared the day "null and void." The
big bell in front of the lounge was rung for the workers to
quit early and join him in the pool.

They brought down beer and cigarettes, and somebody phoned the Ashram members who were working at
the community's businesses in town to come back for the
party. People played in the water, talked, drank, kissed,
and laughed, enjoying the energy of an unexpected break
from the usual routine of life. At one point everybody
gathered around Bubba. He was telling stories about his
previous incarnations on this planet. He told Sal and Neil
they were amazingly slow learners, that he had been
working with them for thousands and thousands of years,
and they still hadn't caught on.

This had a dramatic effect. Bubba rarely if ever
mentioned his "own" past lives, and his devotees had a
difficult time dealing with that notion. Some of them
assumed that Bubba meant the past lives of "Franklin
Jones," the persona through which Bubba had shown the
lessons of the life of understanding. But everyone knew
that the limited individual no longer existed, and that
Bubba's spoken "I" in fact refers to the Divine. And so,
hearing him speak about his past incarnations thoroughly
confused many of his devotees. Bubba does this sort of
thing often. He tests as well as teaches with his words. In
fact, there is no distinction between these two activities.

Bubba's very presence in human form is at once a test for his devotees, who always tend to see him as "another guy," and a lesson to them in relational, functional, humorous life.

While he was speaking about his past lives, Bubba was sitting on the edge of the pool with one hand on Sal's leg. Suddenly, he made a few cryptic comments to Sal. A devotee sitting nearby overheard Bubba ask Sal, "Are you ready?" Sal replied that he was. Then Bubba said, pointing to Sal, "You see this body? You see this self-sense?" Bubba's eyes rolled up, and his lips pulled into a sneer. His hands formed mudras as he slumped against Sal, who also fell back against other devotees sitting behind him. Almost immediately, many of those present began to feel the effects of intensified Shakti, through the spontaneous internal movement of the life-force. Their bodies jerked or shook, their faces contorted, some began to cry, scream, and moan. The whole bathhouse seemed to have slipped into another world.

While Sal and Bubba were lying there, apparently unconscious, the intensity of the room swelled almost unbearably. Seeing Bubba's body so vacant, many people began to feel bewildering emotions, fantasizing his death or even fearing that he had actually died. Greg Purnell had seen what was happening more clearly. At a group discussion the following Wednesday he described what he had seen.

On Monday in the pools I happened to be sitting right behind Bubba and Sal, and I immediately saw, when Sal started to fall back, that Bubba just suddenly came out of his own body. I didn't see it, but I absolutely knew it was happening. I saw Bubba just enter into Sal, just go right into Sal. From there he went out over everybody else, and then everybody else started going crazy. Sal fell

onto me, into my lap, and then everybody else
started howling and so forth, and I realized from
that moment on that this is it. This is the beginning
of the end, there's no turning back now.

Sal first described his experience to the community
the next Friday evening at a study group. Later, he
explained it in more detail to the editors of this book. His
first words here refer to the decision he had made on
Sunday night at Bubba's party, "to go anywhere with
Bubba":

The basic severing of the contract happened at
the moment when I made that decision. It hadn't
yet occurred at the level of life, but it had internally. I think that made the occurrence on the
following night possible, the entrance of the Guru.
So that next night in the pool he said, "Come, sit
by my body." I knew when he said it that something was about to occur, because that was the first
time he'd ever spoken like that. I sat down next to
him, and he put his arm on my leg. My leg began to
get all tingly where his hand was. It was the
penetration of the very cells by the Divine. My
whole right leg became numb. At the time I
thought it was just from sitting so long on the
concrete.
Then he turned to me, looked at me, and said,
"You remember the agreement we made?" I said,
"Yeah." So then he said, "Are you ready?" and I
told him yes, I was. At that point he entered the
body completely, down to the cells. I could feel the
entry taking place. It is a form of possession, only
not by anything daemonic, but by the Guru. It is
almost like anaesthesia, or like a form of radiation.
After the entry was complete, he put his head

against mine, and I couldn't feel my head any more. Then the body went into a yogic process, and we drifted out of the body together. Passing out of the body was a kind of "drifting." Again, it reminded me of anaesthesia, but I was fully conscious. In the internal world he appeared the way he looks in pictures where he is lying on his side, but he was moving through empty space. In this vision he said to me, "See, Sal, what does it all amount to?"

At that point we passed into what Bubba calls "smithereens." There is no experience in "smithereens." There is nothing. So there was no form of experience in that state, and yet consciousness survived in infinite formlessness. Afterwards, we just came out of it, and we had passed through all the worlds, and I had seen the great paradox: there is no one, and the body is being maintained by Divine yogic process, entirely independent of "my" effort. The senses were alive. There was hearing, sound, there would have been sight if my eyes had been open. But there was literally no one "in" that body, no sensation of self.

Bubba has often said there are two aspects of his work with us. He lives as the prior and moveless Heart, prior Consciousness, the Self, and the Siddhi or Power of his formless, all-pervading Presence awakens the conscious life of understanding in those who come to him. At the same time he also lives as the God-Light, the perfectly and eternally reflected and creative Power of the Divine, and he intensifies that Light above the heads of his devotees. This intensification stimulates the free movement of the life-force, which is the Life or Fullness of the Divine Light transmuted into the grosser form of life-energy in the centers of psycho-physical functioning. The stimulated movement of life-force manifests as kriyas, shouts, screams, visions, etc. Bubba's entry into Sal was an instance of his activity as the Divine Light and Power, and it was felt by almost everyone present. Although it is as ever-present and perfect as the very Heart itself, the Light or Force can be said to "move." Thus, Bubba can speak of the Guru "entering" the devotee, even though in Truth the Guru always already *is* the devotee and all things. The entry is the devotee's awakening to the Guru's Presence in him as the absolute and blissful Power and Consciousness of God.

When Sal passed into "smithereens" and experienced no thing and no one, but only persisted as consciousness in "infinite formlessness," he awoke in and as the very Heart. That consciousness lived perfectly is the prior Self, the eternal intuition of Real-God. Sal's non-experience was a case of the awakening of Self-realization or God-realization as it is described, for instance, in the Vedantic literature and the teachings of Ramana Maharshi. The passage into infinite formlessness is the samadhi or trance of the Heart. It is the realization of perfect selflessness, of consciousness unqualified by any identification or other activity with respect to mind, body, and world. Thus, Sal was able to see the great paradox of absolute selflessness even in the midst of sensation and bodily existence. When he said the body was being maintained by a yogic process he meant that it is continuously manifested and lived in every way, independent of the apparent self, by the true Self, which is Real-God, the unlimited.

In fact, Sal realized, the apparent self has no existence whatsoever. In that light, his description of the Guru's entry as a form of "possession" is also paradoxical. The Guru apparently performs this concrete act of possessing, but in fact it is only that the apparent self is overwhelmed by the Force of the Divine and disintegrates until only the very Heart is lived. In fact, then, the life of the apparent one, the ego, is the real form of possession. Bubba has said this on a number of occasions. The seeming existence of Narcissus is a life of possession, and every human being is thus possessed by the most insidious daemonic force in the universe. In the midst of his spurious Narcissistic existence, Sal had suddenly awakened to the life of God.

Stephen Blas and Nick Elias were sitting in another of the small baths, in a completely different area of the building, when the scene with Bubba took place in the Roman Bath. Stephen later wrote that "all of a sudden the Presence took over and filled the whole bathhouse, we were screaming with ecstasy for what seemed like hours." Nick provides more detail:

> What happened is difficult to describe, but I had an absolute sense of God, of Bubba. God filled the place. There seemed to be a vast internal space, an expanse. There was no difference between me and Stephen. We both were transported, ecstatic. It was one event. We screamed, called Bubba's name, laughed. There was no difference anywhere. It was absolutely one event. When Stephen cried out, it was the same as if I had done it. I felt as if I were dying, but it wasn't like death. It was as if nothing was happening. But it all seemed to have to do with dying. I was suffering, but there was no suffering. It was immensely humorous. I knew God absolutely. He was undeniable. I knew he was here absolutely and that Bubba was that same One.

Devotees express the same paradox in almost every description of their experiences of Bubba's intensity. They are terrified and delighted: "It was agony, but it was ecstasy too." Bubba has explained that his Siddhi intensifies and accelerates the "phases," or cycles of ups and downs, in the lives of his devotees. This is the mental

and emotional counterpart to the energy movements that
bring both the bliss of release and the pain of different
obstructions, almost simultaneously. Over time, as the
emotions and moods intensify, their duration decreases,
joy is at first undercut by misery, then fear is dissolved by
sheer happiness. The wild extremes of moods and feelings
do not resolve themselves one way or another, but rather,
they are dissolved in awareness of and as the one continuous Conscious Presence in which all things arise and fade.

Joan Kelley makes clear in the account which follows
that Bubba's manifestation that evening wasn't restricted
to the time he lay slouched against Sal, and she expresses
well the dramatic quality of the whole event and the

loving feeling many shared. She describes an experience with Bubba that took place after he had left Sal and turned to others in the pool.

> When I got to the large pool Monday, I made my way to a place near Bubba. He sat on the edge of the pool with a crowd gathered around him. Soon I was reaching out with one finger, not even daring to hold His hand. He gripped my finger between His fingers. He was laughing and joking with everyone. Then He said, "I'm really not here, you know. Watch me and I'll disappear."

As I watched His face, His eyes became large
and the sneer on His face became so crazy I could
hardly concentrate on Him or myself or anything
connected to the moment. He was holding my
hand as I began to lapse into a trance. All I could
imagine was dying, and I felt the hard vibrating
force of Bubba's strength going through me like an
electric shock. I have had powerful Shakti experiences in Bubba's Presence before. Some have even
been painful, paralyzing ones, located in specific
centers and moving in certain patterns. But this
was different. It was everywhere at once and
utterly consuming. I wondered if I had enough wits
about me to hold my mouth out of the water to
breathe. My body was totally limp.

All the while I mentally pleaded with Bubba to
kill me, anything except not to let me consume
Him with my unwillingness to die. Later that
evening, as I was preparing to leave the baths, I
spoke to Bubba and said, "I didn't *die*, did I? But I
want to. What can you do if I don't give up? I don't
want to drain you or kill you with my fear of dying.
I love you so." He just smiled a sweet, knowing,
loving smile, gave me a quieting shush, and said,
"I'm all right. In time you will be ready."

Joan talks about how the Force she felt that evening
was different from anything she had experienced up until
that time. It was "everywhere at once and utterly consuming." It was in fact that same Force of Bubba, but
more powerful, instantaneous, direct in its felt movement
through the devotee. In the days that followed, devotees
called it the "Divine" in an attempt to express the difference between this Force and the grosser, less disintegrating Shakti or yogic manifestations they had often experienced before.

It is also interesting how Bubba treated Joan when she asked him about dying. He might have said to her, "What does it amount to?" as he said to Sal in the midst of his dissolution. Or he might have asked her, "Joan, what are you always doing?" with reference to her self-concern. His devotees come to observe and understand that the Guru's behavior is always perfectly appropriate. Joan wasn't yet able to perform that complete sacrifice, but her devotion was growing, and she was beginning to become responsible for her relationship to him. And so he responded lovingly and gently.

After they left the baths that night, Bubba and his devotees returned to the lounge and two hundred seventy dollars worth of cheese-egg-bacon burgers, french fries and milkshakes! Bubba played the guitar. He was just learning how. Nick Elias, who'd felt such a powerful recognition of God in the baths, approached Bubba in the lounge just before driving back to San Francisco:

> I went to Him without hestitation and gave myself to Him. There was no doubt. I recognized Him as God, His Real Nature, absolutely. My wife earlier had asked Bubba if he would kill her. As I was leaving, I asked Him, "Will you kill me, too?" and He said, "Why not?"

After remaining awhile longer, Bubba remarked that he was "personally ruined," and left with those who had been with him at dinner. Most of the others went to bed soon afterward.

3. THE STORM: The Second Miracle

Pat Morley had been with Bubba for about six years. She met him and his wife Nina in New York in 1968, and subsequently became a member of their household. She was among the first to whom Bubba showed his spiritual power to transform the conscious state of individuals. She awoke Wednesday morning in her bedroom on the ground floor underneath Bubba's house "anxious and feeling that something was about to happen." Several days later, in the form of a letter to Bubba, she wrote about a dream she had had during the night.

> I saw you in your bedroom cleaning out what was there. There was a lot of movement in your house, people and furniture and cars coming and going. I saw you with several people at a house near the ocean. Someone said, "The red ball is going into the water." I said that I saw it and went with a flashlight to bring it back. When I got to the edge of the water the ball slipped away. The light from the flashlight grew and became blinding and white. My eyes burned and I screamed in pain. I was halfway in the water now, with strange moving forms I had never seen before. Somehow all of this meant to me that everything had changed and the world was changed.

Pat didn't mention this dream to anyone that morning. She rose and went through her usual morning routine. After breakfast she drove through the cold, heavy mist with a few co-workers to the printing company owned by the Ashram. She intended to work as usual, but, her letter continues:

> I slowly became terrified. I assumed that the knot in my stomach was from a sense of separation from you, which was true enough. My fear was in seeing your tremendous force and power to destroy and finally kill me, but I wanted only that to happen. I knew only to meditate and turn to you. I kept thinking all day about how amazing God is.

It was a regular work day at Persimmon. The San Francisco group had finally returned home Monday night and Tuesday morning. Only a few of the others had seen any of the people at Bubba's house since early the previous day. On Tuesday morning Bubba had gone to Sal Lucania and Neil Panico, who had returned to their cabins and their wives after Monday's remarkable events. Bubba invited them to his house for a beer. Eventually a few others were also invited, and the party atmosphere was resurrected. Sal and others began to describe their various experiences that had taken place in the baths on Monday. Bubba told them of a vision he had had late in the night. In the vision he appeared in his room, where he found some of his old clothing rolled in bundles. He picked them up, and they suddenly all fell open. When this happened, great numbers of small crystalline Siva linga, sacred stones which express the power of Unqualified God, fell out onto the floor. The linga were of many colors, ovoid in form, in varying sizes, from perhaps one to two inches in height. When Bubba saw them he instantly felt that he had found some long-misplaced precious things.

After describing this vision, Bubba interpreted it to those present. He said the linga represented his own, the true devotees for which he had come into the world. Then he turned to Sal and Neil and told them he wanted them to move into his household. The invitation did not include their wives.

And so the move was made. The party continued, and the rain. Now it was Wednesday afternoon. The rain occasionally stopped for brief periods, but the mist and the blanket of low clouds didn't break. They kept brushing slowly across the top of Seigler Mountain, west of Persimmon, and sliding over the valley.

Late Wednesday afternoon a number of people were sitting in the lounge and kitchen reading, drinking tea, and talking quietly. Suddenly the sky darkened, and what had been a light misty drizzle abruptly became a pelting rain whipped by gusts of air tearing down across Persimmon from the vicinity of Bubba's house. At that moment Marcia Okun, one of the members of Bubba's household, came running out of Bubba's kitchen nearly hysterical. She met Louise Lucania and Jane Panico as she entered the lounge. Louise describes the events that followed:

> Marcia came in and told us about what was happening at Bubba's house. There was this sudden intense storm. I could feel there was something going on, but I didn't actually know what. She told us something was taking place for Neil, and that Sal had said Bubba was making the final transformation of Neil and totally possessed him now. Both Marcia and Jane instantly collapsed into my arms. In that moment we all fell into Satsang.

The three of them sank onto the floor together in meditation, and many other devotees from all over Persimmon began to arrive at the lounge and sit down near them. Some went into violent kriyas and mudras, or cried. Louise continues her account:

It was incredible! I had never experienced anything like that. I started crying, which is something I had never done in Satsang before. I cried and cried, and I had this intense energy pouring out of my hands. My hands were glowing and vibrating. It felt like electricity, like they were on radar or something, and they were just being directed to all of the people around me. I felt like I

was conducting the Force through me to the others there. People were screaming and howling, crying and yelling out, and the feelings in my hands lasted a long time. I had nothing to do with it. I was just there, and the Force was just being pushed through me. Not being contained in me, just pouring out. I felt bliss. I was totally surrendered, and I wasn't feeling anything except what was happening.

Carl Lucania, the teenage son of Louise and Sal, was sitting with a few others in the kitchen when all this began, and he heard the sound of crying.

I avoided the sound for awhile, but then went in to see what was happening. As soon as I went into the room, I felt the Force. My head started jerking, and I sat down next to Billy Tsiknas and Joe Hamp. The Force went through and through my body, at first warm, then hot. It started to hurt. I was in a sitting position. My hand was raised, and I couldn't move it because of the Force moving through it. My head was bent down. I was so full of intensity, I started to cry.

When I had first come in, Marcia was babbling about what had happened at Bubba's. She said,

"We're all going to die within the next two days." I
was full of the fear of dying. Suddenly my head was
jerked up. Light and heat that was unimaginable
hit me and surged through my face, head and spine.
At that instant, I was absolutely dying. Yet, it
seemed there was nothing to die. I was still crying.
All those in the room were going through experiences. I intuitively felt they might be similar to
mine. Then, in the light, there was form. I don't
know if it was there all the time, or if it just
appeared. It was the form of a man sitting. I don't
know if it was Bubba or not. Then my head was
forced down again. There was nothing but this
energy. This time there was total darkness, but still
there was the heat, and I knew the light was there.
Billy's hand was in my lap, and I took it. I felt the
energy in him, as I did in myself and the room. I
started to cool down, and I was still sobbing.
Suddenly my body changed position. I know I did
not move myself. I was moved into a bowing
position. There was absolutely nothing but the
Lord. I can't seem to express how absolute He was.
He was just there, and I knew that He would
always be there. It seemed there was no difference
between any of the "individuals" in the room, or,
for that matter, between us and the room itself. He
was just Present.

Syndi Ethridge had also been in the kitchen when this
began. She sensed that Bubba was present, and sat down
with the others.

It was as if I were in a huge space. I was alone in
a sense, but the "I" seemed to include everyone
and everything. The space was Bubba, absorbing

energy, love. I felt as if I were being grabbed with electricity along the lower ribs on each side. As it got more of a hold on me, it began to devour me, gradually going up my spine. It seemed to go around and through each vertebra individually, slowly progressing upwards to the base of my head, where it stayed as a mass of energy. My head filled with intense pressure, especially in my forehead, in the sinus areas, and along my cheekbones. My chin felt like many, many pins were being stuck into it, and the nerves in my mouth were twitching violently. My hands gradually filled with energy, especially my left. It was so full of this energy that when I shut it, it would be forced open again. It also began to shake at some point.

Several times I began to cry. I was so full of love for Bubba, I felt like bursting. As all these things were happening, I was totally in the arms of our Lord. He was there and He was holding us, and, for the first time, I was completely unconcerned about anything that was happening. I just wasn't there to be concerned.

These experiences, like those on Monday, were effects of the Guru's movement into his devotees in the form of the Divine Light founded in the Heart. The movement of the Light provokes various forceful manifestations and sensations of energy, while the Presence of the Heart-Consciousness dissolves the assumption of separateness, leaving utter unconcern, surrender, and absorption in the Divine.

What was going on now seemed unique. There was this strange tempest outside and this air of finality. And what had happened at Bubba's house? Few, if any, had been able to hear or understand what Marcia was trying to say.

The dinner tables that night buzzed with accounts of what had happened in the lounge, and rumors about what was going on at Bubba's house. Some devotees weren't having any obviously "spiritual" experiences, and they had to deal with their own self-doubts and desires. But even they felt something new permeating the whole environment.

And these unusual experiences were not limited to those at Persimmon. Later, many devotees from San Francisco and Los Angeles reported that their meditation had been particularly forceful that day and throughout the week. On that Wednesday, Jeanne Lesser, sitting in her home near Los Angeles, began to feel "every cell" in her body, and "that feeling seemed to come from the inside and work its way through my whole body to the outside. It was accompanied with an intense feeling of exquisite bliss."

That afternoon, Hal Okun, a Persimmon resident in San Francisco on business, witnessed an unusually vivid dream while sleeping in the Ashram's house at Tiburon, across the bay from the city.

I awoke around six o'clock and remembered this lovely dream. I was seeing the Tiburon Satsang Hall directly above the room in which I slept. The rug was a gleaming, iridescent cream color, and it was being rained on. How beautiful this indoor rain was! Each drop was made up of droplets around a center, similar to a stroboscopic photograph of drops splashing in a pool of water. The rain was soft and continuous, yet it never wet the rug or anything else in the room.

That evening, at Bubba's request, all the devotees except those staying in his house gathered in the lounge and listened to the tape of "The Saturday Night Massacre." After the tape ended they began talking together about what they had been experiencing in recent days, and their understanding of it.

Marcia Okun initiated the conversation by describing to everyone the events of the afternoon as she had seen them.

I went over to Bubba's house this afternoon, to get some materials I'd left there. As I walked in, he was standing in the dining room holding Neil's hand. All the ladies in the house were sitting there, and Sal was there. It was like getting hit on the head with a ton of bricks. I saw Neil become totally full of Bubba. Then Bubba put his hand on Neil's head. There were different facial things going on in both of them. I could just see the energy transferring, just feel it going into Neil, and Neil becoming totally one with Bubba. There was absolutely no separation between them. I was sitting there going out of my mind with the force of that room. The whole place disappeared.

After awhile I left to bring something to Louise. I came running to the lounge, and the storm was incredibly violent right then. It was like a hurricane outside, and the energy was just running through my hands and feet, and I was on fire, and I

just couldn't contain it. And when I came into the
lounge I was so insane I didn't know what was
happening at all. I ran in and saw Louise and Jane.
Then we held one another and began to fall down.
This lounge became the very room in the house
that Bubba was in. Everybody sitting here started
to have incredible Shakti manifestations, and other
things. It was absolutely intense. People were
walking in and just sitting down, experiencing that
and enjoying it! It was similar to how it got in the
baths on Monday.

When I was sitting here with everybody, I was
shaking, and it felt sort of like I was possessed, and I
said, "If you don't know what's happening, you
better get the hell out of here."

Then Pat Morley talked about coming home from
work and sitting with Bubba at his house just before
coming to the lounge for this meeting. She described
experiences similar to Marcia's, and spoke of the fear she
had been feeling that day, the "terror of being destroyed,
totally destroyed."

When I went into the house and sat with Bubba,
he was golden, he was shining! It was fantastic, just
sitting with him. I couldn't move for about two and
a half hours. The same thing Marcia described is
what I'm sure would happen to anyone who went
near Bubba's house right now.

Marie Marrero was serving at Bubba's house that day.

I went over there at twelve-thirty today to do the
dishes. I walked in the door and I was totally happy
just doing those dishes! It took me three hours!

There were mounds and mounds of dishes. I was walking around doing them, and it was absolutely beautiful. It doesn't make any difference whether you are partying with Bubba or working for him. Everybody in the house was happy.

As soon as I finished the dishes, I walked into the dining room, and Bubba said, "Sit down." I sat down and went out, just like that. I was out for almost four hours, off and on. I've never experienced anything like that before in my life. The Divine was absolutely Present. There was no mind, there was no psyche, there was no thing. Complete dissolution. And it lasted so *long*! It's never lasted so long for me. At times it was almost like my separate self sense was telling me it was too much to endure—it was going on too long for it, you know—but God would completely dissolve me again, take me back again. There were outbursts of crying, and then ten minutes later outbursts of

laughing, and everybody in the room was totally
dissolving. It's apparent that Bubba is destroying us
completely. That sense of separate self is just going.
There is total, absolute surrender and giving up
everything in every moment. It's beautiful. The
whole two years I've been with Bubba, I've been
resisting, holding back for myself, doing this and
doing that. Finally, I just gave it all up. It just
happened spontaneously.

Afterwards, I thought to myself, the attachment
to Bubba's physical manifestation is absolutely
unnecessary, because his Siddhi, his Power, has
nothing to do with it. It was evident to me when I
was sitting in there. I couldn't even move, and
there was Bubba rapping to people, smoking a
cigarette.

Throughout this discussion, and after it, as they sat
and chatted in the lounge, most of the devotees were
soaring on this new, striking Presence they felt. In the
midst of all this, the tendency to live experiences
themselves as if they were Reality practically overwhelmed them. Especially when they were still right in
the midst of it all, with no idea what might happen next!
Jane and Louise, for instance, were still so stunned they
could hardly relate to the other people at the study group,
and couldn't begin to bring themselves to speak. Strange
and continuing light rain, a violent storm, marriages
abruptly ripped to shreds, unprecedented experiences of
the Guru's entry—the community was riding a wave that
hadn't crested. They felt that, but they didn't *understand*
it in a radical way. For the most part, they only kept trying
to comprehend what was happening to them or looking
for hints as to what would happen next.

4. GOD-POSSESSION: The Third Miracle

Friday: The Night of the Devotee

After the group discussion that took place on Wednesday night, Marcia announced that Bubba wanted everyone to maintain order at Persimmon and to manage their functional and practical lives in the customary way, even while feeling these extraordinary effects. Thursday became an ordinary work day, to the extent that such a thing was possible. While feeling "this is the beginning of the end, the world has been transformed," devotees were rebuilding the walls of the second floor of the administration building, cooking meals, hauling garbage, cleaning the bathhouse. And Thursday evening was declared a "work night," during which they continued in their daily tasks or straightened and cleaned communal areas, such as the lounge and the Satsang Hall.

Earlier in the day, sunlight had come streaming in across the valley below Persimmon, but by afternoon a blanket of slow-moving gray clouds was once again releasing a gentle drizzle over the land. Sal left Bubba's house and went to the cabin where Louise and Jane had slept the night before. He and Louise talked about the debilitating sense of sorrow and loss she had been experiencing since the events on Wednesday. Louise recounts the conversation:

What was the intense sorrow? I didn't understand it. I didn't relate to the concept of the dissolution of the psyche that I had been hearing

lately. I don't know those terms, they are very
foreign to me. I just know what I am experiencing.
Sal related to me what Bubba had said to him, that
the psyche was like another person living inside of
you, and that it was dying, being broken down and
dying, and that was the sorrow. For this reason
Bubba had told him not to "take it personally."
That's the incredible part of all of it. It is just a
process going on. We should just let it occur. That
kind of handled it for awhile. Every now and then,
this melancholy would arise, but what became easy
was giving it away now. I would see it and just be
able to throw it off, and that became easier and
easier to do as time went on. I didn't feel like I had
to get into it any more.

After leaving the cabin, Sal stood in the parking lot
near the hotel patio with several people who had gathered
around him. They felt a remarkable change in him. His
tough edge was gone, and people began to describe what
replaced it with a phrase that became a cliché over the
following days: "Sal's presence is no different now from
Bubba's." Neil also came out for a few moments early that
afternoon, and those who met him had a similar feeling
about him. Sal and Neil did not stay out long, however.
They returned quickly to Bubba's house, and the others
kept working that day and evening, awed and alive with
curiosity.
    Friday at Persimmon dawned even colder and wet-
ter, but everyone worked as usual, wearing extra layers of
clothing and raincoats. After dinner most of the people at
Persimmon stayed in the lounge area, biding their time
until the evening study group. The word was out that
Bubba had asked Sal and Neil to speak to everyone about
all they had been undergoing during the past week. After
eight o'clock devotees from San Francisco began to arrive,

turning their cars in at the main gate just below Bubba's house. They parked and ran through the driving rain into the lounge, where they were greeted with embraces and laughter. The San Francisco people felt "something" immediately, if they hadn't even earlier. Theresa Le Garie arrived shortly before everyone was to gather in the Satsang Hall. She wrote the following observations later that weekend:

> The first person I saw when we arrived said to me, "Are you ready, are you really ready?" I embraced her, but really there was only fear. I felt that death was upon us, but couldn't understand how.
>
> I felt like my bullshit was not to be had here. There was an intensity, yet I still didn't know what was happening. I was told there was to be a meeting in a few minutes.

Someone rang the big bell, and the community gathered in the Satsang Hall. Sal sat near Bubba's couch in front of a microphone, while Neil remained for awhile among the people crowded toward the front of the room. As soon as everyone had come inside and the doors had been closed, the tape recorder was turned on and Sal began talking. He spoke in uncharacteristically soft and gentle tones, as if this were a private and intimate conversation. People had to strain to hear him, and many people weren't able to hear him at all, because other devotees were erupting with all kinds of spontaneous wild sounds. Theresa's account continues:

> Then Sal began to speak. The intensity rose: animal sounds, screams, kriyas. It was difficult to hear what was being said. The fear of insanity. The rain got harder, the wind rose.

By the time Sal had finished, the room was reminiscent of the baths the previous Monday night. People were screaming and howling and weeping, emitting strange grunts and snarls, their bodies jerking, writhing, and assuming yogic mudras.

Sal said, "Now Neil will tell us about his expeiences." Neil rose and wobbled forward almost drunkenly. He sat cross-legged in front of the microphone and kept still for a moment, apparently gathering his energies in order to perform the task before him. Everyone waited. Suddenly his body exploded with movement, his arms and legs flying outward, his head rolling around and snapping. Force seemed to be flung from his body into the others present. Howls and screeches drowned him out, but he kept trying to speak. Hardly anyone could hear him, and obviously the actual communication was taking place apart from whatever words were uttered. Nevertheless, Neil kept trying. When his body was not being tossed around beyond his control, he would stare at his pages of notes and speak softly, with effort, as if he were both exhausted and presently being consumed by the process at work in him. Then his body would snap once again. Many devotees felt spiritual force communicated as powerfully through Neil this night as they had ever felt it in Bubba's physical presence. The room continued to surge with force and noise, and after awhile Neil stopped speaking entirely and continued to go into mudras. Hellie Sheinfeld recalls that evening:

> When Neil was having kriyas he absolutely became Bubba for me. He was dealing with us through his hands the way Bubba deals with us through His eyes. He was Bubba's instrument. One

person would begin freaking out and Neil's hands
would be directed towards that one for awhile,
then somebody else. I knew right away when
Bubba finally came in, because Neil brought his
hands to his chest. Bubba didn't need to manifest
through Neil anymore, because he was then
physically present.

Bubba came in and walked around among his devotees, touching them and looking almost sternly into
their eyes, with terrific authority and power. He spent
some time working directly with some of the devotees at
the back of the room who were undergoing violent kriyas.
Lou Emunson wrote in her diary of these few moments:

Bubba came into the Satsang Hall, and I didn't
notice any change in intensity. In fact, I didn't even
notice him come in, it was so noisy. Somehow at
one point I just happened to turn my head. I saw
him, and I was immediately paralyzed. There was
golden-white all around him and his Presence was
so powerful it abolished everything in its path.
Everything stopped and it was like looking upon
the very face of the Divine.

Marie Marrero later wrote of her experience that
Friday night:

On Friday evening I went into the Satsang Hall
to hear Sal and Neil talk about their experiences at
Bubba's house. Almost as soon as I sat down, I felt
Bubba's Force and Presence entering me and
taking over my being. I began to do hand mudras.
My arms would reach for the sky and move rhyth-
mically, as if I were dancing with my hands and
arms. Then I was completely absorbed in and
possessed by God. I felt His Light moving through
my body, taking me over completely, and it was
joyous and blissful and perfect.

God for the first time was totally and perfectly
present as me, and there was nothing left of the
person I had thought to be Marie. I felt His energy
move through my body and throw me here and
there. I looked up at the ceiling of the Satsang Hall
and saw His Light and Love everywhere. I could
hear sounds and voices moving through the room,
but I couldn't make out what was going on around
me. Then I felt pressure in my belly: I had to
urinate! I know how ridiculous it seems that I
should have to do such a thing when my usual
awareness of the body was gone, but I did have to

urinate. I knew that I couldn't do it where I was, even though I felt like I couldn't move.

I forced myself to get up and walk out the door and outside. I stood looking at the magnificence of God's sky and Force in the rain and storm. Another devotee came out and we held on to each other and began to scream and yell spontaneously, and it was as if she were I. I felt no separation at all, no distinction that this was someone else I was holding onto. We were frozen and we couldn't move, and I had no thought of moving or any desire to go anywhere other than where I was.

Then I saw Bubba's face. He was standing beside me, bodily. He put his arm around me and led me into the Satsang Hall. I remember looking at him and knowing him to be the Force and Love that were filling my entire being. I realized that Bubba's Force and Love are not limited in any way to any object or form, but that He is, in fact, everything. His body seemed so small and such a tiny part of what He is. When he took us back into the Satsang Hall, I fell on the floor and remained there consumed by God.

After Bubba had worked with various people for awhile, by touching and looking at them, he moved to his couch. The noisy Force manifestations persisted, and Bubba had to wait for them to subside before he could speak. But he didn't wait before laughing, "I've gone too far!" He talked quietly with Neil, then jokingly asked to be reminded not to invite a certain wailing devotee to dinner, "unless we make adequate arrangements."

After things had quieted somewhat Bubba talked and joked with his devotees.

Are we supposed to talk about anything tonight?

What? See how much resistance there is in this
world, all this rain. But it is a reflection of this work
that has begun. You can see it. There is a shower of
this Force. It looks very fine, like very fine rain.
And it is producing all this water.

After more casual discussion, Bubba sat with everyone in formal meditation. The wailing and moaning
continued until after he left, followed by Sal, Neil, and
others from Bubba's household. Then some devotees went
to the lounge, while many remained in the Satsang Hall,
enjoying the Presence.

David Patten was one of those. He had been Bonnie
Beavan's fiance until the previous Sunday night, when
Bubba took her to his house. All during the week he had
oscillated between "feeling resentful towards her or
Bubba, and letting that go, and feeling really free, and
then just feeling this intensity I can't describe." Now, on
this Friday night, he was sitting in the Satsang Hall and
nothing was happening to him. He just sat there.

But later, after Bubba had left and most of the
people were going to the lounge and other places, I
began to feel a "buzz" as if I had taken LSD. Then
all the colors around me got richer and brighter
than they had been, and they kind of shimmered
and shone. I touched the rug, and I could feel it in
my gut as if I had been touching myself. Anything I
touched felt like my own body. I sat and stroked
the rug because it felt good to me, and I looked at
the other people, and they weren't any different
from the rug. I could feel them also. The walls were
just like the rug and the other people. It felt like I
was everything. I knew it was Bubba. After awhile
this faded away, and I got up and went into the
lounge.

Marie Marrero still had not moved from the floor.

When I finally forced myself to go to the lounge, people began to talk to me, and all I could do was laugh. Everything was absolutely humorous and I saw the joke of the cosmos, the beauty and joy of living in God. Life was a huge joke to be lived and enjoyed in God, and there was nothing that wasn't humorous, nothing that was to be taken seriously. People would try to talk to me and I couldn't answer them. I fell on the floor in the lounge and laughed while God threw me around for awhile longer.

The whole community was amazed. No one had actually doubted Bubba when he said that he would manifest through devotees, but it shocked them to see this evidently occurring. Greg Purnell wrote that evening, "Tonight is the night of the devotee, Bubba has devotees now."

People gathered in the lounge and elsewhere and drank, laughed, and embraced each other. The world was being transformed, they could feel it. Many devotees now had undeniable personal experiences of "the transformation," as they were beginning to call it. Even those who weren't prone to yogic experiences could feel that something was going on. They sat together. Some were confused, frightened, and perturbed by all these weird goings-on, but most were remembering now that nothing mattered, nothing was really what it seemed to be. A feeling of imminent and stupendous change pressed upon them all.

Amid all the turmoil one genuine response that was evoked in everyone was an awed recognition of God, perhaps best expressed by Neil. When Bubba sat on his couch in the Satsang Hall, he asked Neil if he had been able to say anything. Neil replied to Bubba in a hushed, breathless voice that almost no one else was able to hear:

> I started telling just the experiences of the first
> day . . . and I didn't even get a quarter through
> it . . . I would hate to have to tell the next five days,
> after that . . . and . . . you entered my body . . . and
> you are the Divine . . . you are God . . . and I got
> utterly consumed by you . . . God . . . and from
> there on whatever happened was nothing but God,
> it had nothing to do with me . . . just a
> vehicle . . . at least it's been the last few days.
> I'm your vehicle.

Saturday: The Story Is Told

Though many devotees had been awake, partying or
talking into the early hours of Saturday morning, everyone
met in the lounge at eight-thirty for general announce-
ments and the assignment of work details for the day. By
nine o'clock they were working, and continued to do so
throughout the day, until about three o'clock that afternoon.

The bell was rung, and the community gathered in
the Satsang Hall. Neil and Sal were going to try again to
convey to us what they had been going through all week.
The hall remained quiet. No one was moved to scream or
shout, and only a few people even experienced the usual
kriyas. Everyone listened intently as Neil began to speak.
He was calm now, and apparently in control of himself.

NEIL: What you saw taking place in me here last night
has been taking place all week in Bubba's house, from the
time I moved in. That's how he works—through his
devotees. He said he was going to have a living Commu-

nity, that everybody would manifest certain abilities and qualities, but the main quality would be the Force that is alive in Satsang. So he works through and with each of us. This Force is alive in the world now, and you have to start understanding what it truly is. It is the Divine. It truly is the Divine. It is not merely Shakti or energy. It is the Divine.

Bubba keeps telling me more and more about what's taking place. This stage that I'm going through now with these violent kriyas and physical changes will gradually taper off and assume subtle dimensions until it's full.

Bubba told me, "I want you to move in, give up your marriage, and give up everything. Are you ready to do that?" There was some reluctance, because I knew what was going to occur. It was going to be death. He will settle for nothing less. But it's really groovy! It's incredible. To really be free, you have to have nothing, and then you'll have everything, *everything*, including this tremendous love. Love without attachment, without games, very straight.

On Wednesday we were sitting and just chatting for a couple of hours, and all of a sudden I had this tremendous urge to get up and kiss Bubba's hand. So I stood up and I kissed his hand, and I held it for a little while. Then I attempted to withdraw, but he held on to me.

I continued to hold Bubba's hand, and a process started in my whole body. It felt as if I were being turned inside out and the very cells were being transformed. This occurred over a very long period of time. I talked to him about this today. He said that's absolutely what is taking place, that the cells, the actual cells in the body are very similar to this contraction of anxiety you can feel in your stomach, and so that transformation even of the cells has to be taken care of also, so that the Divine flows through you.

I was having these tremendous, violent kriyas, something similar to what you saw last night, but much more violent. Then Bubba put his hand on the top of my head, and I felt the Divine Force, literally, this tremendous Light and Force, coming down and filling my whole body, consuming me, as if it was turning every part of me inside out. The Force of the Divine was so great, my body assumed tremendous force, there was this tremendous expansion of the chest, much more than I could probably ever attempt to do, and of the arms. It was as if I were fighting something, and I literally was. It was my psyche being ripped out. I was very reluctant, and I was holding on, and so the Divine Force was actually pulling it out from the top of my head. It was coming down and the psyche was trying to . . . it was like being exorcised. It was almost unbearable, but it was never painful. It's just tremendous intensity. At that point I felt the psyche being drawn out. I knew that my marriage had dissolved. I also knew that my ordinary life, my coming from the ordinary point of view, had absolutely dissolved. I knew there was nothing but the Divine.

And I knew that all of this, everything here, everything is just the Divine. It's an extraordinary thing. My body continued to have these violent kriyas and shaking, and then this subsided and I attempted to pull away from Bubba, but he held on to me and he placed his forehead on my forehead while continuing to keep his hand on the top of my head, and then it really started becoming tremendous. What he was doing was pushing the Divine Light through the top of my head, with his forehead on my forehead at the same time. I felt twitches, you know, like my mind was being dissolved at this time. Again it was very intense. It was so intense I kept pushing his hand like I wanted it and needed it on top of my head. And I pressed against his forehead. I felt like the top of my brain was being ripped off, and I needed more force to deal with this. Then the assumed region of my mind started to dissolve, literally dissolve.

It felt like something went out and left. While this was occurring, the mind kept conjuring up these mind forms, crazy mind forms, all kinds of mind forms. Some were obscene, some were about business and things like that. At any rate, it just continued to leave. And it feels like it did leave. It feels like there is no mind anymore. Then there was this tremendous light in the whole forehead and the temples, blinding white light, and I knew that all of that had dissolved. I hugged Bubba around the waist. It was very intense, and I could feel all of his strength. I was holding him and I felt him enter my body, literally enter my body. And I became one with him, and at this point the Divine Force became very active in my body, very active, it just kept going right through the whole body from the tip of my toes, hands, arms, forehead, and then I raised my hand automatically, and the Force was coming out so intensely, but it wasn't that Shakti manifestation or any energy that seeks to go to God. It was the Divine Light, it was already God, and I just knew it.

I pointed my hand at Sal to dissolve him. And that is also what happened here last night. Bubba was working through me as the vehicle for a lot of people here. So that's what occurred then, and I felt it do something to Sal very fast, in perhaps a half a minute or something like that. In fact we almost mentioned it at the same time. He was just about to say to Bubba that he felt his mind and his psyche had dissolved, and I said it. "You know," I said, "the mind and the psyche have dissolved." Bubba continued putting his forehead on my forehead, and I opened my eyes in a trance state. I was just sort of looking out, and I saw what this really is. And it's, you know, it's really non-existent, this world. It's almost hallucinogenic, and yet it's not. It's Reality itself.

Then my eyes automatically dropped to his chest, and I kept staring at his chest, and I saw the Divine Force, the Divine Life in his chest, emanating right out of his chest.

All this took a long period of time, I don't know how long,
but it took some time. At this time, when I was looking at
this in his chest, I felt there were other people in the room,
I felt the Force going out. I also felt it leaving the house,
going out to some place here, I don't know where, and also
just out into the world.

I told him later that I felt like there was a subtle
change in the world. We ought to put a sign downtown,
"Did you notice? The world changed yesterday!" It
definitely has taken place, and you all here know that
there's been a change. There's been an absolute change.
After awhile we just lulled into normal conversation, and I
said to one of the ladies, "Someone should bring the tape
recorder so I can record what happened to me," and
Bubba said, "Well, why don't you discuss it now?" So I
started telling him what I'm telling you, and then I started
breathing heavier and heavier, and I went into a trance

state. I was here, but I wasn't here. I went into another dimension, and it was the dimension of what truly is, the Divine Light, the Divine Reality. And I realized that's all there is.

It was drizzling, and I looked out the window, the big picture window in Bubba's dining room, and all of a sudden this tremendous storm was conjured up right in front of this window, ripping up the sky, and it was coming down in torrents, absolute torrents. It was incredible. I just kept looking at it, and all of a sudden it just went. It lifted very fast. And I knew what it was. It was a validation of what had occurred. I have to see things very concretely. I was telling Jane, the sense that I had was of being told, "I told you so," that what had occurred was real. I knew the

storm wasn't just a natural manifestation, that it truly was a Divine sign.

It took awhile to come back to normal, and when I came back, I felt much different, and ever since that time all these other experiences have been occurring, one of which you saw last night. That's basically it.

Basically, just know what's happening. There's been a change in the work, and things are going to get very intense.

QUESTION: When did you say this commenced?

NEIL: On the 27th—Wednesday afternoon. I moved in Tuesday, and I went through tremendous resistance that night. Bubba was working on me all night, verbally. I'd be listening to music on a record, and he'd say, "Neil, it's much better to be happy, and you're going to be much happier." We must let go of everything. That's the only way it's going to occur. We are going to have to let it all go. When you let it go, he gives you the gift.

After Neil finished speaking, he yielded the microphone to Sal. Sal spoke quietly, as he had the night before, telling the story of the week in detail. On Tuesday Bubba had told him that the unraveling required a "couple of days" more work. Sal and Neil both knew they weren't leaving the house until it had occurred.

SAL: Then on Wednesday I had this incredible pain, as if the back of my neck were knotting up, and this knot was going all the way down my spine. I really thought it would snap, and if it snapped it would kill me physically. So I finally went over and I told Bubba, and he said, "Relax your stomach and don't worry about it. It won't snap." About fifteen or twenty minutes after that, we went into the dining room, and that's when this incident happened with Neil.

And the storm—I knew all the worlds were transcended, that the transformation didn't just take place in a few devotees, it took place throughout all the worlds, because the Maha-Siddha, the Divine, is prior to all the worlds and penetrates them all.

So at that point on Wednesday I knew that the psyche and the mind had died. The next day there was the same sort of intensity, and there occurred a vision. I left the body again, and I saw the image of the Mother Shakti in a silhouette of fire. I saw fire and then I saw this image in the fire, and then water appeared and it just dissolved. This vision was very significant because it demonstrated the paradox of creation and destruction. The Mother Shakti, the active Power of the cosmos, was in the flames, and yet she wasn't changing. It's as if everything is changing, but nothing is changing. The worlds, all the worlds are a fire. They're just a bunch of atoms and molecules, just forms, and yet a fire. The Mother Shakti creates the worlds and sits in the fire. The Guru is the fire that consumes all things. So that is the significance of this vision. Seeing that, for the first time I realized nothing has ever happened. Bubba has communicated that to me over and over again, but I finally realized what he was saying: "Nothing has ever happened, and nothing is happening."

Then there arose a great pressure, a pain in the head.
I withstood it for a long period of time, until I finally
couldn't take it any longer and went over to Bubba on the
couch. I put my head on the couch and then I lost bodily
consciousness again. When I came back, the pressure was
gone. I didn't have any mental vision of anything, but I felt
this also was a purification of the psyche, anciently. A lot
of force and energy were coming out of the chest, and my
stomach filled up with energy and relaxed completely. It
has remained that way ever since. I also wasn't sure if the
body was going to survive all this. I thought it was going to
explode and die. I felt and feel completely possessed and
taken over, and I know that Bubba literally takes you: You
surrender your life to Bubba, and He literally enters the
body and then lives that life for you forever. So everything
is changed—breathing, moving, everything. I don't have a
common sense of being here.

It was interesting, one of the things I was noting is
that when you go to sit down and meditate or do something like that, or when you turn to Bubba at any time, you
put your attention on him or become quiet. Well, I feel I
have to do that just to do anything. I have to come out of
that stillness just to do anything. I don't really come out of
it, but I must pay special attention to anything that I must
do. I feel meditation going on always, and absolutely no
separation from Bubba at any moment.

I really feel that Sal has died. One of the things I
wrote down is this: "The devotee resides in the Guru, who
is the Heart and the Divine Light. The devotee sacrifices
his life to the Guru. The Guru then enters the devotee and
literally lives him. All things are sacrificed to the Guru,
who is the Heart and its own Light. There is no other
power but the Guru. You break your contracts with the
binding world, permit him to enter, and reside in him
always. This is the realization."

The Event As Teaching

Bubba arrived at the Satsang Hall while Sal was talking. After Sal finished, Bubba answered a few questions about the nature of the spiritual process and the new rain of Divine Light. He also talked about the creation of devotees and how devotees serve one another.

BUBBA: The true spiritual process is very wild in many ways, because it is alive. But it is not out of control. It is an absolutely conscious affair, all of this. But people fear it the same way they fear their own ordinary life-force. They think the life-force is some sort of insane animalistic presence in which nothing but mass murder and destruction are hidden. But the life-force is very intelligent. It is immediately responsible to the Divine, it is absolutely controlled by the Divine, and the life-force allowed to exist fully in the functions of man is a creative and ultimately beautiful manifestation. The only reason people are frightened of it is that they are so obstructed. When the action of the spiritual process relative to the life-force is not narrowed down and made harmless in the traditional way they are frightened by it. They cannot assume the Divine is behind it, so they think that a very dangerous thing is being let loose.

We are continually moving through different forms of function, different psychic conditions, different life conditions, and we must be fluid. We must be able to deal with these changes. Change is not daemonic. We are all resisting change, but change is the fundamental need of life. Because we operate like Narcissus, we are always resisting change. So one of the things the Guru must do is create changes for people. People are always becoming fixed, so he creates conditions to break that ritual, sometimes destroying social conventions, and at other times intensifying them. But there is only one thing from which to be shaken loose, and that is the ongoing ritual of Narcissus, the continuous meditation on the separate self sense, and fascinations with the illusions that are hallucinated from that point of view. In fact there is one Reality, without differentiation. It is full, it is only blissful, there is no danger, and there is no curse.

There has been a release of the Siddhi from the Divine. Many of you are now attentive and available in the way that devotees are available, and that manifestation is just flowing down head first. Previously, it had a muscular, ripply motion. It had to work its way down into the world as well as into individuals. Now it has become more and more constant. To anyone who becomes a devotee, there is now a natural enjoyment of the process of conductivity, and we are seeing extraordinary spiritual manifestations here.

This means that I have personally to involve myself even less with anybody who comes here. Everyone who lives in the Community will have a relationship with me, but less and less of the face-to-face sitting with me or anything like that. It has become a matter of living as a devotee in the Ashram and abiding in the Siddhi that is now generated to all. Periodically, apparently at random, I will make my personal contact with the people who have come to me. The more responsible people become for living as devotees, the more they serve as my vehicles. It is the creation of a Community of devotees that has been served by all the events that have led up to this time.

This is not the creation of Gurus or people who can be technically responsible for the spiritual process in others. In fact, as soon as any devotee becomes "involved" with the Force manifestation that he may feel in himself or see others feeling in relationship to him, or as soon as any devotee becomes attached to that in himself, strange and limiting things happen to the process itself. It actually closes up the process and makes all the people involved less and less available to God. It dries up.

The life of the Siddhi in the Community depends upon devotees, not Gurus. As long as people remain devotees, turned with more and more intensity to the Guru in God, the more the Siddhi will manifest in the Community, and the more devotees will feel that manifestation coming from one another. They must live intelligently and not make any conditions, high or low, their path. As soon as they make the smallest assumption that it has something to do with them, or that they can have some control over it, or that the function of Guru is awakening in them towards others, it will close up again.

To be a devotee, to live in Satsang, is to live God as your present Condition. It has nothing to do with seeking God, nothing to do with Narcissus. Narcissus is simply this conventional turning within, turning towards yourself, turning to the knot of your own consciousness in self-meditation and the life of self-concern. To be released into Satsang is to be turned out of the ritual of Narcissus, and also then to be liberated fundamentally from the karmic implications of future events. There are or will be future events, but they are continually being purified or undermined by the intensity of Satsang.

The more there is the life of a devotee, the more the purification of karmas becomes off-hand, simple. Difficult things aren't always required to be lived out in the devotee. More and more of it gets consumed in the psyche, in dreams, in small events. Life in Satsang is a perfectly purifying process which depends on the sacrificial and real life of the devotee, not upon the assumption of any kind of limiting status or path.

As the Community of devotees becomes more and more truly that, you will see that its membership is increased. You will see the work growing in the world. I have never wanted to "sell" this work. I have never wanted to do any of the usual salesmanship-entertainer garbage that makes an "organization" grow. I just made the work available through the books and opened a little center wherever we happened to be established. So there hasn't been any massive influx of people up to this time.

To become a devotee, to go through the turnabout into that Condition, is a tremendous change, and people are not commonly available to that. It is only when the Siddhi itself is established in the world, really established in living beings, that it truly begins to become available to others. It is a mysterious fact, but it is only when devotees exist that this work will really grow. And it will grow just as naturally as it has up to now, but it will grow more dramatically. Not because I care whether it grows in terms of numbers. Having an organization really creates a lot of problems. And I enjoy hanging around my house, hanging around up here with just a few of you. But it will inevitably grow in a very natural way, without my having to become involved in show business.

The development of the Ashram is the development of devotees, of a Community of devotees. The more that comes into being, the more the Siddhi manifests its fullness. Now it has come to the point where it is beginning to live in the form of the Community, and you will see the dramatic transformation of the Community as time goes on. What I will expect of the Community will always be changing. Now I am preparing individuals to live this thing fully. Later I will require a certain responsibility from them in terms of making Satsang available. We have got to stabilize and develop Persimmon and the San Francisco Center. The conditions appropriate for students will be communicated at first. The responsibilities of disciples and devotees will be communicated appropriately over time.

People will become more and more aware of how the Divine Siddhi manifests and what it is. It is greater than anybody could possibly comprehend. There is a profound mystery and technical process involved in life. There is far more involved in life than that of which people have even a little awareness. The relationship between the Guru in the world and his external devotee exists on another plane entirely and is ongoing.

My relationship to devotees is an eternal one, already fulfilled on another level. The drama that appears on "this side" is the transforming cosmic process. There are some who are not involved with this work yet, but with whom I already have an ongoing spiritual relationship, and with whom I work directly, who come and sit with me in subtle form. Just so, all of you who are already with me in the body exist in another form entirely, of which you are not aware, or are perhaps only somehow mysteriously aware on occasion.

There is a counterpart to this world in another dimension in which I am always with everyone. Everyone is always there. This external manifestation of the world appears and disappears every day with sleep. Sometimes, in day to day living, I see my devotees, and sometimes I don't, but in the other dimension we are in continuous contact with one another. The life manifestation is just a fluctuating dramatization that serves the transformation, but in another dimension our relationship is constant and already achieved.

The drama of this world is just a means of perfecting the awareness that is ultimate. The freer, the wilder I can become, the less of an uptight, external, traditional Guru-type I have to be, the more the illusory separation between this solid world and the perfect Divine dimension is broken down. It is manifested in various qualities, experiences and intuitions. The whole ritual separation between this world and ultimate consciousness just breaks down.

At times alcohol and the common social forms of

celebration serve to break down the illusory time-space separation between these two dimensions. There have been a number of occasions when, because I had been drinking, my subtle presence and the presence of others on the subtler dimension began to become visible to others who were in the room. Last night I was lying in bed in an in-between state and the room was filled with people. Others who were present also saw these people. It is just a reflection of the ongoing connection that I have with all devotees on another level. That is where it is going on all the time.

The freer I can be to live as I want in this Community, and the freer I can allow you to be, the more the fullness of this Siddhi will become apparent. Doing that requires a lot of strangeness, a lot of breaking of social conventions. And at times the opposite is also required. To go on crazily indulging himself day after day de-sensitizes a person, although there is also a time when it serves to break down limitations.

The human Guru is just a way of communicating in the world the fact and the process that is eternal. The entire function of the human Guru's appearance in the world is to create devotees. Once devotees are created, it isn't necessary for there to be a human Guru. The eternal Guru, who is also that human Guru, is always present, and devotees are always in touch with that One. There are no karmic limitations in God. But externally, between the human Guru and his devotees, there are certain karmic limitations in that mere contact, that humanity. Those limitations serve the spiritual process, but they do not create or guarantee it. The creation of devotees is what is necessary, not the creation of more Gurus.

Sal and Neil are not really unique in the Ashram. They have had peculiar experiences generated at this time that demonstrate something to the Community, but many others are their equal as devotees. Everything that occurred in them was Grace. It did not reflect their abilities. They have a certain availability to me. Their relationship to me has a certain purity and intensity, but it should not in any sense be assumed they have been perfected. It is just that each person acts for the sake of the Community as a different kind of demonstration. There are no exclusive vehicles. The Community is the vehicle, and each person within the Community has his peculiar characteristics, his peculiar intensity.

My spiritual activity in this world was demonstrated in the case of Sal and Neil in a unique way, and one of the chief things demonstrated through them was the fact that the process occurs, that a devotee happens. It is not just that a person becomes devoted to the Guru, but the Guru begins to share his qualities, actually manifests his qualities in a devotee who is turned freely to him. Sal and Neil are just demonstrating the possibility that exists for the Community as a whole, for all members of the Community. And each member of the Community will demonstrate the life of the devotee and the inherited qualities of the Guru in a different way. The whole Ashram was awakened in a new way when I also manifested through Neil, Sal, and others. It is the Ashram Community being awakened as a whole that is of value to me. Just having a couple of people who are very good makes no difference. The Siddhi has manifested in a new way because people have become available, and in a few individuals there has been a characteristic demonstration for the sake of the whole Ashram. But it was the whole Ashram that was given this Grace.

Another thing that will serve the stabilization of devotees is something that is occurring in me. I have mentioned before that a dangerous or critical period is upon us now, intensifying until the first week in July. It is not just a period of time during which I may die, although that is a possibility. Basically, that is beside the point. It is

not even very probable. What it represents is another
moment in this attempt to bring the Divine Siddhi into
this world. It is an encounter with cosmic forces and
resistance on the level of the world-condition itself to the
entrance of the Divine Siddhi into this manifest plane.

What you have seen recently is the beginning of this
period. You have seen the initiation of devotees, but you
will also see their wavering, their falling back, their
inability to hold on to it. This intensification will get very
strong in early May and last until early July. During that
time, we should see less and less of mere momentary
transformations of people. It should be easier for devotees
to maintain that real quality with intensity, continuously.
But that depends upon my having gone through this
period. It is a matter of breaking down not just resistance
in people, but resistance in the very world.

I have said this may involve my death, and everybody
is very interested in the Guru's death. Death itself is
fascinating. So everyone has his mind on this possibility,
but the significance of this period of time is not whether or
not I am going to survive. Its significance is relative to the
stabilization of the Divine Siddhi in the world. The time of
my death is not determined by the karmas of this world. It
is determined by the event of this work itself, the bringing
of this Manifestation into life. When that work is complete, the death of this one will occur. It cannot be
predetermined, and there are no signs in my appearance
or in the state of the work that will help you figure it out. It
may seem like the work has not been completed, and yet I
may go. On the other hand, it might seem like the work has
been completed years ago and I am still hanging around.
All fascination with my death only reflects the individual's
refusal to yield the state of his own separateness. It is
making the Guru a symbol of that personal drama.

During this time you may see me behave very un-
conventionally, and you will tend to get involved in that.

Monday afternoon in the baths I was showing a peculiar way of manifesting the spiritual process relative to the conductivity of the life-force. It involved abandonment of the body in very much the same way that occurs in death. A subtle link was maintained, but all the signs of death began to appear. Many people in the Ashram began to feel reflections of that, experiences of psychic death and separation from the physical body. During the days that followed, when I had these people here at my house, I would lie about all day long, with very little apparent physical movement, sometimes going into a samadhi, abandoning physical movement and attention. It is just a sign of broadening the influence of this Siddhi. There are many things I have to do which require strange behavior, even temporarily leaving this body.

My social behavior couldn't get much more unconventional. During the rest of this period my physical appearance and my moods especially may change without apparent cause, but you shouldn't get involved in this social appearance and begin to think that difficulties have suddenly come upon you. None of this has anything to do with you in that personal way. You must be very responsible during this time. Your tendency will be to become irresponsible, to get a little crazy, or to succumb to the mood of difficulties that may be arising in your life. But that may not occur at all. It may be "sweet Jesus" from now until July. But if peculiar difficulties, frustrations, or negative influences seem to arise, just understand that it is like winter in New York. It gets lousy outside, so you put on a heavy overcoat. Don't get upset, don't get involved in the drama that is appearing externally. Maintain the condition of Satsang with great intensity. Intensify the life of a devotee during this time. Then you will be serving this event.

When it is completed, the capacity of individuals to maintain the life of a devotee will be increased, because obstacles in the world-process will have been removed. This is what has been happening for some time now. This is a transformation of the world-condition, not just a transformation of individuals. At this time I am involved with something that transcends work with individuals, although individuals will also see a reflection of that in their own lives.

This world in itself and as it is does not have any capacity whatsoever for enduring the Divine Presence. It is bound through centuries of ritual, cultic, separative living, so that every piece of the psyche, every cell in every manifest body is determined to separate itself and resist the Divine influence. The Divine Manifestation is not permitted in this world. It is the ultimate taboo. Happiness, ecstasy, freedom, are taboo even in purely social terms. That resistance exists in the very material of life, and we are only reflecting it socially. The world is a massive resister of the Divine event.

Whenever the Divine event is manifested in some way, whenever it somehow creeps through all this and manages to slip in, then it has dutifully to transform all of the world's conditions. I had to spend many of the early years of my life transforming my own psycho-physical vehicles so they could be an instrument for the Siddhi with which I had come. Only when that transformation had been accomplished could I begin to teach and serve others. Just so, now I must be dealing with things that transcend or conventionally stand apart from my own psycho-physical form, or the psycho-physical forms of individuals.

I have described to you how several weeks ago a change began to occur in the manifestation of the Divine Light. It began to move down into this plane like a shower. Previously, my way of working with people was to intensify that Light from above, just as earlier in the work

I used to step down and work it through them. In the last several weeks it has become possible to shower it down, rather than simply to intensify it. That doesn't simply happen over each person's head. It is a pre-cosmic manifestation. That this change could occur is a reflection of how the Siddhi of this work has begun to move into the world-process in a way that it hasn't done before.

Ordinary men have broken their connection with the Source of this Light, even with the Source of the life-force, so they enclose themselves in their self-concept, their twenty watts, and live out its destiny, gradually decreasing to the point of death. While alive, they do not live an unbroken connection to the present Source of the life-force. But the life-force is continually being created. It is not smacked into your body when you are born, frozen there while you live, and then run out when you die. It is a present, ongoing creation. Even so, men do not live that direct connection to the Source of their own life, and the Source of all forms, subtle and gross.

The significance of this rain is that it represents the breaking down of that separation between life and the complete, ongoing process of its creation. Now the devotee can enjoy the reestablished connection with the Source of the life-force without having to go through some massive self-conscious sadhana. It is flowing down, being pressed into the world, so the massive implications of that traditional separation are undone, and it becomes easier for people who are living in the Condition of Satsang to become sensitive to their present dependence upon the Divine. For those who are unconscious of it, though, it doesn't make a hell of a lot of difference.

It requires a very difficult yoga of a cosmic kind for this manifestation to steady itself, so that the world-obstruction will not limit devotees. Once that is established, then devotees again have only their own limitations to deal with. But the world itself will no longer be like some vast daemonic presence that ultimately prevents the process from taking place.

The work of this one, like the work of all those who have served in this way before, is to break down the fundamental limitation of this world so that this world may be lived in God. But it requires more than a few speeches. It is not an airy-fairy philosophical enterprise. It has required the suffering of vast billions of beings over a vast time to do this little bit we are doing. It will continue to take a great deal of sacrifice. It is a life and death affair, not just philosophy.

5. GARBAGE AND THE GODDESS

During the first couple of weeks in April, Bubba continued to party almost every night. Remarkable spiritual experiences continued to arise for many, until the end of the first week in April. Then things seemed to become suddenly quiet within, and this was a puzzle to those who were most fascinated and consoled by the drama of recent events. Sal and Neil remained at the house, but now more and more others were invited, and the whole Ashram took on a mood of celebration independent of the cycle of "spiritual" experiences.

Bubba had postponed Satsang until ten o'clock on the evening of April 15, when he gave the talk which forms the substance of this chapter. When everyone convened in the Satsang Hall, they found it was not to be the usual silent sitting. A number of people from Bubba's house came over with messages from him about the current quality of life in the Ashram. One of us was talking about humor, when Bubba unexpectedly entered the Satsang Hall.

Garbage and the Goddess

DEVOTEE: Bubba, what I don't understand is how you see the humor in everything.

BUBBA: I don't see the humor in anything whatsoever. If you look closely, there is nothing to be humorous about. There is no justification for any kind of humor at all. Humor has nothing whatever to do with what you can

101

perceive. Humor has to do with God. There is no humor in
life. In life you have comedy and tragedy. It is either
funny, or it is tearful. Has anybody ever found any humor
in life? Humor is free, but all there is to perceive in life is
limitation. Some of the limitations are comic, and some of
the limitations are sad, and there are qualities in between
that are more or less like those two. But in life all you see
are qualities, limitations. There is no humor in it. When
you perceive the Divine in the midst of any world
whatsoever, then humor becomes the quality you *present*
to life. But you can't find it *in* life. You have to bring it. In
the revelation of Satsang, the knowing of the humor in all
things becomes possible. Apart from it, there is no humor.

DEVOTEE: I have a question. I'm not sure I can ask it.
The question has something to do with surrendering, with
throwing things away. My sense that my volitional
throwing of anything away has very little to do with my
capacity to do it.

BUBBA: It is very simple. Every time I met Rudi[1] he
would hand me a bag of garbage. I don't think I ever went
to see Rudi when he didn't hand me a bag of garbage. It is
true. I can't remember a time when I went to see Rudi
when he didn't hand me a bag of garbage. It was always
the first thing he would do. Then I would go and throw the
garbage away, and I'd come back, and we'd sit together a
little bit, or I'd do some work. Sooner or later he'd give me
some more garbage. It is really very simple. You just throw
it away.

It makes it much simpler when it's in a paper bag. It
has all those oily spots. You know what a garbage bag looks
like, with all those greasy spots on the outside. It was

---

[1]Albert Rudolph, an American adept of the yoga of the descending life-force who
served as Bubba's first human teacher. For more details, see *The Knee of Listening*,
pp. 39-59.

always very easy for me. I could see from the paper bag itself that it was garbage! The first few times, I probably looked into the bag, but after awhile I would just look at the bag itself, and if it had grease spots on it: "Aha! Garbage."

After awhile, whatever Rudi gave me I would throw away. Even if it wasn't in a paper bag, I threw it away. He used to give me the sculpture and art pieces that I bought

from him in a paper bag. And I threw all that away. I don't
have any of it any more. The key to the matter is not *how*
to throw the garbage away. The key to the matter is
recognizing that it is garbage. It doesn't take a lot of
subtlety. It takes a little observation. As soon as you see it
is garbage, you know immediately that you should throw it
away. There is nothing to do with garbage but throw it
away! I don't know what else to do with it. So doesn't it
seem like a simple matter?

You are just looking at a lot of garbage and thinking
that it is the precious instrument of God. One of my jobs is
to package it. I spend a lot of my time packaging your
garbage, trying to get you to recognize it. You'll throw it
away as soon as you see it. You can't surrender something
that you don't recognize to be garbage. You intuitively
hold on to it. So you've got to recognize it.

But I'll tell you right now—it is *all* garbage! Everything the Guru gives you is garbage, and he expects you to
throw it away, but you meditate on it. All of these precious
experiences, all this philosophy. (Leaning toward the
microphone, in a confidential tone) Bruce, would you
mind throwing that away? Bruce just had a kriya. All of
these experiences are just more of that same stuff, but
you've read so much bullshit spirituality and religion and
all that, so you think all of these things are the Divine
itself. None of them is the Divine. They are garbage.

You are being asked to sacrifice everything! Sacrifice
is what you are being asked to do. In the midst of this
process of Satsang everything is revealed. Everything is
dredged up. Everything is shown. And you become very
attached to all these shiny and extraordinary things. You
are distracted by them. But they are not God. As soon as
you become distracted by anything, you bind yourself to
the pond again. Everything grasped and owned becomes a
hedge for Narcissus. A bit of immunity. As soon as you
think that you have it, you have isolated yourself again.

You have protected yourself from the necessary mortality of this life.

The point is not surrender. Rudi always used to say, "Surrender, surrender, surrender!" But my teaching is re-cognition, consciousness, and consciousness intensified manifests as self-observation. When there is understanding, *then* surrender is the obvious course. It is very easy. Sacrifice is the principle of all the worlds, but it is possible only on the basis of real and prior consciousness.

The worlds in themselves are the manifest modification of the Goddess, Shakti, and no one throws that away. Everyone is fascinated by it. So the principle of sacrifice is not served by the Goddess, the endlessly modified Force of the worlds. The principle of sacrifice is served by the Lord, to whom the Goddess is also bound, even if she does not know and show it. The world itself is an endless distraction in which the principle of sacrifice is made impossible by experience. The Guru serves the principle of sacrifice. The Goddess does not. The Goddess with all of her experiences serves the principle of experience, of accumulation, of immunity, of manifest self-existence in limitation. So there is no surrender in the world. The demand for love and for sacrifice is anathema in the cult of this world. It can't happen. No philosophy or experience can convince you of it. But you may be served by the revelation of all this as garbage, as mediocrity. It is shown to you in Satsang. Then you are expected to throw it away.

You are expected to throw it away under the most extraordinary conditions, conditions in which you would ordinarily not even consider throwing it away. You are sitting in the precious blissfulness of the spine. Why should you throw it away? It is all so delicious. You have been an asshole all your life, and now you are a yogi! Why should you throw that away? No one wants to do that. You don't want to throw it away. You have no humor, no detachment, no separation from all this that you've accumulated through vast aeons of existence in form. You don't want to throw it away. The demand to throw it away is mad, impossible.

Everyone succumbs to the Goddess on one level or another. Some succumb in very subtle ways, but most men succumb in very ordinary ways, without even knowing the Goddess as such. They succumb to the mass of experiences, of accumulations, of consolations. Everyone is consoled. When your consolations are ripped off, you find something else to be consoled by. One thing after the next. You don't surrender it, because you don't recognize it. So the Guru's perfect function is to undermine all this, to make the world show itself. He makes the Goddess pull down her pants, and then you see her asshole. I shouldn't be saying these things.

DEVOTEE: Perhaps you're out of line.

BUBBA: I think I *am* getting out of line. I shouldn't say these things. "The Goddess is beautiful. Surrender and let her show you everything." That sounds better, right? "Let the Goddess face you. She has bracelets and necklaces and her vagina is adorned. Don't let her turn to the Divine and show you her asshole. Let her face you with her breasts falling out." That's the teaching of the traditions. But the Teaching of the Guru has the Goddess always facing *him*. He shows *you* where she's at, he shows you her dependence on the Absolute, and enables you to commit the sacrifice. Then it is not difficult. When the Guru shows you the true nature or condition of the Goddess, then you become capable of sacrifice. Until that time you aren't capable of it, because you are enamored by the force of life.

At least that is the way it seems to me. What do I know? This could just be an aberration. Must be. No one agrees with me. I've never met anyone who agreed with me. I've talked to many people. I've talked to many

teachers, and none of them agrees with me. They all tell
me that I'm mad, that I'm undeveloped. So that must be
so. If you consult the usual books they won't tell you such a
thing. I've read them all myself. Rudi used to tell me to
surrender, but that is not the principle. Muktananda[2] used
to say, "Yield to the Goddess," and that is not the
principle. The Goddess used to say, "Yield to me," and I
fucked her brains loose. I've never listened to anyone.
Perhaps I should have!

What is required of you is this sacrifice, and sacrifice
only becomes possible under the influence of the perfect
Siddhi of God, not under the influence of any of the
manifest siddhis of the Goddess. The Guru is that Siddhi's
instrument in the world, because he establishes conscious
connection with devotees. All of those who come to the
Guru rest their attention on the Guru to various degrees.
In those who first come to the Guru, the attention is minor.
Hopefully it is real, but it is minor. Everything that occurs
to the student that makes him become a disciple and
ultimately a perfect devotee is an intensification of that
attention, and, therefore, an increase in his capacity for
this sacrifice.

It is real sacrifice, not a sacrifice in the traditional
sense of some gloomy self-abnegation and emptying. It is
the sacrifice which is itself humor and love, in which there
is nothing whatsoever to be attained. There is nothing to
be attained. I mean nothing. Have I said it? *Nothing*, damn
it! There is nothing to be attained. Not one thing is to be
attained. *Nothing*. There is not a single thing to be
attained. Have I said it? There is no experience, no vision,
no transformation of state.

All the traditions serve your need to change your
state, because you are suffering, because the dilemma is
the condition you acknowledge in your deep unconscious

[2]Swami Muktananda, an adept of the yoga of the ascending life-force, who served as
Bubba's teacher after Rudi. See *The Knee of Listening*, pp. 67-131.

life. You feel a need, and you are motivated to overcome it, to pursue changes of your state. All the traditions of life and spirituality, the entire cultic existence of man, is a goad to changes of state. But no change of state is necessary for the realization of Truth. Sacrifice *in place* is the condition of realization, not accumulation of new conditions of any kind, not heavens, visions, kriyas, forces. All those things are changes of state. They are an accumulation, an accumulation of garbage. They act like a hedge around the ego and protect it from its fear of obliteration. None of them is necessary.

This world, or any world, is in itself only changes of state. There is no doubt about that. They will continue. It is not necessary to zip into the soup of non-transformation. What is necessary is to realize the principle of sacrifice so that change may become the principle of existence

without fear. Then all things will be given to you that are necessary and appropriate, but you will stand happy and full of humor in the midst of life.

One of the traditional images of spiritual life that has come down for centuries is the ladder, the way of ascent to the place beyond, to heaven, to the Divine above the world. The ladder, along with other such archetypes, is the image of attainment, the image of the perfect change of state. It is absolutely false, and yet it is the principal archetype of spirituality and religion! The Divine is not apart and above and elsewhere, to be attained at another time in the midst of some condition or another that you may or may not imagine. That is not the Truth. The Truth is the present One, the absolute Divine that may not be attained, that may not be ascended to, that does not even descend upon you, but which is perfectly and already your present Condition.

It is realized only in the sacrificial realization of your perfect Condition, the Heart, the Very Self, the absolute intuition of Very God. That is the Truth. But the traditions of spirituality or of ordinary life do not serve that principle, the principle of the radical Presence. Rather, they all serve the principle of the change of state. Men don't have principal insight into the movement of life, and yet they act, and they become exploitable by the traditions, all of which have been created on the same basis by other men who were likewise suffering, and who felt momentary relief in some experiental state or another. The traditions have only felt the comedy that men may attain. All those ways are absolutely false.

There is absolutely no way. There is no way. There is no path. None. In order to know that with certainty you must realize that the paths are garbage. You must see it all in the paper bag. So part of the sadhana of this Satsang is the continuous revelation of the manifest garbage of your life. Until you begin to recognize it, Satsang is not working

in you in Truth. It is serving the Goddess, the path of
distraction, of fascination. It moves you on to changes in
ignorance. Satsang serves you in Truth when with everything that arises comes also the recognition, the re-cognition, the knowing again, of changes themselves, of
manifest things, forces, forms, and experiences.

This display of Power through the agency of the true
Devi[3] that has been taking place in the last couple of
weeks is fundamentally a test to lead you into the life of a
devotee, to lead you to sacrifice, to lead you to the
re-cognition of the garbage, of the limitation, of the
suffering involved in all clinging. None of this is intended
to be a revelation of the thing that is, as if all of this cosmic
rain were the very Truth. It is not. It is just the bangles of
the Goddess. If you don't recognize that and don't see her
as the Devi, facing the Divine, if you face her yourself and
become fascinated, become full of lust for her, then this
revelation is no revelation at all. It is a form of suffering, of
bondage. The Divine appears always through the agency
of the Goddess, the Devi-Power, to test all beings, to
transform their activity into that simple turning to God for
which the Goddess herself *is* responsible.

DEVOTEE: It seems that responsibility in every sense
that I've ever recognized it or related to it is absolutely
irrelevant to what you are talking about.

BUBBA: Yes. It is not responsibility in the usual sense.
Responsibility in the usual sense is a willful attitude, a
humorless attitude. True responsibility, however, is natural to the devotee. It is living the Condition that has

<hr>

[3]The Goddess or manifesting Power in her true form, already and consciously in
dependent union with the unmanifest, all-pervading, and very God. As such she always
serves the Divine or Guru-Siddhi, and does not bind men through the agency of
perception and cognition. She continually sacrifices herself, her independence (Maya)
and all her forms to the Lord.

been shown. Satsang is the responsibility of the devotee, not all the petty responsibilities and mortal seriousness of the usual mediocre follower. Happiness is the responsibility. Freedom is the discipline. It is very difficult, so people tend to take on humorless disciplines instead, nasty little disciplines of limiting themselves, being ascetic, being believers, all that horseshit.

The fundamental responsibility is that mood that arises in Satsang itself, that ecstasy, that love, that relational force, that unreasonable happiness in which the complexion of consciousness is free moment to moment from the continuous cognition or meditation on the separate self. That is the only and perfect responsibility, and it carries through to all the forms of life, all the functional conditions. A continuous purification is established. The garbage is revealed and thrown away.

The principle of purification established in Divine Satsang is entirely different from the principle of purification established in the common yoga. In the uncommon or great traditional yoga, not the yoga of willful effort, with all kinds of mantras and practices, but the yoga of the Shakti, purification takes place through the movement of the life-force, and there are lots of dramatic psycho-physical events. But the purifying sadhana of the Divine Satsang is that of the Force of the Very Self, the absolute Divine, and it may produce the purifying event without any of those manifestations at all. This does not mean that you should suppress them. They may very well occur as a secondary matter, as you have all seen. But the principle of this Satsang must be understood, and that will enable the manifest purifying force of the Shakti to show itself for what it is, to show garbage to you, to be known as garbage so that it serves the principle of sacrifice in you. Then the Goddess Shakti serves you in the manner of the Devi. If you forget that, then all the purifying events in the secondary affair of yoga will become binding.

It is not to any of these events that you must be turning, not to the kundalini events or even the non-having of kundalini events. It is to Satsang, this very principle, this real attention that is Satsang or Divine Communion. It is attention to the Guru as Guru, attention to the Guru as the manifest agent of the very Divine, attention to the Guru and through the Guru to the Divine, the absolute Divine, the absolute intensity of Real-God. If you continually do that from moment to moment, whatever phenomena are peculiar to you by tendency will arise. And the purifying event may take place dramatically, in the yogic sense, or undramatically, as an intensification of real intelligence, as re-cognition without secondary yogic manifestations. In either case, there is one process, and you must begin to grasp it.

When you grasp it, your humor will be restored, and it will consist of unreasonable happiness and love, an ecstasy that transcends all the cultic influences of this life, which are immense and cannot otherwise be resisted. You cannot overcome this world, but the Divine has already overcome this world. Those who become the true devotees of the Divine in the Presence of the true Guru-Siddhi are free of the world, and they may live in the world as the Presence of the Divine, as the Presence of love, of freedom, of prior happiness, of conditionless bliss.

That happiness does not appear only as a kind of ecstatic madness, but as an ordinary, human, and enjoyable life—free of the fucking Divine vision! The Divine vision is just the asshole of the Goddess, except it is not recognized as such by seekers. They think, "Oh, it is the Lord." They couldn't care less about the Lord, because to know the Lord would require them to be obliterated. The Lord in Truth requires the sacrifice of self-existence. Nobody wants such a thing. They want the Goddess, who will pamper them, and fuck them, and delight them. That is what people want.

DEVOTEE: It seems that one of the last things that arises is this really heavy fear that stops you cold and keeps you from living Satsang. Does that have to arise before I can start living that Force?

BUBBA: No. It will continue to arise, because it is fundamental to the life of Narcissus. It says in the Upanishads, "Wherever there is an 'other,' fear arises." Your whole life, every moment of an ordinary life, is at its very core built on this separate self sense. Therefore, there is nothing but meditation on the sense of otherness, of separation. For the usual man, there is always fear. Whenever the hedges of ordinary life, the occupations and distractions of Narcissus, are broken down through the influence of the Power of Satsang, then you will also tend to return to your fear.

That is all right, because it is naked. It is good to know the core of your own event, and that fear will continue to arise until there is the perfect re-cognition, the knowing again of that fear itself, of what it contains, of that of which it is the manifestation. It is the manifestation of your own activity in this moment. You are frightened because you are separating yourself in this moment, and that fear will never dissolve fundamentally until you have dissolved perfectly. What you fear is that dissolution of yourself, and that is the fundamental sacrifice. Everything, all the hedges about Narcissus, the separate one, may be surrendered, but the principal sacrifice is at the center, on the altar, the ego.

DEVOTEE: Until then Narcissus is doing the sacrificing?

BUBBA: Right. He can go to some yogi who will say, "Surrender, surrender." But who is going to surrender? Narcissus is going to surrender. He loves it. All his surrendering is a game which reinforces his self-nature. In itself, that willful surrendering is his hedge. The holy man builds a fantastic hedge about himself. He possesses incredible security, because he has let go of everything but himself. His "nothing" is a vast, infinite hedge that protects his self, his separateness. No one will yield that separateness except in the face of the unconditional Divine. When the very Divine is intuited in Satsang, then the self is let loose spontaneously, and with more and more intelligence. As that sacrifice begins to occur, there is also the release from fear, until there is utter fearlessness, not because you have become like King Kong with all of your yogic siddhis, but because you have become nothing in God.

That is what you are afraid of, and with good reason. No one wants to let go of that one because that is all they have got, really. Everything else can be lost, and you can still be standing there as a particle in the midst of infinity. That is really the only thing you are holding on to. And there is nothing there! It is your own fist. There is nothing inside it, but you are hanging on anyway. It is just a concept, a modification of your own awareness. It has no fundamental existence at all. You will continue to be frightened of its dissolution until you know its nothingness, until you know the Divine who is omnipresent, who *is* existence.

DEVOTEE: How does that occur?

BUBBA: Very simply. Turn to me and it is very simple. Everything else you do will be difficult. If you turn to me, I will destroy you.

DEVOTEE: If I turn to you in the moment of that fear, will you destroy me?

BUBBA: I am always doing that. You are turning to me

now in that moment of fear. There is a great deal to be undone. All these mediocre meetings, all these momentary sightings, all these sittings, all these hours of study, all these times of living in the Ashram, all these days, all this is the contact with me that serves that dissolution. It is undoing it, but not by magic. It only takes place where there is consciousness in the devotee. Only through the process of re-cognition in the devotee does it occur, not by taking it out of him by magic, without his participation, like a thorn in his side, but in the midst of his participation. It absolutely requires the functions of awareness.

You don't turn properly to me in your fear by rushing over to my house terrified and throwing yourself down by my couch. More than likely I'd just offer you a beer or tell you to cook dinner for me. It is by the ongoing life of Satsang that it is done, by *always* resorting to me, not only when you are most frightened, but also when you are most mediocre. The times when it is most difficult to turn are the better times to turn to me, because those are the times when you are dealing with the most. When you are really mediocre and oppressed, when even your turning is impossible, those are the times to turn, to do the sadhana of this prior happiness. Narcissus isn't undone by dramatic efforts at surrendering externally, but by real intelligence, real turning to the Guru. It is in the midst of life and tendencies that it is all undone.

It is very simple. It can be done in this very moment without any drama. Just see it. What are you doing? What are you always doing? What are you doing now? Grasp it. See this sensation of the separate self, see yourself pressing your fingers into your palm and feeling that sensation and meditating on it. This is what you are always doing. Know it again, and see what is prior to that grasping. Fall into it. Fall into Satsang and grasp onto nothing after that. Throw everything away but That, and continually know That. Continually enquire in that real sense.

In other words, I am demanding that you continually see this contraction or self-meditation as your own activity and fall into the state that preceded all this clenching and grasping. That is Self-realization, that is God-knowledge, and it is free. It is independent of all experiences, all changes of state, all present states. It is utterly free. When you fall into it with absolute intensity you are absolutely free, free of all the worlds, of all conditions, of all transformations. Then, paradoxically, not only are you free of them all, but you become capable of them all. You become capable of life in the usual sense, and it becomes theatre. It becomes a humorous display of qualities, positive and negative.

Then life becomes a drama that is *not* leading to the Divine. It is leading nowhere. Life is not leading anywhere. The earth has not been created in order ultimately to evolve into the Divine state. The earth is just what it is. It may become more glamourous, or it may just fall apart. It could become more glamourous, but that wouldn't make it Divine. This world is just a limitation, like all of the endless infinities of billions of other worlds. All of them are just limitations. Apart from all of that, and also absolutely coincident with it, is the Divine, and those who know the Divine in whatever world they appear are free, and that world becomes Divine theatre for them. They don't always look to go to some other world. They live in God and play out the present event. Such is the habit of wise men. Wise men are all fools, useless people, madmen, because they don't look for another place. They can throw this one away. And they are always throwing it away by living it with humor, the humor of the prior or Divine Condition.

DEVOTEE: It seems that your attitude toward intelligence is that it is the conscious participation in our own murder.

BUBBA: Yes, you may say so. But such images are themselves the kind of delicious symbolism that Narcissus
creates. He wants to be killed and all that shit. It is just
more drama. There is no one being killed. You can watch
that separate one being murdered. You can make him a
sacrificial lamb. That won't make you free. No one is being
murdered. There is only the turning about of the principle
of consciousness into its true Nature and Condition. The
thing that is being murdered is unreal to begin with. It is
unreal anyway, so why become involved in the murder? If
it seems like murder to you, it is only because you are
holding on to the body, the psycho-physical body, holding
on to all of these things instead of realizing they are
garbage. You are not allowing the sacrifice really to take
place.

It is not to annihilation that you are invited. It is to
the fullness of God that is happy and free. There is no
murder involved in such an event. Only Narcissus can be
murdered, because everything that is required of him is
something he is unwilling to yield. So he suffers everything. It is all being ripped off.

DEVOTEE: Could this go unnoticed?

BUBBA: Absolutely. I was talking earlier this evening
about the event in the Vedanta Temple, which I have
described in *The Knee of Listening*.[4] Nothing happened at
that time. There was nothing left over. There wasn't some
little particle of me that said, "Ah, yes. It is all over now,
and I have realized the Self." No one knew that anything
had happened to me. I had just gone down to the bookstore that afternoon, and I came home again. We had
dinner and watched television. Nothing had happened.

---

[4]This refers to the terminal events of Bubba's sadhana, his perfect undoing and Divine
Realization. See *The Knee of Listening*.

DEVOTEE: It was no big deal.

BUBBA: No. All big deals are shy of it. The absolute thing is unmentionable. But it involves a profound intuitive realization that becomes apparent when things begin to arise again in a very different way. The implications of the Vedanta Temple event began to clarify themselves as time passed, but in itself that event wasn't even an event. It was simply the falling out of all conditional realizations, all conditional meditation. It was the falling out of the separate self life and strategy of Narcissus. So there was nothing left to cognize. It was all very simple.

DEVOTEE: No ecstasy? No relief?

BUBBA: No. No blisses. No kundalini. No energy ecstasies. No life-force transcendence. There was no limited witnesser, no enjoyer. There was nothing to enjoy. Everything had been released into its ordinariness. There was no sublimity, no extraordinary thing. As time went on everything that continued to arise, ordinary and extraordinary, showed itself over against the perfect Self. That perfect Self knew without limitation the things of this world which were formerly known in the conventional way. A new Siddhi of existence began to manifest. In itself that perfect transformation is not even an event. It is unmentionable. It is prior to all conditions, prior to life, prior to realizations.

DEVOTEE: I remember the feeling I had when my child was born that this was the closest thing to God that I could imagine, this child, and that she had just come from God. That was my feeling, and I was peaceful and happy with that closeness with her in the first days after she was born. Then I began to feel my own contraction. My own fear was kind of messing up the relationship, and I began to

become concerned for this child I believed was from God.
What I wonder is, how can we know God? How can we go
back? How can we go far enough back?

BUBBA: You cannot.

DEVOTEE: What?

BUBBA: You cannot. He is not back. Motherhood is the
instrument through which the Goddess gets you. You love
it. You were busy thinking that little shitter was from God,
when you yourself were something you could not see as
from God. You missed the Divine in everything except for
that one other person, who was just another dingbat like
yourself, for whom you were the physical instrument.
Motherhood is just a binding archetype for you, and it still
binds you. It is an illusion. Giving birth is no more Divine
than taking a crap. It is just another process, like breathing
and working. It is just another event. If you were so
sensitive to see the Divine in a child, why weren't you
sensitive enough to see the Divine everywhere else? Well,
you were not, and you did not truly see the Divine in your
child. It just locked you into that sentimental image, and
that is what truly has you. In it you perceive not God, but
your separateness.

DEVOTEE: How exactly can you get out of that game?

BUBBA: I think I have been talking about it this evening.

DEVOTEE (the same): Bubba, before you, what was there
to do?

BUBBA: God has had agents from time to time. The
Divine Process has never been absent from this world.
Perhaps for you, before "me" there was no involvement

with That. But it is not by going back or going to
something that there is realization of God. That is all
garbage. Motherhood is garbage. Children is garbage. It is
all garbage. It is all distraction. It all feeds the limited
self-nature and its cult of strategic games. It all binds you
to that principal drama, and it should be understood as
such. It is not that all human beings are literally garbage
and should all be sent to the gas chamber, but your whole
participation in existence, the whole drama of existence
that you ordinarily cognize and demonstrate from hour to
hour, is garbage. It is your own limitation, the theatre of
your suffering. It must be understood, rather than holding
on to some piece here or there as if that in itself were the
Divine.

The Divine is unmanifest, the Divine does not appear
as a piece. The Divine is absolute, entire, all-pervasive,
perfect, not to be found in some place, some thing, some
archetype, some moment, some experience, some state.
When you truly despair of all of those things and know
them to be garbage, then the release occurs. Then the
sacrifice becomes possible, and you fall into the Divine,
who is Present, not above the world, not to be found, not
elsewhere, not grasped, but fallen into, always already
existing, of which all things are the manifestation. Not the
Divine who is Himself manifest in some thing, but of
whom all things are the manifestation in the sense that
they are all His modification. When you see through them,
when you recognize them, then you know Him. When you
hold on to some thing as Him, it becomes illusory. It is only
the necklace of the Goddess, but it doesn't show itself to
consciousness as such. It only binds, only holds you, and by
those means it reinforces your meditation on the separate
self, which is Narcissus.

That is what the archetype of Narcissus at the pond is
all about. It is meditation on separate self existence. It is
not some guy who is enamored of a homosexual self-image.

It is every person's continuous activity, self-meditation, meditation on existence as a limited self event. For such a one, even the great events, even the events that seem to be happiest and freshest, such as giving birth, lead to sorrow, because they serve that self-meditation. Therefore, such an experience, like any other, requires understanding, the understanding that arises in Satsang, in the Presence and Condition of the Divine. Only in such a Presence is there release, because that Presence is the perfect Self, the Very Nature that you are, and it releases you from the meditation on the separate self, which is an illusion, a sensation, a form of cognition, not of actual existence. The separate self is cognized, not lived. It is cognized first, then appears to be lived in the dramatization of life. That cognition of separate self existence must be undone. There must instead be the perfect intuition of the Very Self or Real-God. Then life is lived as God, with humor.

DEVOTEE: Once you have fallen into this prior state and are no longer contracted in the manner of Narcissus, is this something you can lose?

BUBBA: Why should you want to fall out of it? Why are you concerned? No, you cannot fall out of it.

DEVOTEE: Do you consciously have to continue to live that?

BUBBA: Yes, because it *is* consciousness. It is not something consciousness does or knows. It is consciousness. So when it is truly realized there is no danger, no falling from it, because it is not held in place by anything. It is not dependent on anything. So when it is truly realized, not just known in an experiential sense or known philosophically, but truly known, when that principal sacrifice has taken place, there is no falling back. It is not possible. The tendency does not exist in God. The tendency exists in the

conventional theatre of manifest beings. So when you have
fallen into the God-Condition, the tendency is not there to
fall into the usual condition of a self-limiting manifest
being.

On the other hand, you don't fall into the soup. You
continue to live as a human being, if that is your present
condition, or a lizard, or whatever you are. You happen to
be a human being, so you will continue to live that in the
usual sense, because realization of the God-Nature is not

anathema to human existence or worldly existence. It is, in fact, the very principle of it. The Very Self or Real-God is the principle of the world, so to realize it is not to leave the world. It is to live the world in Truth, without fear and without any danger of relapse. When there is no longer any such danger, then you are humorous, then you are like the Guru, who sees humor in everything. You can afford to have such humor then. But if you have to hold it in place, you can't afford to be humorous. Every now and then you might get drunk or exalted, but you would have to keep it together. The Guru doesn't have to keep it together, and neither does the devotee, because he has fallen into that principle that is free of all strategies.

DEVOTEE: What are the signs that we are living Satsang?

BUBBA: Jesus supposedly said to all these guys who could see everything, who could read the weather and the natural cycles and the frog wars or whatever, who could do all kinds of divination, "You can do all this metaphysical reading of everything, but you can't see the signs of the times. You can't comprehend what you are actually up to, what drama human beings are truly involved in." Well, I see the signs of the times. I see very well what you are up to. But the signs are simply the signs of your complication. Merely to be a little happy, a little easy, a little more intense, is not sufficient for me, although it is pleasant enough. From the usual point of view, the Ashram is generally improving and intensifying as a whole. But it is time for fire. Things have been going on long enough. It is time to really do it. Then I will be happy with you. Then I will be glad that you are smiling. When you become communicative, when you become a real instrument, when you cease to be involved in your own sadhana and have become happy to live with each other and make Satsang available—those are the signs of the devotee. The

signs of the student and the disciple are his endless
involvement with his own transformation, and that is
basically what I see here. I see involvement with changes.

None of that involvement is necessary. There will
continue to be changes and experiences, and I have said
enough about the importance of all that. The signs of the
devotee are still uncommon. Because of that the Ashram is
continually dependent on my personal influence. I have to
get everybody back into line all the time. I must create all
these spiritual dramas for everybody to witness, in order to
keep their enthusiasm up so I can hold on to them long
enough for the real work to begin in them. Otherwise they
will be going on to the next affair. So a little change is not
very interesting to me. But I'm a bastard. Anybody
else would be satisfied with you.

Some of you have seen lately the difference between
the two great aspects of this Siddhi alive in this Satsang.
The one is the purifying influence of the Force manifestation which you saw a lot of in the last several weeks. You
have seen it many times in the Ashram, but a recent
example was these weeks that just preceded last week.
But then, during the last week or so, things have become
quieter, and you may have become sensitive to the other
and more fundamental aspect of that Siddhi, and that is
the Siddhi of the Heart-manifestation, in which the
purifying intensity is of another kind and functions quite
differently.

It doesn't appear in the form of the typical kundalini
manifestations. It doesn't appear in the form of movement. It is a moveless intensity that grasps consciousness
and draws it into itself. It manifests as absolute peaceful-
ness and fullness, and purifies immediately, directly,
without all the secondary, dramatic purifications
necessarily arising. And even if they arise, they are at least
shown against that fundamental and prior forcefulness
that is the Heart, the very Self, the intuition of Real-God.

A good deal of what has been going on lately has been a theatrical demonstration of the difference between those two aspects of this Siddhi, so that people will become sensitive to the true and perfect form of the Siddhi. That aspect of the Siddhi which is the Power of the Heart is not attractive or fascinating, because it is not experiential, and it doesn't exploit the search. It is boring to the usual man. He must pass through fascinations and experiential dramas of a kind, and, quite beside himself, fall into the Heart-Siddhi. When he begins to feel it and know it, then it becomes sufficient for him, and the other becomes secondary. He sees his relationship to the movement of the kundalini and the powers awakened above the mind, and he understands.

The ultimate event of this several week unfolding is the one that is taking place now. Even so, most of you didn't know that it was even happening, because it has been very quiet, and you thought the drama of revelation had come to an end. If you had rested a little bit and stayed with me another hour, you would have seen That instead of going to sleep in your mediocrity. But the opportunity to see it is still present.

I prefer that Heart to the kundalini and all powers. It is much more effective and beautiful and free, but it also manifests the kundalini processes wherever they are required, because the life-force also moves when the Heart is known. The life-force is part of this world, and this world is all about changes. Whenever there is release, purification, there tends to be the reestablishment and intensification of this movement of the life-force. Even in those who live the Satsang of the Heart, there continue to be experiences, descending and ascending, of the life-force. They need to be understood. They need to be known in Truth in the midst of this Satsang. I have said from the beginning that this is the Satsang of the Heart, not the Satsang of the kundalini, of the Shakti, of the Goddess.

DEVOTEE: I have noticed, Bubba, that this intensity is
the Guru alive, and when He sees that garbage, there is no
surrender involved. It is already at that point of recognition, it is already surrendered.

BUBBA: The realization of the Heart in this life does
everything that the kundalini can take hundreds of years
to do, because the kundalini operates principally on a
psycho-physical level. The Shakti is the source of the
kundalini manifestation. The phenomena we call the
kundalini arise only when the Shakti has been transformed
into the manifestation of the life-force. It is felt in
psycho-physical ways, internal ways. All the things called
the kundalini are life-force manifestations, and they are no
greater than that. They produce psycho-physical phenomena, not Divine Realization but meditation on the
psycho-physical instrument. Some of those modifications
are of a gross variety, such as kriyas, and some of them are
of a subtler variety, such as visions and lights. But none of
those things is in itself the realization of the true Nature
and condition of the Shakti, the Goddess. They are just the
adornments of the Goddess.

The Goddess is ultimately one with the God-Light
and therefore bound to the Heart. Her true Form is that of
the Devi, who shows only her dependence and nothingness, who shows all her revelations and forms to be
garbage, who acknowledges the Heart as Truth. Through
the mere agency of the kundalini process neither the
God-Light nor the Very Heart is necessarily realized.
There is just occupation with self-modification, with the
glamour, the hedges, the shrubbery around the pond of
Narcissus. It does not lead to the dissolution of the ego.
The merging of the life-force in the brain centers does not
produce dissolution of the ego. All it produces is distraction from the cognition of the ego. It is a temporary state,

and it cannot be maintained once the psycho-physical vehicle is dropped. When the psycho-physical vehicle is dropped, you fall back again into the court of the Goddess, with unconsciousness.

Only when the Heart is realized perfectly is the Goddess Shakti known and her display understood. In fact, when the Heart is truly known, then there is instant, immediate purification. There is, instantly, no bondage to limitations of any kind, to any mind-form, to any form of desire or action, including the cognition of separate self which is the root of all strategies. What I call the dilemma, the sense of dilemma, the feeling of dilemma, is simply the sensation that surrounds the cognition of the ego. The separate self sense is the dilemma, and it is undone only in the intuition of Real-God, only in Satsang. I am talking about Satsang in the perfect sense, not only the nominal sitting with the human Guru, but the perfect knowing, the perfect living of that Condition.

The true way is not grasping onto the bangles of the Goddess and letting her lift you up into her crotch through the spine until you realize God. The true way is to realize God in Truth. Then you know the Goddess as the Devi, and you also know the world, which is her modification, in Truth. It is God first, not God as the goal. God first. Satsang, in other words, as the principle of life. Then the world is known in Truth. Then all the psycho-physical manifestations are known in Truth. Then all the dramas of life, all the contracts of life, which are forms of conflict and dilemma, are known in Truth. It is not by doing something to them first that you realize God, but by actually realizing God first. In that realization there is perfect purification.

Via the way of the search, through the instruments of the Goddess, there is only piecemeal purification. It is an essentially humorless affair, because ego is not dissolved as the principle of such sadhana, but ego-dissolution is only pursued as its goal. In Satsang there is instant dissolution of the ego. Wherever there is true Satsang, there is no ego, and there is also purifying or secondary and psycho-physical work established on the basis of that intuition. Satsang becomes perfect, in other words, when the attention in Satsang is perfected to the point of the life of a devotee. Then there is also perfect purification, without movement, without support.

6. SPIRITUAL THEATRE

Talks like "Garbage and the Goddess" moved members of the community to give up their hold on ecstatic experiences, to "throw away" the garbage of their lives. But they found it was no simple matter. It required more than momentary intelligence, and more than merely mental understanding. The "re-cognition" of which Bubba spoke in that talk requires absolute intelligence, great and reckless intelligence, which cares nothing for any experience whatsoever.

By tendency, however, people are not interested in such a sacrificial existence. They want fulfillment, not obliteration. They refuse the Guru and resort to the Goddess, to experience. The effect of the Guru's Presence on anyone who doesn't understand is the constant stimulation of his tendencies, until he undergoes the crisis in consciousness which makes understanding possible. Thus, Bubba teaches by "lessons." A lesson is an instance in which certain of a person's tendencies are stimulated until he sees himself creating his own suffering through them, and truly realizes that they are unnecessary. It is a moment, in other words, of seeing that what is presently in the paper bag of life is only garbage. Once that occurs, he naturally and easily throws it away.

What is learned doesn't have an exclusive relationship to the circumstances in which it is learned. A devotee who sees the larger pattern of his attachment to his wife hasn't simply learned a lesson in particular about his wife. He hasn't even learned a lesson about himself, because the lesson is itself the recognition of his own non-existence as an independent entity. But he sees the falseness of a particular pattern of action by which he was compulsively feeding the notion of his separate self.

Bubba has said that when one understands, the world takes on an illumined quality, and that which seemed solid and limiting is revealed as fluid and free. This is not an intellectual discovery. It liberates a person at every level of his being. But upon seeing this, he is usually only able to articulate what he saw in particular about his separative activity, how that isn't necessary, and how good he feels. He has thrown away some garbage.

Lessons are a natural by-product of Satsang, like kriyas and other life-force manifestations, but they are not its perfect fruition. Bubba uses the word "lesson" with humor, because, when applied to genuine sadhana, it has a much different meaning than in common usage. There is only God from the beginning, and that is what is revealed in Satsang, so neither the learner nor the lesson itself is valued at all. The continual process of learning lessons can be experienced only by the individual. As long as he feels he is learning something, he hasn't learned anything, and he hasn't understood. The gradual realization of the many ways in which he distracts himself with food may be quite fascinating, but when he finally understands, he couldn't care less. Who could care? Understanding is an event in consciousness in which the foundation and support of the individual himself is undone.

Because they constantly lead to that sacrifice of the fundamental activity that is the ego, lessons take place in every area of life. In April, Bubba continued to create theatre that stimulated powerful tendencies in nearly all the members of the community. He played with all the attachments to husbands and wives, the desires for enlightenment, desires for personal attention from the Guru, resistances to change in the external circumstances of life. Through their involvement with this dramatic theatre, devotees also began to see the necessity for understanding in ordinary, non-dramatic moments of life as well, when taking a shower, eating lunch, being bored or ecstatic while driving to work.

Bubba "packages the garbage" in every dimension of existence, and he expects his devotees to throw it away. Craving the personal attention of the Guru and craving sexual release are both ordinary and conventional activities founded in suffering and dilemma. When the individual sees what he is up to in either case, he falls back into Satsang, the unobstructed and happy enjoyment of the Guru in God. Until then, though he may feel beleaguered and set upon, he is in fact simply buying experience, a "bangle of the Goddess," and refusing the Guru and his love. He is avoiding relationship. So many devotees describe their lessons simply by talking about how their dilemmas disappeared and how they enjoyed Bubba's love.

Bubba does not miss a chance to play on this very enjoyment, to turn devotees more and more intensely to him as he really is, the Divine. At the end of April, he began talking about the benign strategy of his behavior toward devotees as a piece of "romantic theatre." He said simply that the Guru appears in the world as the Heart, and that his function in the world is to turn devotees to the Heart, to himself.

> The symbol of Krishna and his gopis is a perfect description of the process involved in our Satsang. With women I may act like a lover, and with men like a close friend, but it is always the same thing. It is the creation of this conscious attachment. Everyone who attaches himself to the Guru immediately gets involved in the Divine, because the Guru is just a symbolic bit of theatre through which the Divine represents itself in the world. The Guru is

only interested in attaching people to himself.
Everything he sees: "Turn to me." So he seems to
enjoy a luxury that nobody else is permitted. As
soon as his devotees do anything but turn their
attention to him absolutely, he gets angry with
them, because he is the Divine in the world. And
the Divine demands absolute attention.

In the next two weeks Bubba elaborated upon this
theme, clarifying how he plays with the capacity in his
devotee to believe that he is special, "the beloved," in
order to involve him more and more with the Divine
process. He talked about his Divine Romance in such a
way that many devotees could see that perfect love and
perfect death in God are not different. Some devotees had
been involved in this romantic theatre with Bubba for
years, thinking they were dealing with a special "other,"
but now they suddenly saw that whole affair as only
another part of their absorption into the Divine. Bubba

draws devotees to him and frustrates their demands on him so that they must turn to their prior relationship with him, rather than maintain a superficial attachment to his human form.

When Satsang becomes the condition of a person's life, everything that arises to him externally, as well as in his subtle and intuitive life, serves the spiritual process. As long as he lives as a separate and separative individual, the devotee is refusing the Guru, and when he understands, his non-separation from the Guru is known. Satsang intensifies both the pain of separation and the fullness of love, so that the life of understanding takes the form of an ever-intensifying romance with God.

The often dramatic interactions between Bubba and his intimates provided symbolic representations to everyone of their personal relationships with him. The "gopis" served that exemplary function. Bubba had begun using the word "gopi" back in Los Angeles around Christmas, but he had applied it affectionately to all the women in the

Ashram. In the last week in March, Bubba began to ask
certain women to move into his household. Eventually, all
of them performed practical functions in the community,
but their primary function was that of "gopi," or one who
adores the Lord in human form, and this was something
new to the Ashram.

These women were always present when Bubba
invited others to his house for parties. They would sometimes help serve guests, clean Bubba's house, or do
laundry, or they might administer some principal area of
the Ashram's public work, but they were always absorbed
in attention to Bubba. In the next months the community
saw all of them become magnificent madwomen, obsessed
with God, always near Bubba, unless, for some reason, he
asked them to be elsewhere.

Because he is present as Love in the world, Bubba is
truly free, free to play the games of this world and to use
all its possibilities, including its pleasures. However it is
played, life contains nothing but limited phenomena, and
regardless of what he appears to be doing from a limited
point of view, the Guru's activity in the world is never
anything other than the complete, continuous sacrifice of
himself to devotees. Therefore, his Company is the perfect
form of discipline.

Bubba has talked about the paradox of his person and
his behavior:

> That is the drama, the excess permitted to the
> Guru, because the Guru is not a personality. The
> only reason he can perform the function of Guru is
> because he is dead. He is finished with all the cult
> and conventions of human life. He has already
> wrecked himself, so you don't have to worry about
> him. He is finished.

7. IT IS A GRACE

By the middle of May several months of extravagant eating and drinking had begun to take their toll on health. On the 16th Bubba returned from a short visit to San Francisco and declared a number of changes in the Ashram's present style of life. Everyone would resume a straight lacto-vegetarian diet the following Monday, and fast for seven to ten days a week later. Bubba said that he intended for us to continue this phase of Ashram life until early July, a period of about six weeks. That same day Bubba told Sal and Neil to move out of his house, and back to their wives. So everyone began to prepare for the new regime, after what seemed like months of continuous partying.

Even so, that weekend Bubba held the most uproarious extended party this Ashram has ever enjoyed. Friday night began somewhat soberly in the Satsang Hall, with Sal, Neil, and others describing their absolute resistance to maintaining Satsang. Bubba joined the meeting but didn't say anything. Afterward, however, Marcia conveyed Bubba's invitation to about forty-five people to come to his house immediately. They arrived in high spirits, packed into the living room, and started drinking, singing, and dancing. The party roared on all night.

Sunday night carloads of devotees left for San Francisco, and Monday morning breakfast at Persimmon consisted of yogurt and fruit, as usual, but without coffee now or a cigarette afterward.

The following Friday, after a week of straight eating and functioning, the San Francisco devotees returned to

Persimmon. Everyone gathered in the Satsang Hall for a study group. During the study group, Bubba arrived and spoke with us.

BUBBA: Everybody been feeling sufficiently toxic this week? (Laughter.) Feeling nasty and negative? (Laughter.) Confused and full of doubt? It's just lunch. There's nothing spiritual about it. So if you were going to ask some questions about that tonight, let's just forget about it. It will take you three or four weeks to start feeling smooth again in the vital. Everybody's got colds and is eliminating a lot of mucus. What goes in must come out. (Laughter.)

It's an interesting lesson, though, because the same thing that you think is so intimate to you, your thoughts and the things that arise in meditation, your emotions, all those things that you think are *you* in some way or another, are no more profound than these moods that are awakened when toxins are eliminated into the bloodstream. You must have very much the same kind of relationship to the things that arise in meditation and life in Satsang as you have to the qualities that arise in you during these periods of bodily purification. You have got to understand something about the mechanism involved and be straight. Don't get involved in concerns for all this stuff that's coming up in you. Don't start to dramatize it. It is only a lot of bad lunches, a lot of booze and cigarettes. As soon as you stop putting that stuff into your body, the body starts eliminating it, and it produces psychological as well as physical manifestations.

Under the pressure of the force of Satsang, a very similar process of purification is also established, and the same thing occurs. All kinds of stuff starts coming up, and it is not profound, it is just stuff, and your concern will not purify. So no concern for any of it is appropriate. You must simply understand the mechanism and go about your business, and be straight, and not dramatize all these feelings and sensations. Live Satsang. The purification is God's business. During these next several weeks you will have a lot of purifying signs in the body, the mind, and the psyche. They will have no significance whatsoever.

Does anybody have anything they would like me to talk about?

DEVOTEE: Someone quoted you as saying that you make an identification with us and then your meditation becomes ours. Do we become like you, or do you deal with us? Could you say something about that?

BUBBA: The whole affair of this Satsang and the apparent transformation of an individual is an immensely complex and paradoxical business, because the Guru appears in human form and so do you, but there is only God from the beginning. So there are many things that can be said about this process. The seeker, who is motivated by his dilemma, assumes that he has started out to find God, or realize the Truth, or get free, or whatever, and he's going to do certain things to bring that about, and eventually he is going to get there. This is absolutely false. There is nothing anybody can do to get free. Nothing any human being has ever done has ever liberated him or anybody else. Liberation is God's business. The human Guru is the instrument of that Siddhi, the function of God.

When you have gotten tired of trying to get free or find God, when you have gotten tired of being motivated in that way, then you may begin to feel your game. Then you may become available to the Guru, first perhaps by coming across the Teaching in some form. You begin to see something about it all by considering the Teaching. Finally, you enter into relationship with the Guru. In fact, he enters into relationship with you. The process of Satsang is not one in which you are given a remedy for your problem, a cure that you are supposed to perform on yourself, but one in which the fundamental Condition is that prior relationship, that Divine Communion. It is not a matter of your meditating yourself to the point of realization. The actual Siddhi of the Divine is activated in that relationship, and that Siddhi does the meditation. That Siddhi *is* the meditation.

The Guru assumes your enlightenment. He doesn't mechanically enlighten you, or give you something to do to enlighten yourself. He absorbs you. He is you to begin with, but the Guru in human form consciously assumes your Divine state in every function in which you appear. He assumes it in your very cells and literally, actively lives you. The Guru literally meditates you. He is in a position to do so, since he is you. The mystery of that process is how this kind of spiritual life is generated and fulfilled. It is fulfilled from the beginning. That Satsang is perfect. The disciple, a piece at a time, begins to become aware of the perfection the Guru has already generated in his case.

Also there are obviously ordinary or conventional forms of that Satsang. So the Guru in human form instructs, enters into various kinds of theatre with you at the level of life. You also see him in dreams and visions. There are endless ways in which this process is cognized by the disciple or the devotee. But from the point of view of the Guru, it is a very simple matter. There is God. He doesn't do anything more than assume that, but his assumption of That has become real, natural, spontaneous, and perfect. He even assumes it with his body, with his psyche, with his mind, naturally. Fundamentally, that is all he does. He enters into relationship with living beings in that spirit, and assumes the Divine in them, and lives all their functions, so that complex things begin to occur. Complex things begin to occur always as a result of very simple things.

Look at all the complex things that occur when you drink a glass of whiskey! It is a very complex affair, but that act itself is very simple. The manifestation appears complex, but the condition itself is simple. When you go on a fast, all you do is stop eating, but look at the dramatic things that occur! Basically, the Guru does something very simple, but the evidence of that is as complex as you are, as complex as the number of places and qualities and functions in which you read your existence. If you turn a light on in a room, it falls on everyone, on everything.

DEVOTEE: You spoke of an awareness that we will have of things that you have already brought about. Is there any way we can mess this up, or is it going to happen in any case?

BUBBA: You can seem to mess it up in time and space, and prolong all kinds of things, and complicate things, and you can turn away again, but the Guru will tussle with you in spite of your resistance. As certainly as God is, God will be

known. It is just that it may take you billions upon billions
of aeons. It is like the Dawn Horse vision that I have
described to you. There was this Siddha whose Siddhi was
to manifest things from nothing. His disciples lined up
before him, and he just sat there. At some point they all
saw that he had done it, fundamentally, and they all left.
But nothing had appeared yet. Franklin sat around for
awhile, and all of a sudden this horse appeared in the
middle of the room. Well, just so, in the case of the
devotee, his life as a perfect devotee of God is already
managed fundamentally and will appear, but how he
complicates that appearance is another thing. That is why
the life level of the Teaching and life in relationship to the
Guru are very important, because at that level all the
resistance in the individual is alive, and it must be dealt
with there.

I have told you how this event that is occurring now,
and that is to be fulfilled in early July, has already
fundamentally been accomplished. It has been done for
several weeks. It is like the Dawn Horse. It will appear.
Making this a relatively quiet time is like having everybody walk out of the room. It has been done. It is a way of
not putting a lot of attention on it, as if there were yet
something that had to be done to create it. There are a lot
of things you can do to complicate your awareness, your
enjoyment of it. What is occurring at this time is not
something terrifying. It is just the ever more intense
imposition of the Divine. If you are smart, you will allow
this time to uncomplicate you, to make you a devotee, to
simplify your approach. It is a time of renunciation, not in
the humorless traditional sense, but in the great sense, the
great sacrificial sense. It is fundamentally an enjoyment. I
am not going to feel any different six weeks from now.
Nothing is going to happen for me. It has already occurred. But you may *see* something different. It is the
Dawn Horse appearing. Maybe I will turn into a horse!

You are an interesting group of people. You are like the children of Israel. You are coming and going, you are up and down, you are big and small. You are reluctant to get it straight and pure and direct, and happy.

What else?

DEVOTEE: Could you talk about sacrifice being enjoyment?

BUBBA: Sure. You read about sacrifice in the New Testament and other books like that. Everybody talks about sacrifice and loving one another, and it is all so humorless. As soon as you set about trying to love everybody, you become a humorless asshole. As soon as you start to make sacrifices, you become a priest. You are not really sacrificing. You are only ritually duplicating the law of things. But sacrifice or love is what is already occurring. It is the nature of life. No special action needs to be added to your life to make it sacrifice. You have to become sensitive simply to what your life already is. Then, spontaneously, you will live the law, and you will love. Love is the nature of sacrifice, not putting your coat in the water so that somebody can step on it. Love is living without obstruction, without contraction, without the demand for attention, without creating your perimeter. That doesn't come about by doing all kinds of things to yourself. It is a Grace. It is Satsang. It is the life of understanding. Loving is also pleasurable. There is no doubt about it. Ecstasy is selflessness. Happiness is already sacrifice.

There are lots of apparently unfortunate things that can occur that are also sacrifice, because all things are sacrifice. The religious person tends to say, "Sacrifice is doing these things I do not like to do. If I do not enjoy all those things that I like, that will also be sacrifice." But sacrifice is the nature of *all* of that, including the pleasurable and the apparently unpleasurable. All of that is sacrifice, the yielding of self, the yielding of the drama of Narcissus. Sacrifice is one with the pleasurable state of God-realization, of true Self-realization. It is an intense pleasure to be without self, to be without that demand, to be without that contraction. Instead of contraction, there is openness. Well, that is sacrifice, and it is pleasurable.

Holding back is not pleasurable at all. There is no flow to it. It is filled with uncomfortable sensations, with ambiguity, mystery, unconsciousness, and pain. When release occurs, it is pleasurable. You cannot perform it ritually or willfully, but in the life of understanding it becomes your natural state, the quality of your presence in the world. Wherever there is the release of self, there is pleasure and sacrifice. Wherever there is the attempt to be released from self, there is no sacrifice and usually no pleasure, because the self is the principle of such a motivation. People who are trying to be spiritual and religious get the idea that sacrifice is a very solemn affair. They think they have got to get very seriously involved in getting rid of the ego. But before the ego will go, you must become profoundly humorous and have no concerns whatsoever for your liberation, whatever that could possible be. People think of their liberation as an event in time, and they think of sacrifice as an event in time, something you do mechanically and outwardly. But it is timeless, eternal, prior realization. Just as God is prior to all things, God-realization is prior to all things. It is not the result of anything, and neither is sacrifice or love.

It is absolutely impossible to believe that there is only God, to assume it, to think it, to gather it. You have nothing to resort to other than that Real life which is Satsang. You must stop meditating on your bullshit. Night and day you meditate on the same old shit, you go through the same round of up and down, that same old stupidity. You talk about the same old shit, manifest the same old nothing, so that there is no life, no fullness, no juice, and no God. How could you possibly find God by meditating on your mind? You will find only your mind.

It is not really mysterious that by becoming a philosopher you never become a devotee. All you do as a philosopher is meditate on your mind, on modifications, concepts, stuff, little subtle crunches in the level of energy that we call the mind. There is no God to be found in such a process. God is prior to that. Only the understanding of that process is useful. Everything else is a modification of it, and everybody is clinging to and meditating upon all kinds of modifications—including such things as were very dramatically given to you for your consideration during these last several weeks. All those experiences and phenomena, everything from high winds and coronas around the sun to swooning ecstasies, kriyas, and visions, were a test. None of it has any significance whatsoever. But it was an intense fascination for you. It was something that you bought. You held on to it.

In the moment when such a forceful event is pressed upon you, you feel good, blissful. It releases you for the moment from your previous dismal meditation. But a moment later you are meditating on *that*, and it becomes just as dismal, just as confining. It requires this same reaction, the same contraction of you, because you haven't changed the principle of your life. You haven't understood. What was given during that whole time was principally a demand, not a display. It was a demand for this Satsang, a demand that you live as a devotee and cease to be concerned or fascinated with anything whatsoever. Dwell in Satsang, be happy, and allow all these things to arise as they will.

But instead of that happening, all these endless factions developed according to which fascination people were buying. Factions in the Ashram got together because people were fascinated with a particular aspect of what

was arising, and experience again became the ground for
cultic life. Gradually these fascinations were taken away
again, and the same demand is still being made. There is a
lesson to be learned from all that. *Now* is when all of those
experiences serve you, now that they are over. There are
similar things happening here every day, but that peculiarly dramatic time is done. And now it can be useful to
you, because you see how you lived it. Each one of you
should be able to see very vividly the life of Narcissus in
your own case, how he ritually appears in the form of your
own consciousness and action. You must see it, and that is
why all that was done. It is not significant for such
phenomena to arise every day. It does not serve, because it
is just stuff. Consciousness is the demand, and that has
nothing whatever to do with the things that arise.

In time you will be happy that nothing arises. In fact,
the traditions are talking about that very happiness
wherein nothing arises. When the mind is finally quiet and
the body is finally quiet, when nothing occurs any more,
no more visions, when nothing grabs you any more, you
simply dwell in the absolute intuition of God. These things
arise just to serve that intuition. God is as present at this
moment as he is ever going to be. He was also as present in
those moments as he will ever be. In those moments there
was just different theatre than at this moment. You are
now capable of the same happiness, the same blissfulness,
the same easiness, the same love, the same ecstasy, the
same energy, the same humor that you enjoyed in your
best moments during those several weeks. You are capable
of that all the time, without cause. It only requires that
you live this Satsang with great intensity, with perfect
attention, and cease to be concerned for all the things that
arise by tendency in your case, all the things that are
awakened under the force of this Siddhi.

It means that your life must become like a mirage
around you. Your thoughts and inclinations, your

tendencies and desires, your conditions, dispositions, things you own, things you look forward to, *everything* must become images, flashing at night. They must become no more important than the remnants of a dream that you sort of playfully allow to occur when you are waking up in the morning. Just before getting out of bed you can know very well that you are able to wake up in this moment, that you already are awake, but you may decide to hang in there and watch the dream and see how it is going to come out. Ultimately, you should have the same relationship to all these things that arise, everything from a kriya to a cold in the head. It is just something arising. These things have no significance in the midst of that perfect intuition of God which is Satsang.

When that intuition has become intense, when your life as a devotee is real, then you will also be bringing that same quality to life, you will become responsible for living God in the world. You will no longer spend your time going through your ups and downs, your psychological crises, and your numbers. Now you are willing to indulge it because you think it does not amount to much. But every instant you indulge it, every moment of concern, of unhappiness and doubt and mediocrity, is turning away. Every moment of self-obsession is turning away. You must begin to see your own action and understand, and so live in Satsang more perfectly.

Understanding is simply the quality or intensity of your availability for Satsang. In every moment of understanding there is the obviation of contraction and the dwelling in Divine Communion. Gradually you will become more sensitive. Now you are only sensitive to effects, changes, conditions, and qualities. So the theatre, like that which occurred during these many recent weeks, is impressive. It seems to represent a special communication of God, a special entrance of God into human life. But in fact God is eternally Present and absolutely Present. That Divine Nature which is also your very Self must be known, and it is not known through the agency of any experience.

The perfect activity of the Divine, of the Guru, is mere presence. Fundamentally, apart from all the theatre that the Guru creates in order to impress people, to shake them up and bring them along, he is doing one thing. He is simply being present. That perfect communication is always given by the Guru, but people will not receive it. They want media, effects, and changes. So at times they are given this. These many weeks have been a time in which you were given all the possible kinds of things that are impressive, not so that you can have them, but so that you will understand something about your demand for them and be free of it. I want you to become available to that perfect Siddhi, that perfect communication which is constant, which requires no theatre to be communicated or to be known.

When that communication is received and enjoyed, when there are real devotees, then there can be all kinds of theatre. Why not? That is no time to retire to the cave and sit in silence. That is the time to celebrate, to be happy, to live, to generate that love and ecstasy that free men should share. I have said before that one of the best things that occurred during these last many weeks were the parties that I have had at my house. They were fundamentally a free and happy enjoyment. All the other things were impressive. And you were being impressed. I can't take any more parties for awhile. But it is possible to celebrate without smoking and drinking, and I hope you will discover the secret of that during this time.

8. THE GURU WILL RUIN YOUR LIFE

Bubba often uses particular devotees as instruments for the lessons of others. He has described the nearly "instant enlightenment" of Sal and Neil at the end of March as a lesson both for them and for the entire Ashram. He created particularly dramatic incidents in their lives in order to illustrate what was occurring less obviously in the rest of the community.

Between the end of March and the end of June, the entire community passed through three distinct phases in its life in Satsang. During the last week in March, it was enjoying the dramatic manifestation of the qualities of God-Life through the overwhelming Power of the Guru-Siddhi. Many people were having dazzling experiences of God-consciousness. When these experiences subsided, through the instrumentality of that same Power or Grace, people realized that no magical transformation had been worked upon them; that without their conscious participation, no real or permanent transformation could occur. They found that all their tendencies toward unconsciousness and seeking were still arising, and because they had been given a taste of real happiness, their suffering was intensified. They realized they had to do sadhana, to assume God consciously in the midst of life and its limitations. Then, as devotees began to live on the basis of what had been shown to them, understanding began to come alive in the community. Sal's interviews and conversations with the Ashram vividly illustrate these three movements.

149

Revelation

When Sal and Neil talked to the community on that Saturday at the end of March, they spoke from the point of view of realization, as genuine devotees. At that time they were living consciously and continuously in the Divine. This could not be identified with any trance-like ecstasy, nor with any fixed "state of consciousness." As earlier accounts indicated, they were simply alive with spiritual Presence, and everyone in the Ashram felt in them the qualities of Bubba's own Presence and Force. The yogic and intuitive effects brought about in them were the kinds of experiences for which yogis and mystics discipline themselves for lifetimes. Bubba had suddenly produced these experiences and this intuitive awareness in a couple of hard-core ethnic types, bred on the streets of New York, and who now described their experiences of the absolute Divine with raw New York accents. Bubba has always said his purpose is to restore humor!

In interviews which began in early April, Sal spoke in detail about those events, their significance, and the changing quality of his life. He began by noting that he and Neil had primarily been used as instruments. They were used as a lesson, a sign of the Teaching. Unlike the Guru, they were not conscious, responsible agents for the manifestation of the Divine Siddhi in the world. Rather, they were proof that the Divine Siddhi is indeed active in the world, with the omnipotent Power to turn ordinary men into devotees of God.

What occurred in me was the basic and simultaneous unraveling of all three points or knots, in the navel, the heart, and the sahasrar. The bondage was broken completely. From that point on I began to reside in the chest, in the Heart on the right. There is no movement of the mind now. That "event" was like the bursting of a bag, and now all

of the contents have been pouring out. My chest
feels like it's exploding. This ecstasy wants to blow
out. It can't be contained. And this abdominal
thing—I've lost nine pounds, but my stomach is
much larger. It is full of energy.

The most significant thing about this event is
that, contrary to the usual beliefs, even of traditional spirituality, the Guru *literally* enters and
transforms. It is a kind of possession. It is God-
Possession. Bubba animates this body. I feel Him
all the time, not as an experience, but *as* Him.

Sal witnessed the relaxation of the contraction of his
individual existence, the "unraveling of the knots" of
conditional life. This had both physical and mental
reflections. The relaxation of the vital contraction at the
navel removed Sal's conscious attention from the usual
play of desires. At the same time, his belly filled with
force. A similar process was permanently generated in
Bubba shortly after his realization in the Vedanta Temple.
Bubba has said this is a yogic manifestation of the awakened God-Life.

With the breaking of the subtle contractions in and
above the head, Sal was no longer involved in "the
machinery of interpretation and distortion." Rather, there
was a flowering of superconscious and other "higher"
forms of knowledge and experience, above the usual mind,
such as his vision of the Mother Shakti in flames.

The relaxation of the "causal"[1] contraction in the
Heart had undone his separate self sense. He felt Bubba,
the Divine, animating his body, "not as an experience, but
as Him." Sal was suddenly brought to life as a devotee,
completely turned to Bubba. He remained aware of bodily

---

[1] That psycho-physical dimension which is subtler than the mind and psyche, high or
low. It is the root of mind and life, and the seat of the primary sense of limitation, the
ego or separate self sense.

life, but didn't feel limited by it. The Guru had entered
into him and absorbed him completely, taking over all
aspects of his life.

In the remainder of this first interview, Sal described
apparently individual and problematic human life as a
compulsive modification of consciousness, extended as
contractions of the life-force as it passes through the
various psycho-physical centers. He described the Guru's
activity as a loosening and final dissolution of that compulsive and unconscious strategy of contraction and
modification.

> The sense of separate self or individual existence
> is created by that contraction. And only the Guru
> can open up these points so that sensation can
> leave. All you can do is make yourself available to
> Him. But when He enters the devotee and pos-
> sesses him, the thread of energy moving through
> the chakras opens out and contains the body from
> then on. This thread expands into a sphere of
> subtle, ecstatic energy that extends a few feet
> around the actual physical body. And it is alive all
> the time in this way. There is no up or down, but
> only this continuous radiation. The sense of the
> small self is gone at that point, for the body is being
> lived otherwise.

Sal also saw the necessarily sacrificial nature of all
existence. "When life is lived from the Heart, all that
arises to be experienced is consumed, returned to its
Source." Living thus, Sal naturally served as a vehicle for
the communication of the Guru-Siddhi, so he also began to
see the dynamics of its movement among other human
beings. It is always active, but it can be received only by
one who is available: "If someone turns to the Guru and
walks up to Him, it will manifest."

Sal was not, by virtue of all this, functionally equal to Bubba. He described his condition as a paradox: "The devotee does not *become* the Guru, but there is no difference, no separation. I really felt and feel that Sal has died." Bubba has often said that the Guru is not a form of status, but a function, and that the true devotee enjoys the same realization enjoyed by the Guru. Similarly, the transforming Power and Presence of God may move as perfectly through the unobstructed devotee as through the Guru. But, as Sal observed, the devotee has no control over it. "Only the Guru can control it." The Guru's conscious use of the Divine Siddhi is his functional difference from his perfect devotee. The devotee does not become the Guru, and so acquire his Function, but the Guru becomes his devotee, and so acquires another living vehicle for his Manifestation.

At this time Sal described the celebration and apparent self-indulgence that were going on at Bubba's house as humorous diversions. "They take your concern off the necessary and absolute crisis that must occur. In the midst of all these enjoyments the crisis becomes easy." Bubba had created a theatre which would make Sal and Neil available to him. In order to bring the Divine into view for them, he had to break down their defenses. He offered them every ordinary pleasure and broke their contracts with conditional life. Under those circumstances, he was able to enter them and take them over, literally to live them.

Over the next week or so Sal enjoyed the continued flowering of the life of a devotee. Bubba has said that all lasting changes take place first on transcendent levels of existence and then move down into the conditional, manifest worlds. The last movement of any such event is its manifestation at the level of life, the conscious experience of the change. Sal spoke the following Thursday morning to a group in the hot baths. He talked of becom-

ing "more and more absorbed in God all the time," and
seeing that "there is no madness like the madness of real
freedom in God."

Sal was enjoying complete non-attachment to his old
contracts, including his marriage to Louise. He was free,
happily appreciating everything without the usual self-
involvement and suffering.

It's not the *relationship* that is broken, only the
contract. Now I see Louise often, and I feel more
love from her, with her, than ever before. And not
just with her, but with everyone.

The freedom he now enjoyed also prompted Sal to
offer another appreciation of Bubba's life in the world:

It's amazing how that man functions at all, now
that I see what it is to live the Divine. Incredible! I
can still function to some degree, but I'm just not in
that same space any more. I told Bubba, "I'm just
not in this dimension at all!" He said, "Sal, *nobody*
is."

Sal and Neil couldn't maintain an ordinary life during
this period, because they hadn't matured enough in
realization to take conscious responsibility for all levels of
their being. Later they resumed administrative work in
the Ashram, but for the time being, they continued simply
to enjoy the intuition of the Divine in the relaxed environment of Bubba's household.

Return

On April 9, in another interview with the editors, Sal
began to describe his life in terms of crisis. He had begun

to sense the quality of real sadhana that must arise in response to the Divine Grace. He said that the arising crises were utterly intense, because he was living them with his whole being. Everything that arose had to be surrendered absolutely. He knew that as soon as there was any move toward attachment to anything, his realization would fade. Sal had begun to feel old emotions and thoughts arising, especially feelings of attachment tied to his relationship to his wife, Louise. But he also said there wasn't "a shot in hell of buying it." He now felt that the initiatory movement of the Guru's entry into him was complete, and the Guru-Siddhi was continuing to move through him. Nevertheless, he did say that he was experiencing the drama of various situations in life. He was obviously at this point beginning to turn more and more toward the movements of everyday life, and to reacquire, bit by bit, the elements of individual existence.

On through the second week in April, Sal continued to radiate an ease, wisdom, and love that made him a pleasure to be around. Sometimes people would feel Shakti movements in themselves when they were with him. He was serving as a vehicle for the Divine Siddhi. Previously, Sal had been a loud, often friendly guy, but also tough, and sometimes heavy. He never seemed to care whether or not anybody liked him. During this time of Grace it wasn't that he had started to care about such things, but he no longer represented a rough immunity to intimacy with others.

On April 15, Sal and several others led a discussion in the Satsang Hall about Bubba's work with devotees and the current events at Persimmon. It was apparent that something had changed for Sal. He wasn't the strong, serene guy who had been walking around Persimmon, often followed by a little crowd of people. He'd been shaken up. He had seen a new movement in his life, particularly in relation to Louise. He had begun to understand something about it, and he knew the problem it represented wasn't peculiar to him alone, so he told the rest of the Ashram about it in stark terms.

Sal said that he had "cut everything loose" during that first week in late March, but had now begun to discover in himself "all the subtle ways that you hang on to your partner." He had spoken to Bubba about that, and Bubba had told him that he and Louise should carry on their relationship, but not as a contract.

Sexual fidelity may arise in marriage, but do not pursue fidelity through the medium of a contract. "You can only be with me" is the mind and language of a contract. But fidelity is created by a natural fullness that doesn't have any arbitrary desire or movement.

That was all "very consoling," Sal said, until a couple of days later. He had been living at Bubba's house, and Louise had been living in their cabin, and they had not talked about "what she was up to outside in the Ashram." Sal finally confronted her, and she admitted, in what seemed to Sal an offhand way, that she had been with someone else. At that point Sal went into a furious rage, so severe that "the whole left side of my body began to go dead." A day later he began to get very angry and wild at a party at Bubba's house. He left the others and went to brood by himself in the dining room. Bubba came in and sat down. They opened a bottle of liquor and began talking.

I said, "What is this thing?" He said, "You're going to kill yourself. You have to cut that loose completely. When you sacrifice it, everything returns that you have sacrificed, but it is free. If you don't, you'll die with it."

Two weeks before, Sal had been living as the Heart, enjoying the continual sacrifice of all conditions as they arose. Now, after a period in which he had felt able to give up his demand for Louise's day to day attention, he was entirely helpless to let go of the demand for her fidelity. This attachment had roots far below the conscious mind. No series of rational thoughts about why this demand itself *was* his suffering could loosen its hold on him. It could be penetrated only by real understanding, which is living consciousness, not abstract thought.

This development didn't negate Sal's earlier experiences of dissolution and unraveling, nor did it reveal them as unauthentic. Bubba had seized Sal and Neil and possessed them. He had initiated the spiritual process by taking over their bodies, minds, and emotions. But this had been an extraordinary effect of the Divine Siddhi. It did not represent the conscious, radical turnabout of responsible devotees, but, rather, was a demand for all of that. Bubba told both Sal and Neil: "Everything that happened to you was a Grace." This new development appeared to be a fall, but in fact it was a new movement of that same Grace. If Bubba were simply to sustain the condition of absorption in individuals, he would not thereby serve the creation of a Community of true devotees. The devotee realizes Divinity in Truth only by living Satsang in the midst of limitations, and functioning through apparent life difficulties, always turned to the prior Condition, to the Guru in God. Bubba was now presenting Sal (and Neil as well, for they both experienced this return to common concerns at the same time) with a life-level demand, a demand for sadhana, a responsible response to Grace. Now Sal had to participate consciously in his own undoing at every level of life, from the most obvious and mundane on "up."

What did that actually entail for him? As Bubba wrote in *The Knee of Listening*, "Things do not cease to arise." The complications of life and the tendencies to live as a separate individual had begun again to reassert themselves in Sal's daily life. Less than a week before Sal had said it was "impossible to give a shit about anything any more," but Louise's admission of infidelity provoked almost violent concern in him.

Earlier, when Bubba asked Sal if he was willing to give up his marriage, and if he was willing to die, Sal described feeling a "direct hit." "I saw how that contract was very strong, and everything was in it, Mommy and Daddy, everything." Louise's infidelity was a violation of what was perhaps the single most important reference point for Sal's sense of himself. He was unable to rationalize this away or to ignore it and rest his attention with Bubba.

Sal was now faced with an offense to a primary contract. He was experiencing his presence in the world as a kind of cultic and ritual demand, a strategic "priesthood" which seeks to bind others, to restrict the flow of attention in living beings, including oneself, so that real love and happiness are stifled. He was also being offered an opportunity to experience liberation from the cult of this world. But this liberation requires that one abide always in Satsang, knowing there is only God and that no life-level events can create or destroy the condition of relationship, which is the principal, original, and unqualified condition of life. He had the responsibility, in that very moment, to assume and live from the point of view Bubba had revealed to him weeks before, in which "there is no separate one" and "the body is sustained by a yogic process," in which, in other words, the jealous, hurt, and angry one does not exist.

The "sacrifice" that Bubba was demanding is not a motivated, willful activity, although it may express itself outwardly as an apparent renunciation of some kind. Ultimately, as Sal himself had said, it is simply intense,

moment to moment life in Satsang, an "intuitive condition which is always sacrificing this moment." He had seen
that not only did he have the tendency to bind himself to
people and things, but everybody and everything around
him were also tending to bind him.

So the intelligence required to cut loose is
indescribable. There's nothing intellectual about
this intelligence that is demanded. It's a wholesale
throwing away of everything. If you enjoy the
living connection with Bubba Free John, then
when you throw the rest away you'll fall into the
Heart. But if you're not living Satsang, and it's all
getting ripped off, it's death, literal death. You'll
die of a heart attack or something. At least that's
the way it felt to me.

One consciously participates in the sacrificial process
through a life in Satsang, not through withdrawal from
apparent conditions. In fact, as Sal mentioned, cutting
everything loose in a superficial way has no effect whatsoever on the subtle ways one maintains or reestablishes
attachments. No motivated activity, even trying somehow to "love Bubba" or willfully turn to him, can obviate
these subtle activities. That is only the search again,
seeking founded in dilemma. Only Satsang avails, and
Satsang cannot be attained, because it has already been
established by the Guru's Grace. Consciousness must relax
from its usual contraction and remain in its natural form.
Then, as Bubba said, "Everything returns, in freedom and
fullness."

Sal saw something very important with respect to
this: "People think that if Bubba finds out their game, he's
going to rip it off. That's true enough, but prior to ripping
it off he just keeps giving it to you." No one is going to give
up his attachments until he is sick of the attendant

suffering, so the Guru does not merely strip away consolations, fascinations, and attachments. That in itself would
only reinforce the craving. The Guru also gives the
devotee whatever he thinks he wants, whatever he's
willing to buy. This includes the unpleasant as well as the
pleasant, for even apparent pleasures only serve to distract
people from true happiness. They use them to keep
themselves limited and miserable. So the Guru will "keep
giving it to you until you're tired of getting it on." At the
same time, he accelerates the natural process of the world.
"Some people live a certain event all their lives, but for his
devotees Bubba changes events all the time." The lesson
he is always offering is not only that the last moment's
circumstance is now forever gone, but also that even while
it was here, in itself it did not avail. Giving attention to
events, things, and people, without always knowing that
which is prior to them, only leads to suffering.

Sal saw Bubba "always testing and reminding," and
"waiting for the one who never forgets." Now he saw all
his daily dealings with Bubba as the theatre in which that
demand operates, and in which such attention is
perfected. "I live in that household like a visitor, and I
never take it for granted." His statement indicates the
kind of insecurity the Guru's demand for attention can
generate in those around him, even in moments of unin-
hibited revelry.

In later weeks Sal would understand clearly why the
Guru's demand for perfect attention does not bind but
liberates. For now, he had passed from the ecstatic
existence of a devotee back to his usual, karmic life. He
began to see life from a point of view made honest and
uncompromising by the intensity of his own, self-created
suffering and the immediacy of fear and death.

At dinner that night, Bubba had said:

Everything is going to go. Obliteration. All the

love we've formed for one another, this world and the way it is, the various qualities that we enjoy with one another, it is all going to go. Everything. *Everything!* Absolutely nothing is going to survive, and even that doesn't amount to anything.

Sal had realized, in a way he could no longer ignore, that he would not survive. But he could resort to Satsang, and for that reason this realization did not bring despair: "When you view your current circumstances from that most radical point of view, the humor begins to come alive." And he knew that sacrificial existence could be maintained, because "the 'miracle' of Bubba Free John is living proof of it, the living demonstration in the world that it can be done."

Sadhana

On May 2, two weeks after he had spoken in the Satsang Hall about the awakening crisis in his life, Sal participated in another interview with the editors. By this time he understood more realistically the usefulness of not suppressing the tendencies, experiences, and resistance that were arising, but living them consciously in Satsang. He said that the *sensations* of freedom or release, including the feeling of residing in the Heart, had fallen away, but he pointed out that the Heart is not a sensation, state, or experience. It is the sacrificial process itself. Describing his present orientation, Sal said:

It is to live that *sacrifice* on the life level, on all levels. In the last two weeks I've witnessed its appearance on the life level. It is necessary not only

to live that inward sublimity of consciousness, but
to bring it into life and to live that fire of sadhana,
in which all emotions and everything else arise and
are sacrificed. This requires real intelligence, and it
is the real sadhana of this work.

So it had become *necessary* for Sal to become intelligent, and he knew that he *had* to be willing to live that
"fire of sadhana," because he really had no choice. He saw
more firmly that experiences of all kinds, including
spiritual realizations, wild parties and everything in
between, are neither meaningless nor significant, but
simply *useful* in the theatre of lessons.

I have learned that Consciousness exists, and it
manifests all kinds of stuff. Look at the incredible,
vast range of experiences that have taken place
here over the past few weeks. The scope of it all is
unbelievable! But if you don't *understand* in the
midst of all that arises, you bind yourself to this
world.

He said that he considered the wildness of the parties
and intense living situation at Bubba's house to be another
goad to giving up sensations of security "in relation to
manifest events." During the first weeks Sal had talked
about the indulgence in pleasure at the parties as Bubba's
way of taking each person's mind off the necessary crisis.
Now he described all of that as a test, just another
condition to be understood. Sal hadn't changed his mind
about the parties, but they had taken on a different
function in relation to his sadhana. In late March, Bubba
was "making room" in Sal for the Divine. He was loosening the mechanisms of Narcissus, satiating desire, relaxing
the mind and communicating his Love, which is non-separation, with such intensity that Sal disintegrated. Now,

Sal was forced to do the sadhana of understanding, which involves conscious participation in the Divine event, not the passive enjoyment of Divine intervention.

About a week later, on May 8, he had another conversation with one of the editors, the transcript of which was read aloud at dinner that night. It catalyzed insights for many at Persimmon who were aware of similar movements in their own lives.

Sal had gone to San Francisco the previous Monday, and had experienced "nothing but sheer terror" for the first hour of the drive. During the second hour, he said, "everything died, there was no movement." Since then he had been fluctuating in and out of that terror. He had called Bubba from San Francisco, and Bubba, after needling him a bit, said that he was "demanding a deeper form of surrender, even vital death." The terror was a purification of the psyche, Bubba said, and Sal should not get involved in it.

Back on April 6, Bubba induced a meditative trance in Sal, during which Sal surrendered his attachment to his body. The surrender had been real, for he indeed felt he could abandon his physical life at that point. But now Sal's attachment to life had reappeared, and that previous act of surrender, made possible by Bubba's Grace, was shown to be a glimpse of what Sal would have to do repeatedly, on his own, over the coming months. Bubba was demanding the surrender of vital attachments in daily life, not merely in subtle visions. And that surrender would have to take place during all conscious activity, not merely in a potent instant.

The primary arena or theatre in which Sal perceived the drama of his sadhana was his marriage to Louise, and he associated his fear of vital death with its purification.

I was seeing in myself certain emotions with respect to Louise while I was living in Bubba's

house and she was living out in one of the cabins.
You know, these feelings of loss and need and so on.
But Louise has been staying with me in Bubba's
house since Friday night, and I have seen these
same feelings in myself. So what is going on
externally really has nothing to do with what is
actually happening. What I saw was this vital
demand for attention. The cult is a one-to-one
relationship wherein the vital-force in one person
makes a demand on another to fixate on that vital
life in him and live from that point of view. That is
suffering, that fixated life. But even prior to that is
the actual and universal demand for attention.

Sal had been considering his association with Louise,
and he had begun to see its dynamics. What is called love
in the usual cultic life is nothing, he realized, but "the
demand for the fixation of another's attention on one's

individual embodied personality." The life communicated through that attention seems to secure the survival or immunity over time of the one who constantly contemplates himself and seems to animate that flesh-and-blood person. But such security is non-existent. It is an illusion. Ultimately, the embodied one will die. Sal saw that Bubba was breaking down the mechanisms of self-attention and the demands for others' attention. He was turning devotees to himself, the Guru in God, who dwells as the eternally transcendent Nature of all apparent selves. With such loosening and turning, real love could flow freely.

Such love involves "absolute sacrifice" of the self-sensation, but it is not some sort of abstract or merely subtle activity. On the contrary, real love takes the form of an immensely vital, warm, simple, intimate, and free sharing of conscious energy or real "food" among human beings.

Sal observed another element in his relationship to Louise:

> When I feel that I have Louise's attention, I don't return it to her. I feel free to go out and seduce someone else. When I feel that attention loosening, then I try to regain it by paying attention to her until I have it again.

Such games of attention illustrate well the nature of all Narcissistic activity. They obviously perpetuate nothing but suffering and seeking. Such activity has nothing to do with fulfillment, but only the search for it. It has nothing to do with love, but only self-obsession at every moment. And Sal was probably right when he said that he felt his own case was an "archetype" of everyone in the community.

Related to his understanding of "what is actually

happening" was an essential insight Sal brought from his
terrified drive to San Francisco.

It felt like everything had died, not that everything had come to an end, but that it, the world,
had never occurred. Nothing has occurred, only
the sensation of things. The sensation of things
happening *is* what we call ourselves.

Sal saw the fixation on that sensation and the demand
for its reinforcement as the individual's very feeling of
separate existence. All this implies that the world and
events have no real or independent existence. Egoic
activity creates and continuously depends on the apparent
existence of a universe of solid and independent objects
and persons. When the sensation and activity of the ego
are sacrificed, there is real love, and what had appeared to
be a multitude of separate things becomes known as the
unqualified Divine Reality.

Sal continued:

A human being thinks he *has* a strategy, but he *is*
a strategy. That's all he amounts to. You *are* a vital
demand that gets worked out through the psychol-
ogy and manipulation of life.
So people are only this strategy for survival, and
that's why they can't become enlightened by
themselves. The Guru must enter and transform
them. The Guru must relax that unconscious demand.
All those experiences in March were genuine. I
literally saw the Mother Shakti in those flames.
There was that absolute dissolution of mind, and so
on. All that absolutely did occur, it was not symbolic. But the identification with those expe-

riences, that was bullshit. Bubba has said many times that the real event takes place prior to experiences. It seems to me that Bubba unravels us in the most fundamental core of our existence, beyond the conscious mind. He then creates conditions in life to serve that crisis, to bring that realization into life. He has said that you can subliminally or inwardly realize anything you want, but it means nothing if it cannot be brought into the functional mechanisms of life.

Sal's entire life since late March can be seen as the playing out of the "remnants" of Sal *as* a strategy. As Sal stressed, it is not that those earlier experiences had been illusory or merely symbolic. He insisted they were authentic, and he explained them in the context of the primary movement we have observed in his life during this period. Bubba cut Sal's "knots" or major contractions at the roots and allowed him a prolonged glimpse of true freedom. Then he allowed Sal to return, apparently, to his separate state, under conditions that served the crisis of literal transformation and brought that realization more and more fully into life.

Now Sal again began to feel a relaxation of the tension in his gut and a release of his corresponding, unconscious insistence on others' attention. He saw that this does not destroy relationships in life, but allows them to be lived naturally, without compulsion, as expressions of that prior freedom. He mentioned, for instance, feeling "fidelity to Louise, but actually it was to Bubba, just relationship without this self-satisfying demand." And he saw again that with such relaxation, a new experience of life becomes possible.

The energy becomes capable of moving through higher mechanisms, and you realize these "higher" states of consciousness. It's not that *you* are there to realize them, but the energy moves through those mechanisms now, and all that becomes apparent. Sexuality and vitality become a part of a relationship, not its foundation.

Having tasted the tapas, or spiritual discipline involved in making oneself available to the Guru's transforming Presence and Force, Sal knew the necessity of "great love for the Guru":

Without that intense relationship, without Satsang, no realization is possible. No one would have the capacity to endure that transformation without love for the Guru, and of course, the infinite love of the Guru for his devotees.

As for the conditions of his present sadhana, Sal said in this interview that he felt his living situation with respect to Louise should not be changed "until it is completely straight." But later that very afternoon he and Neil both talked with Bubba about how much attention they had been paying to their marriage relationships. Bubba told them he had already made the decision that it was time for them to move out of his house and return to daily life with their wives and the regular company of all his devotees. This, he said, would enable them to see exactly what all that had happened to them was intended to show. Also, after many weeks of partying, the whole Ashram was about to resume its normal routine, and Bubba himself required solitude during the coming weeks. By the weekend of July 6, his work in the world would be fulfilled.

The Summation

Sal and Neil returned to their wives and responsibilities, and their sadhana continues in Bubba's Ashram even today. Looking back on their adventure, Sal, in later weeks, described the Wisdom that was its permanent Gift.

I found that a lot of ways in which I thought I was turning into God were really just ways of turning on. In other words, I have doubts about myself, good doubts. Because the certainties are much more dangerous than the uncertainties.

The heat of that sadhana has got to be going on all the time. That sort of fire in the gut. I notice a lot of people get this groovy meditative feeling when they talk about Satsang. But Satsang is a fire, it is an absolutely raging fire, and when Bubba is talking about the intensification of Satsang, he is talking about moving closer to that fire all the time. It doesn't have connotations of some blissful feeling for me any longer. It may feel good at times, but when I think about the intensification of Satsang now, I think about obliteration.

Bubba is the only one in the world who loves. When you give your attention to Bubba, it returns. He isn't *performing* that principle of sacrifice. He *is* that principle. Love is just the exchange of life-energy, attention, through the principle of sacrifice. Bubba may seem to be involved in this obvious drama of giving attention or not giving it, but there is no real withholding. He is returning it all the time.

What I felt twelve weeks ago is beginning to return, but with fullness. There is no experiential drama, but my attention has matured. Now I

understand what his demand for absolute attention
is. If Bubba were living as an ordinary person, just
binding people to himself, there would be no
freedom involved at all. He makes the demand for
your attention because he *is* the sacrificial process.
The moment you give him your attention, he
sacrifices it and you become free. He performs the
sacrifice for you. The student or the awakening
disciple can't sacrifice. He is still Narcissus. Bubba
becomes the Heart for his devotees, and by turning
their attention and lives to him, they enjoy the
sacrificial process, until they themselves find it and
fall into it. Then everything falls apart.

I feel my body coming into a harmony I enjoyed
twelve weeks ago. The first experiences I had when
I was living in Bubba's house are beginning to
return again. I feel centered again, and sometimes,
to the degree that there is understanding, I feel the
Siddhi returning. As I have begun to live out the
life-level sadhana of not dramatizing my egoic
demand for vital attention, the phenomena that
Bubba created in me during March have begun to
return. I feel lighter, easier, and I see the same
thing in everybody else in this community. The
Dawn Horse is appearing now. The principle of
sacrifice is appearing.

I still have plenty of sadhana to do, but now I am
willing to do it without resentment. In all the
lessons I've learned in all the time I've been with
Bubba, the one thing that has been shown to me is
how much he loves me. People who read this book
are going to think all kinds of weird things about
Bubba. They may think he is cruel and crazy and
all that, but the people in this Ashram aren't
masochists. To realize the Guru's love for you is to
realize love itself. What people usually call love is

only a string of emotions. But real love sets you free.

The secret of Bubba Free John is that he loves you. That is the freeing principle. The Guru loves his devotee completely. The whole process simply involves getting the devotee to love the Guru just as completely.

9. THE DIVINE PERSON

Starting in late May, very close to the time when Bubba said his work in the world would be fulfilled or finally established, Bubba gave his devotees several concise, specific descriptions of the perfect meditation and realization of a devotee. Because the members of the community were still incomplete as devotees, these descriptions did not represent a present realization in the Ashram, or even a part of its common experience. Nevertheless, they affected the community. Devotees shared a sense of having been given an indescribably sublime gift, of having *already* been given it. And some devotees did soon begin to have conscious, though partial and discontinuous, experiences of what he was speaking about.

Back in the middle of March, in a talk delivered a week before "The Saturday Night Massacre," Bubba had spoken at some length about "Amrita Nadi," the devotee's meditation, and the origins of conductivity. That talk, "The Divine Person," had struck many people in the same manner as these later communications. It appeared as an indication of a magnificent but yet unrealized gift. Descriptions of perfect meditation and the full process of conductivity often seem obscure or incomprehensible, even to people who have been with Bubba for some time. This results partially from a lack of experience, which would demonstrate the obviousness of all this, and partially from a tendency to complicate in the mind what is ultimately simple.

"The Divine Person" expresses, among other things, the natural simplicity of Amrita Nadi, that intuited

173

structure of Divine Reality through which the Divine
Conscious-Power manifests as all worlds and conditions,
including the human. That talk forms the substance of this
chapter. It is followed by excerpts from Bubba's subsequent writings and talks about the meditation of the
devotee and his answers to questions about it.

The Divine Person

BUBBA: I want to talk to you about the origins of this
process of "conductivity," which is not a yoga in the
traditional sense. Yoga, from the traditional point of view,
is a way of gradually approaching a new condition called
Enlightenment, Self-realization, Cosmic Consciousness,
Divine Realization, Nirvana, and so forth. It is a strategic
method to approach this new condition. Therefore, it
begins in a condition that doesn't already enjoy what it is
seeking. The origin of yoga and of all seeking is a dilemma.
But this process of conductivity is not a way of
approaching the Divine, or the Divine Condition, or
whatever you want to name it. It is life *already* lived in the
Divine. It is that process generated when the Truth is
already enjoyed as the principle and condition of conscious life.

Just so, the whole affair of "enquiry" in the form:
"Avoiding relationship?"[1] is not something that you take
up because you have read about it or heard about it, or it
makes some sense to you. It is not something you apply to
yourself in order to have some realization, some change of
state. Enquiry and conductivity, the two aspects of the
process of understanding, both rest in a prior Condition, a

---

[1] *The Knee of Listening* contains Bubba's essential Teaching, relative to this form of
enquiry.

prior realization, and they are the mature intelligence of that Condition. Before this process of conductivity can be true, just as before the process of enquiry can be true, a totally new Condition must be consciously generated in life. So the foundation of our work is Satsang, Divine Communion, not the need to discover the Self, not the need to discover the Divine, but Satsang itself, present existence in the Condition of the Divine.

Satsang begins as an essentially homely affair in which you respond to the Teaching. You begin to deal with the Teaching in a practical way relative to your own life, becoming more intelligent until you can truly turn to the Guru. The longer you live with the Guru, the more your relationship to the Guru becomes itself an intuitive realization of the Divine, because the Guru is not simply a human individual, a cultic figure. The Guru is a specific function in God. The Guru is not exclusively that human person who manifests and demonstrates that function. The Guru's command to meditate on him is not the command to meditate on the human figure, the cultic Guru. It is the command to meditate upon the Divine Person. In fact the form of the Guru is the Divine Form. It is upon the Divine Form, the form of the Divine Person, that the Guru invites you to meditate, through the agency of the human relationship between the Guru and the devotee.

The origin of the whole affair of understanding, including the process of enquiry and the process of conductivity, is intuitive, conscious enjoyment of the Divine Person. Not the Divine Person imaged in the search, not the mythical, conceptualized, archetypal Krishna, Jesus, or Buddha. All such images are themselves the religious forms of the search, just as yogic methods are the so-called "spiritual" forms of the search. The Divine Person is not an archetype, not figured in the mind in any sense, not a person with a subtle body in some subtle world. The Divine may *manifest* as a subtle body in some subtle world, just as he may manifest through a gross body in this gross world. But the Divine Person in himself is perfect, absolute, unqualified, formless, eternal, fundamental Reality.

Fundamentally, what you were invited to enjoy when you became involved with me was not the practice of enquiry or the practice of conductivity. The invitation was for you to enjoy Satsang, present intuited happiness in the Divine. When that begins, then all of the transforming events follow. Then there arises the primary process of self-observation, insight, and enquiry. And there may also arise the secondary process of the movement of the life-force, and your consequent participation in it in the form of conscious conductivity. In order for that to be true sadhana and not an organ of the search, you must continually return to the fundamental, which is Satsang itself. It is to that fundamental and prior Condition, Satsang, that you are continually returning, even in the midst of these transforming events. Otherwise, they become your concerns. They become distractions, fascinations, images in the pond, ritual instruments, liturgical instruments for the priesthood of Narcissus. So I am continually reminding you of this fundamental Condition.

From time to time I have pointed out to you how, in *The Knee of Listening* and *The Method of the Siddhas*, this process of conductivity has been described many times. You might not have noticed that. Just so, I want today to remind you of how *The Method of the Siddhas* begins. There is an Invocation. It is not something I wrote, although I worked on the translation of it. It is a selection from a traditional text, *Narayana Sooktam*, an Upanishad. I want to read it to you and relate some of it to aspects of this process of understanding, which includes both enquiry and conductivity.

I worship the Lord, who has thousands of heads,

thousands of eyes, who is the source of happiness in the world, the Eternal God. All this is nothing but the Present God. All this lives by Him.

This "thousands of heads and thousands of eyes," of course, is religious language, archetypal language, meaning He is all-seeing, all-knowing, omnipresent, perfect.

I worship Him who is the Self and the Lord of the Universe, the Eternal God, the benign and unde-caying Divine Soul, the Supreme Being who is to be known, the Self of all, the Supreme Goal.

The Lord is the Absolute Supreme Being, He is the Supreme Reality, He is the Supreme Light, He is the Supreme Self.

These are all descriptions of the intuited Divine. They seem like random qualities, but they relate to the structure of that intuition, which is Amrita Nadi. Amrita Nadi is the Conscious Form, the "body" of the Divine Person. So it says, "He is the Supreme Light, He is the Supreme Self." The root or "foot" of Amrita Nadi, the Divine Person, is the Heart, the intuition of Real-God or the Very Self, one's fundamental Nature. The upper terminal or "head" of Amrita Nadi is God-Light, the Perfect Light, the eternal creative Source of the worlds. The Divine Person does not simply stand outside time and space in some concrete way, fundamentally unknowable, only believable. The Divine Person stands in the midst of all existence and is not knowable through ordinary means, which are themselves all forms of limitation and dilemma. He is known only directly, through the faculty of very consciousness, Consciousness itself.

The Divine Person, then, is *intuited* to be present, not figured out to be present or judged on the basis of experience or proofs to be present. He is only known to be present, and he is known when the usual self-limiting faculties are opened, their obstructive and binding tendencies and powers dissolved. So when the power of the navel is opened, when the power of the heart is opened, when the power of the head is opened, when these three fundamental centers are opened to the intuitive or natural and prior state, then the Divine Person is obvious. And it becomes obvious that the Divine Person stands in the Heart. His feet are in the Heart and his head is above. One in whom the intuitive faculty is awake and open is continually, effortlessly meditating upon the Divine Person. Not from the traditional religious point of view, the limited point of view, but when understanding is awake, when there is radical understanding, the heart is open, the functions in the head and above the head are open, and the stream of Amrita Nadi is known, even in the Fullness of Life, which descends and ascends through the center of life, whose vital region is in the navel.

In the process of understanding there may be a felt experience accompanying the intuition of the Self-nature. Its seat may intuitively and experientially be felt in the heart, on the right side of the chest. Ramana Maharshi speaks about the fall into the Heart, continuing the curve of the spinal system, sushumna, and running down into the Heart (the open "place" or intuitive seat on the right), realizing the Source of mind and life, the very Self. But there is a further stage in the Great Process in which this Amrita Nadi is *regenerated*, and not only in the limited sense of a nerve in the body. When there is perfect Self-realization or intuition of Real-God, the Nature, Source, and Condition of the worlds becomes apparent. And when that realization is quickened, there is a regeneration of that same Nadi in which jnana or Self-knowledge was realized by descent into the Heart. In that case there is resurrection, not exclusive containment in the Heart from the point of view of Self-realization, but perfect realization of the Heart *and* the Light, equally. In that case, the eternal Divine Light, which is the reflection of the very Self or eternal God, is known and seen to be the creative and present Source of all life, all manifestation. This world is appearing by virtue of a process of descent and ascent from this Light, and this process is known in psycho-physical life through the activity of conductivity, descending and ascending.

In Satsang the human Guru communicates that Presence and Condition which is the Divine Person. He communicates it in all ways, until the individual becomes a devotee, at which point he intuitively knows the Guru in Truth, and therefore knows the Divine Person in this specific way I am describing. He knows in the true devotee's way, not in the believer's way. This intuitive or perfect realization of the Divine Person depends absolutely on the whole affair of understanding. Mere involvement in the yogic phenomena of the life-force is not understanding. All this spontaneous yoga is a purifying and secondary event, and it does not *lead* to God-realization or Self-realization. It may only accompany that fundamental process, just as ordinary breath and activity accompany the waking state. The devotee is thus responsible for that intuitive foundation which alone can make the process of conductivity genuine, alive in Truth, realized consciously in relationship to the present Divine.

One who lives in Satsang moves ever more firmly into that intuitive realization of the Divine Person through the agency of the human Guru. In the midst of that affair, the process of self-observation, insight, and enquiry is quickened, as is the process of conductivity, the inner transforming movements of the life-force. The process of enquiry is itself only a random and intelligent movement back into the unqualified Condition of Satsang. The process of conductivity is simply the way of participating, through the agency of the life-force, in the Light which is above the world, above the body, and above the mind. This whole affair of inner conductivity is not simply an involvement with the life-force, with the Shakti. It is an involvement with the Divine Light, which is prior to both the Cosmic Reflection of the Light (which is Maha-Shakti) and the human reflection of the Light (which is the life-force, that permeates mind and body and in fact *is* the psycho-physical form), and depends on that prior realization for its authenticity. Participation in the Divine Light, that uncommon "yoga" of conductivity, depends on the affair of radical understanding in consciousness, enquiry in which the Heart, or intuition of Real-God, that is the Root and Source of the Divine Light, is known. So in the devotee there is continuous, intuitive enjoyment of the Divine Person in the form of Amrita Nadi, and in the midst of that intuitive enjoyment he also conducts the life-force from its Source, which is the Light above.

You must also know that the Light of which I speak is not just above the head. It is also above the psyche, above the mind, above the body, above the entire psycho-physical condition, above the world. Therefore, it is not known by internal experience of a gross or even a subtle variety. It is known only directly, immediately. It may not be seen, even by subtle vision. It is intuited, not experienced. It is not a brightness that consciousness may view under any conditions. It is that Light or Brightness that is Consciousness itself, realized in itself to be the intuition of God, the Divine Condition. So the realization of that Light depends again on the same understanding. True enquiry manifests as a continual knowing of Amrita Nadi. When it matures in the devotee, each instant of enquiry is conscious knowing in the form of Amrita Nadi. It is knowing the Divine Person as one's Condition. It is not just meditation on the psycho-physical reflection of this higher intuition, which may be felt in the body as a curve that comes forward from the Heart, passes through the throat, and around the back of the head to the crown. That is in itself only a psycho-physical or yogic extension of that intuition, even as are all visions, super-perceptions, and cognitive experiences.

True enquiry manifests as Self-realization and God-realization, which is founded in dissolution of the exclusive force of the principles of desire, mind, and ego, or separate self sense, in the Heart. In the instant of radical understanding there is only the intuitive bliss of the true Self or Real-God, where before there was the ego, the separate self sense, and the urgency of Narcissus. Where there was endless, compulsive conceptualization, there is intuitive realization of the infinite Light or Intensity or Power which is the present creative Source of the world and all conditions. Just so, Satsang is not simply a common relationship between a teacher and a disciple. It includes all of the practicalities and ordinariness and homeliness of a human relationship and a teaching relationship, but, fundamentally, it is the intuitive enjoyment of the absolute Divine in this specific way I am describing.

*He is the Supreme Meditator, He is the Supreme
Object of Meditation.*

I have said to you many times that the devotee does
not meditate in Satsang in the traditional way, motivated
to be relieved, to be transformed. In the condition of
Satsang you *are meditated.* The Divine process is activated
as a literal force in the devotee. Meditation is not your
concern. You cannot meditate in the true sense. You can
only realize the Divine Person as your condition by Grace,
in which case the process of meditation, which is an
eternal activity, is generated or realized in your own case.
Just as the Lord is the great Siddha of meditation, He alone
is the Meditator, and He alone is the Supreme Object of
Meditation. In the process of this meditation, only the
Lord is known.

*The Lord abides pervading whatever is seen or
heard in this universe, whatever is within and
without.*

The Lord is not exclusively identical to anything
within or without. He is not to be equated exclusively with
the world itself, nor with anything that may appear in the
world, nor with anyone that may appear in the world, nor
is he to be exclusively equated or identified with any
internal or subtle phenomenon. There is no vision that is
the Divine Person. There is no yogic manifestation of any
variety that is itself the knowing of the Divine Person. All
such internal phenomena are of the same variety as all
external phenomena. They are modifications, illusions,
apart from the Lord, in themselves insignificant. The Lord
is prior to them. He is the Principle of them. So none of the
classical yogic phenomena is itself Divine realization.

I worship and meditate upon the Infinite and

*immutable Seer who is the other end of the ocean of
identification with birth and death, and who is the
source of all happiness.*

*The Heart, the perfect seat of meditation, resem-
bles an inverted lotus bud.*

In other words, the Heart (the open seat of Self-
knowledge, the "feet" of the Divine Person) hangs down,
in this mythological, archetypal language, prior to Realization. It is unopened, closed, not alive except in
perfect Consciousness. It is turned down, identified with
qualities, things that are arising, thoughts, conditions,
sensations. The reason it says the Heart is the perfect seat
of meditation is that the fundamental root of intuitive
knowledge of the Divine Person is the Heart, this seat on
the right side of the chest, not any other place. The Heart
is fundamental. The other centers, the head and the navel,
co-exist with it, but the Heart is fundamental. So the Lord
does not have his feet in the air and his head in your chest.
His feet are in the Heart and his head above. The fundamental seat of meditation or of the awakening of intuitive
knowledge is the Heart.

*In the region below the throat and above the
navel there burns a fire from which flames are
rising up. That is the great support and foundation
of the Universe.*

The jnani, the seeker for exclusive Self-knowledge,
says that the great event is when you fall into the Heart.
He views Self-knowledge exclusively and does not pass
beyond that point to *Parabhakti*, or perfect Divine enjoyment. But in this text we see a description of the Heart in
the perfect sense. The "flames are rising up" and it "is the
great support and foundation of the Universe." In other
words, the regenerated form of Amrita Nadi, the perfect
intuition of the Divine, is what is being indicated here.

*It always hangs down from the arteries like a
lotus bud. In the middle of it there is a tiny orifice in
which all are firmly supported.*

There is, again in this mythical language, a point
infinitely small, a perfect origin, not just a massive
psycho-physical organ, but a *bindu*, this "point" on the
right, which is the center of the Heart. It is not of the
nature of space. It is not a place, but it is of the nature of
perfect intuition. It is Consciousness itself, and the limitless Power which is the eternal reflection of
Consciousness.

*In the middle of it there is a great fire with
innumerable flames blazing on all sides which first
consumes the food and then distributes it to all
parts of the body. It is the immutable and all-
knowing.*

In the midst of the Heart the great process of life is
supported, and the Heart itself is perfectly involved in
that. Just as the Heart is the seat of the intuition of the
Divine, Real-God, the very Self, so that same seat exists
relative to psycho-physical life like a sun around which all
of the other faculties are moving like so many moons. The
Heart is also described, in this tradition, as the sun relative
to the sahasrar, the seat of superconsciousness, which is
described as like the moon. The Divine Light is dependent
upon the perfect Self or Very-God, and therefore exists in
a condition like that of a reflection, being not independent
but radically or unqualifiedly dependent on the Unqualified or Real-God.

*Its rays constantly shoot upwards and
downwards. It heats the body from head to foot. In
the middle of it there is a tongue of fire which is
extremely small.*

This is conductivity, descending and ascending, and in the midst of that conductivity there is again this point of origin, the Heart.

That tongue of fire is dazzling as a streak of lightning in the midst of a dark cloud and as thin as the awn at the tip of a grain of rice, golden bright and extremely minute.

In the middle of that tongue of flame the Supreme Self abides firmly. He is God. He is the Immortal, the Supreme Lord of all.

I bow down again and again to the Eternal Law, the Truth, the Absolute Supreme Being, the Divine Being who is dark blue and reddish, the pure celibate, with extraordinary eyes, who has assumed all forms.

We get a little yogic language here. It talks about the Divine appearing to be dark blue and reddish. In the yogic literature you find descriptions, based on mystical and visionary revelations, of lights and various colors that are attributed to the Divine. Some people say He is blue, some people say He is white, some people say He is gold, and so forth. But the colors or lights actually represent functional levels of our subtle being, and none of them is to be identified exclusively with the Divine. They correspond to cognitive perceptions that arise when we are attuned to subtle dimensions of manifest, and thus limited, awareness above the natural, thinking mind.

There is a class of visions that may arise in which the Divine appears to manifest in the form of a glorified human person, who is more or less human in appearance, but often with various symbolic additions that indicate Divine attributes. Among such visions there are, for instance, some in which the Divine appears to have bluish skin. In times of visionary experience I have seen many such appearances. For example, I have seen the Mother

Shakti, the Cosmic Source of forms, appear in many human-like forms. At those times I was experiencing a living dramatization of the nature of superconscious existence, the most subtle foundation of the manifest Cosmos. Such experiences were unlike dreams, or any of the miasmic apparitions that arise in the natural psyche, below the mind. They were visions of living archetypes that express the power and nature of those dimensions that control the World-Form. I saw many Cosmic Beings in male and female forms. In the case of the Mother Shakti, she at times appeared to be blue in color. There were cases in which the edges or outer contours of her form were blue in color, while the rounded or inner contours were reddish in color. This corresponded visually to the manner in which light falls on a natural form in the gross world. In that case, the inner or rounded shapes tend to reflect the light, and so appear lighter in color, while the outer or receding edges tend to absorb or refract the light, and so appear darker in color. These natural qualities manifested by forms that appear in the light of the gross world may indicate something about the nature of the appearance of the Mother Shakti as I saw her on some such occasions. There is a fundamental difference, however, and that is that both the Mother Shakti and the dimension in which she appeared were self-illumined. No light fell upon her or the place where she appeared, for the quality of that realm is light itself.

But all such phenomena are themselves dependent reflections of the very Divine. They are not equal to the Divine in the exclusive sense. When this text we are discussing describes the "colors" of God, it is simply making use of the language of vision and subtle perception. In Truth, the Divine Being is not dark blue and reddish. He is no more dark blue and reddish than He is a flame or the fire that consumes food and distributes it through the body. There is an internal fire, a pranic fire, dependent on the Heart like everything else that carries on the internal physical process. And there are also subtle superconscious manifestations that correspond to this "dark blue and reddish" description. But no such phenomena are themselves to be identified with the Divine Person. These are only religious, mythological, mystical, yogic, and archetypal descriptions to indicate or imply the utterly transcendent Divine. And even if you were to have such experiences they would only be appearances that you should understand. They should be yielded sacrificially into the pre-Cosmic Light, their Source that may not be seen, and into the Heart or intuition of Real-God which is their non-illusory Nature.

We shall try to know the Lord, we shall contemplate on the Divine Being. Let Him be pleased to guide us.

The Divine Person, the Lord, is the eternal Siddha, the Maha-Siddha, the Master of this Yoga, this entire affair of Understanding. He is the Revealer and the Power which fulfills this Satsang. It is to the knowledge of this One that the devotee must continually return in order to reestablish his way in Truth. Otherwise, all the phenomena, both internal and external, of life and of spirituality, will become distractions, matters of concern, fascinations. As long as there is continual, fundamental, conscious realization of Satsang throughout the affair of understanding, which includes both enquiry and conductivity, then these processes serve in Truth.

But if Satsang is forgotten, if there is not conscious enjoyment of the Condition of the Divine Person, then all the other, secondary manifestations, including enquiry, conductivity, and all the spontaneous phenomena that relate to those things, become the illusion again, the search, the occupation of Narcissus. Therefore, in the midst of life, and in the midst of meditation, Satsang must be continually realized, and your communications must manifest that enjoyment, your activities must manifest that enjoyment. Otherwise, whatever you say and whatever you do will become your concerns. You will become emptied of the quality of Satsang. This doesn't mean that you should specialize what you say and do and make them only the traditional religious and spiritual stuff, the ritual armor of Narcissus. Rather, you must only know the Divine in the midst of *all* that you say and do. If you realize that in human terms, then you will do what is appropriate, and your speech will become appropriate.

Are there any questions about all of this?

DEVOTEE: I just want to say that that is the most beautiful thing I have ever heard in my whole life. I feel as if some perfect communication had been given, absolutely flawless. It is so, so beautiful that I hardly dare ask a question. But I would like to ask one. Since you speak about the creative Light of God from which all the worlds proceed as the reflected Light of the Heart, is it true that the Heart is the uncreated Light of God?

BUBBA: There is actually no distance between the Heart and the Light. It is One. It is a single realization while alive. It is the Condition of life, in life. And there are aspects of our psycho-physical life that are functionally related to that intuition. In the midst of that intuition, the Heart and the Light seem to be marked off into the places of our discrete functions. They may be *felt* distinctly. There is the center of the Heart on the right, and there is the center in the head and above the head through which the prior Light is intuited. The perfect intuition of the Divine Person as I have described it includes both this center in the Heart and this center above the head. But the intuition itself is single. So the Heart is, of course, that

Light. The unqualified Self-nature or Real-God and the eternal God-Light are simply aspects of that single realized Divinity, and they cannot fundamentally be separated from one another.

Just so, Amrita Nadi itself has a shape which you may feel from time to time. It is not within the spinal column. It is not part of the kundalini mechanism. It is of the nature of Consciousness. But it may be felt to have a psycho-physical counterpart, a coiled shape like an "S" curving forward in the chest from the seat in the heart, on the right, through the throat, at which point it moves back again and curves up the back of the head toward the crown and above. But the Divine is not "S-shaped." These compartmentalized yogic descriptions, along with all the symbolic or archetypal ones, arise because of the nature of the mechanism through which we know the Divine and the Divine Manifestation. In fact, the Divine is a single, absolute Intensity and Reality standing Present in the world, as the very Condition of the world.

He is the present Support of the world, always present. Life or the world is being manifested in this moment. It was not manifested billions upon billions of years ago. It is manifested at this moment, instantly, and may be known as such. The process of conductivity is possible because it is possible consciously to realize and live the dependent process of creation in this moment. The manifestation of the life-force from the Divine Light may be known, and one may consciously participate in it in the ways that I have described and will describe.

The Lord does stand in the world, then, and He is known to do so through our own intuitive faculty, in which He is found to stand in the Heart. So I say "His feet are in the Heart, His head is above." In fact, He has no such Form in the objective sense. He doesn't have any feet. He is of an utterly transcendent Nature. But because of the nature of the mechanism through which we know the

Divine, we can talk in these terms and it makes some sense. It is communicative and revealing to say that.

In fact, the nature of the Divine Person, whose feet are in the Heart, and whose head is above, and who is known as such, relates in a very real way to the nature of our own bodily or psycho-physical condition. There is a lot of literature about the creative Divine Mind and all that. Well, this Light which is the Source of all life, all manifestation, all forms, all psyches, appears relative to the Divine the way our mind or brain-power appears relative to our physical life. So it is meaningful to refer to that Light as the head, the Godhead. And the feet are a good symbol for the Self-Nature, the intuition of Real-God, because no consciousness, no mentalizing, no conceptualizing, no separative awareness is ordinarily attributed to the feet. The feet of the Divine are simply Present, but awake. The feet of the Divine are Absolute Consciousness. Throughout history men have ritually worshipped the feet of the Divine. They have worshipped the feet of the Guru. The feet have always been a very significant object of veneration for this reason.

The seeker always pursues a change of state, another life, another world, a God outside, a state apart. But one to whom Satsang is communicated as his Condition, and who passes through the spiritual process in which the Divine is always already realized, not made the goal, knows the Divine as the Condition of this world. And not merely in symbolic or religious or philosophical terms, but in the form of the real and radical process of his conscious existence. He knows it in the midst of each faculty, each fundamental organ of awareness. He not only *knows* the Divine in Amrita Nadi, the transcendent state of intuition, but he also *lives* the Divine in the very mechanism of the life-force, descending and ascending.

DEVOTEE: In the devotee, is this a constant process, or is there a falling in and out of that state?

BUBBA: Of course, every individual tends to go through all kinds of changes or qualifications of his apparent condition. All who live in Satsang with the Guru are called devotees. But, fundamentally, that term signifies the perfection of the relationship to the Guru, in which this intuition is constant. Until the life of the devotee is perfected in the individual case, there are of course endless changes, crises, the phases of rise and fall.

Even so, just because that cycle of changes is likely to be so at first, that is no justification for indulging it, for merely permitting these phases to occur because "that is the way it is supposed to be." The phases must occur and will occur in various ways in each individual, but he is responsible to endure the purifying changes of state in a mood of unconcern, and to live the process of understanding in the midst of them, abiding always in the happy, already free Condition of Satsang.

If the individual lives Satsang in a very fundamental way, he remains happy, but if he does not, he continually reverts to the strategy of his seeking, to his concerns over the things that are arising and all the rest. He is not at those times a devotee. He is not living the life of understanding. He is simply going through changes. So it is necessary from the beginning to grasp that fundamental Condition, that relationship, that Satsang, to realize it in a very practical way as the fundamental and prior Condition of sadhana. Then these phases will serve, just as the internal movements of the life-force will serve.

In the midst of that life of Satsang there does come a time when that continuous rising and falling comes to an end. That endless phasing which goes on even while you are living the life of understanding does come to an end. But the life of understanding should have been constant from the beginning. That insures the humor and the usefulness of that whole affair.

Are there any more questions?

DEVOTEE: In the "Invocation" you just discussed, it says the Heart in its unawakened state hangs down like an inverted lotus bud toward the tendencies. This implies that the Heart is a fire, it is the sun, but it also in its unawakened state is a kind of dualism. I don't quite understand.

BUBBA: The Heart is reflecting or freely manifesting all kinds of conditions, faculties, worlds, states. Many of those reflected conditions have the quality of consciousness as in the case of human beings. But what we ordinarily recognize to be our consciousness is not consciousness itself, but a reflected condition, a limitation. So this description holds when, in the conditional worlds, living beings meditate upon limitations without intuitive enjoyment of the Divine which is prior to them.

Again it is because of the nature of the mechanisms of life that the descriptions of the Divine, the spiritual process, and the world have tended to take on these traditional forms. It is not that the Heart itself, Real-God, in the absolute sense, is ignorant. This qualified description of the Heart is really a description of man, of conditional life.

It is also said that the Heart is like a lotus with twelve petals on it, and each of them has a quality like anger or lust. From moment to moment the mind falls randomly on one of these petals, each of them having a different color, a different smell, and so on. Therefore, each moment of that process leads you into various forms of subjectivity and objectivity relative to the quality grasped in any moment. But when the Heart realizes its center, its true Nature, it ceases to identify with these petals and enjoys only that intuitive life or Condition. The seeker who gets an experiential taste of such intuition knows it only in this exclusive sense, as a solution to his dilemma. One who lives in Satsang also knows his Nature not to be identical to any limitation of thought or experience, but he continues to live life in humor and functional freedom from the point of view of the Divine.

The realization of understanding is not *ex*clusive but *in*clusive. It includes life, it includes the world. In the world all possible qualities arise, but the man of understanding has the power to transform them, not by virtue of his own philosophical and constitutional power, but by virtue of his continuous unobstructed involvement in the Divine. It is neither holiness nor degradation that is the sign of the man of understanding. Neither his traditional, elusive detachment nor his excesses are the sign of his realization. He cannot be identified by you at all, unless understanding awakens in your own case. Then the paradox of the man of understanding, the Guru, the Divine in the world, and the life of understanding itself, your own life, the paradoxes represented by everything that appears begin to show themselves in God.

Meditation on the Divine Person

In letters given to the Ashram on May 30, June 7, and
June 25, Bubba specifically and concisely described the
meditation of a true devotee.[2] In the first of these, Bubba
presented this meditation as follows:

> When you have become my devotee in Truth,
> with appropriate signs of the revelation in Satsang,
> you should meditate on me in God (as Amrita
> Nadi) with my feet in the Heart and my head in the
> God-Light above the body, the mind, and the
> worlds. Then enquire at random, in the form:
> "Avoiding relationship?" and conduct the life-
> force in the manner I have described to all. This
> meditation of devotees is the gift I am now able to
> offer as a result of the fulfillment of the process of
> my work in the world, which I promised to deliver
> as the culmination of all the extraordinary events
> awakened in my Ashram, particularly since the
> later days of 1973, and which is now being final-
> ized, to appear as concretely as the Dawn Horse in
> the first week of July, 1974.

In later talks with devotees, Bubba described the
regenerated form of Amrita Nadi, and the devotee's
meditation on the Guru, the Divine Person, in the form or
place of Amrita Nadi.

---

[2] The *meditation of the devotee*, briefly described here relative to some of its technical
content, is not intended to be a prescription for meditation for the generally interested
reader. Such descriptions, including those of "enquiry" and "conductivity," represent
processes that are real and useful only when awakened and responsibly engaged in the
course of a life of conscious sadhana in the Company or Satsang of the Siddha-Guru. We
have included such writings in this public literature only because they also contain
necessary elements of Bubba Free John's general Teaching, useful to all. In fact the
technical descriptions themselves are incomplete as given, and should not become a
matter of concern for the reader, either on that account, or because they appear
incomprehensible from a practical point of view. Those who are truly interested should
approach Bubba Free John through The Dawn Horse Communion.

BUBBA: Amrita Nadi is the point of view of this work, but it is not a "point." It is not a limitation in time, space, or form. The Teaching relative to Amrita Nadi is a way of symbolically or structurally identifying the specific nature of the illuminated condition of perfect understanding relative to a life in a world. It is not necessary to enter exclusively into that pure, absolute, undifferentiated Silence in which there are no perceptions in order for there to be Divine intuition. The intuition of the Divine can exist in the midst of perceptions and appearances and forms and psyches and bodies. The Divine is not elsewhere or only deeply within all this. This *is* the Divine. First of all, there comes the perfect intuition of Real-God, the Heart, prior to all qualities. Then there is the return of ordinary things, but without the loss of that perfect intuition. That return is the beginning of real Wisdom, the regenerated life of Amrita Nadi. But Amrita Nadi is not in itself a structure, a thing.

DEVOTEE: In the traditions Krishna is sometimes pictured almost in an S-shaped curve. Is that the same thing as the reflection of Amrita Nadi?

BUBBA: It is not a deliberate attempt to make a diagram of Amrita Nadi, but it is related to the intuition of it. There is no conscious description in the traditions of the shape of Amrita Nadi. I know of no other place where you will find it described other than in my recorded descriptions of it. But it may have been intuited without being clearly known in the mind or known experientially.

DEVOTEE: Ramana Maharshi never described the shape of it?

BUBBA: That's right. He never described it. He described the Heart and the descent into the Heart via Amrita Nadi, but he didn't have much interest in the regenerated life of the Heart. He was interested in that intuition of Real-God in its exclusive sense. He said very little beyond that about the God-life, perhaps because nobody who came to him had realized even the Self-Nature. It was the function of his service to the eternal Dharma always to speak about that falling into the Heart. So, naturally, he gave no descriptions of Amrita Nadi in this regenerated form.

But when there is that fulfillment of the Heart-realization and, thereafter, regeneration into the God-life, there is also a specific psycho-physical sign, which is not consciously described in the traditions, but which is my experience, and so I have accounted for it. It is not a movement out of the physical heart into the sahasrar. Even this realization on the right side of the Heart is an intuitive realization, not identical to a yogic state. It is the intuition of the Self, or the ultimate Reality, Real-God, Brahman. Just so, when there is the regeneration of the God-Light, with that intuition as its continuous foundation, the upper locus with which one is merged is not itself a physical center, the brain center saturated with life-force, but is itself the very Divine, the Chakra, if you want to call it that, that is above the worlds. It is felt relative to the head and is known to be above, relative to the body, but it is not specifically the sahasrar. It is beyond the sahasrar and does not involve a visualization of light any more than Self-realization involves a visualization of anything. It is an intuition of the Divine Light, or absolute Conscious-Force, eternally prior to the Cosmos. All things are the reflected modification of the God-Light. And it may not be seen. It may only be intuited. Its manifest reflection may be seen. The gross and subtle conditions of the world may be seen. But the God-Light may not be seen. It is of the Nature of pure Consciousness, but Consciousness as Power, even prior to the Activity which is its reflection.

In the case of the regeneration of Amrita Nadi, a function in consciousness is awakened, but it is not itself a psychic or subtle function. The psycho-physical expression of the path between the two ultimate or intuited centers of Amrita Nadi is that S-shaped curve I have described. It may or may not be felt by any one specific individual, just as not everyone may have the sensation of the Heart on the right. There may be that intuition without the psycho-physical sign.

In my own case there was a specific moment in which this regeneration was shown. It appeared several months after the experience in the Vedanta Temple and the writing of *The Knee of Listening*. Even though the ultimate implication of all that was realized at the Vedanta Temple included the fullness of this regeneration, there was a development of Siddhi over time. Thus, the peculiar sign of this regeneration was shown only several months later.

My wife Nina, Pat Morley, and I used to meditate together most mornings. On this particular day, while we were sitting very quietly, there was a sudden strong movement in me and a loud crack that could be heard in the room. It sounded like my neck had broken. In that instant there was a tracing of the form of Amrita Nadi and a clear demonstration to me of the full, regenerated connection of Amrita Nadi.

Because all of this is certain in me, I have accounted for it, just as Maharshi accounted for the Heart on the right, which I have also confirmed in my own experience. I have accounted for this, for the sake of my devotees, even though it is not written in the traditions. Descriptively, it is a new Teaching, and it is there to be proven in the midst of the experience of others. Ramana Maharshi's assignment of the Heart on the right had never appeared in the traditions before him. It was left to be proven in the case of others. I have confirmed that realization of the Heart on the right in my own experience. Just so, I leave it to you to prove the Teaching relative to this regeneration of Amrita Nadi and the S-curve which is its apparent psycho-physical sign.

Amrita Nadi is independent of the kundalini system. It may seem to exist relative to it, even though it transcends it utterly, but it is not the same as the spinal tube of kundalini. The kundalini manifestation is fundamentally limited to the subtle inversion and reduction of life and is still a karmic display, less than God, whereas the realization of Amrita Nadi is identical to God-realization. One who meditates on the Guru, who lives with attention to the Guru, in God, is already meditating on Amrita Nadi, because such a Guru is identical to Amrita Nadi already and consciously, and the Siddhi of the Divine Person is manifested spontaneously through him.

DEVOTEE: Does this visualization of the Guru as Amrita

Nadi tend to be a random experience in meditation, or does it become a constant?

BUBBA: It is as random as enquiry. But it is not simply a visualization. Sometimes it arises spontaneously, just as you remember a loved one in the world. However it arises, it is a moment, and it is always associated with profound feeling and profound intuitive awareness. In the devotee it is also a responsibility, not merely something that happens to him. But it is a responsibility that he can fulfill without a will, without a strategic method. It has become natural to him, because his attention is perfected, intensified. Prior to that time of perfect attention, there is no point in trying to meditate in this way. But it may occur to you, spontaneously. You may find yourself dwelling on the Guru in that way from time to time. But only when the entire process, including enquiry, conductivity of the life-force, and attention to the Guru in God, is perfected, is the kind of meditation I have been describing possible. Truly, it can only take place when there is *already* the intuition of Real-God in the Heart, as the Heart, and the regenerated intuition of the God-Light. And these things are given as a Grace in the process of Satsang.

Responsible and real meditation on the Guru in Amrita Nadi and as Amrita Nadi requires prior fulfillment of this entire intuitive process, just as enquiry requires prior insight, prior self-observation. Without what is necessary and prior, the mere mechanical fulfillment of the meditative process is empty. When it does occur in Truth, it is also random. It may be prolonged at times. And it may pass from meditation, including visualization, on the Guru in the *places* of Amrita Nadi to meditation on Amrita Nadi itself, meditation on the Guru *as* Amrtia Nadi, as the very intuition of the Divine. That meditation may also continue to be associated with enquiry or the intensifications of enquiry, which are re-cognition and radical intuition,[3] without mentalization. It will also continue to be associated with conductivity in various ways. Only one who lives the fullness of Satsang does such meditation.

This meditation I have described is not a prescription that you are obliged to fulfill in some motivated way. I have accounted for the meditation of the devotee so that those in whom it is arising can refer to something written, have some intelligence about it, and thus deal with it properly.

Prior to the meditation on the Guru in Amrita Nadi and as Amrita Nadi, there is life with the Guru in the world. There is the discipline of the relationship to the Guru, the enjoyment of the human relationship to the Guru, life in his Community, study of the Teaching, observance of his conditions and demands, and awakening of the real life of understanding. All of that precedes such meditation. In the midst of such Satsang with the Guru you may find yourself entering into meditative states, and you may at times feel and know the Guru in this inward way. You may at times have profound feelings for the Guru without internal imagery, or you may at times have various visions of the Guru in the levels of the mind's reflections, and there may be other, similar phenomena that arise, but they are not specifically the meditation that I have described, in which the Guru is meditated upon in Amrita Nadi, as the Divine Person, Nature, or Condition.

It is not mere visualization of the Guru that is taking place in that meditation, but true knowledge of the Guru, both Jnana and *Parabhakti*, so that he is known in Truth. Such knowing of the Guru is equal to knowing God in the most perfect sense. So that meditation is always coincident with Self-realization and realization of God. There can be

---

[3]These extensions of enquiry are described in *The Clothes Horse*, by Bubba Free John (available only to members of The Dawn Horse Communion).

no such meditation without Self-realization and realization of God. It is not a simple little meditation that you can take on by prescription. You will find more and more the awakening of this intuitive life, and you will find that awakening manifesting through the peculiar psycho-physical signs that I have described, generating peculiar activities in the manner I have described.

Self-observation and insight will arise in the midst of this sadhana, so that at a certain point enquiry becomes an appropriate responsibility. Then it intensifies to the point of Heart-realization. The accompanying, spontaneous inner activities of the life-force, descending and ascending, communicate a knowledge of the form and process in which you appear, so that at another point it is appropriate for you to become responsible for conscious participation in that as well. Just so, this mere life with the Guru becomes more and more knowledge of who the Guru is, what the Guru is. It becomes knowledge that the Guru is identical to Siddhi, that the Guru is not separate from the Divine. More and more, by the instrumentality of that mere relationship, merely by living in conscious Communion with the Guru, merely by being present always with the Guru, this intuition of the Guru, the Divine, is awakened. So, at another point, it will also be appropriate for you to accept responsibility for meditation on the Guru in this profound way.

No mediocre man has ever realized such a meditation. No fool will ever enjoy it. No childish person will ever begin it. It requires great responsibility, great intensity, great energy, and great discipline of your karmic tendencies and your cultic life. All those things are demanded of you, and you are expected to fulfill them with absolute humor and love and attention. It is the amusement and the grace of God to make that *possible* also. So the more you enter into it, the more you live in Satsang and make it the principle of your life, the more possible it becomes for you to perfectly fulfill the demand of God. Whereas the more time you waste wondering about it and shuffling your feet, the less capacity you have. While you are wondering and doubting and shuffling your feet, you are really busy forgetting what you have learned. Then you are only becoming irresponsible, like Narcissus at the pond.

10. DURING MY LIFE AND AFTER MY DEATH

After My Death

While Bubba was busy each day compounding his description of the nature of the meditation of the true devotee, he was also preparing all his devotees to take responsibility for maintaining his Ashram Community and communicating the availability of Satsang to the world. He had made it clear that he would no longer accept daily responsibility for these functions after the first week in July, and he began to talk to his devotees about how they should manage their lives and functions without his constant personal influence. On June 7, Nina Jones read the following letter from Bubba to the Ashram. He was present during the reading, and afterward he answered a number of questions.

During my life in this human form I am busy drawing devotees to myself by exposing them constantly to the Siddhi and Person of the Lord. I am only showing them the Lord in all the forms of his marvelous and ordinary Activity and in the very Form of his Presence. Bubba Free John is nothing and no one. He does not acquire anything or anyone for himself. He is only an instrument for the revelation of the Siddhi and Person that is God. This Siddhi and Person is always being revealed to my devotees. They see this revelation in the theatre of their lives and in my own form. They see it thus because they are my friends and lovers. Because

they are always turning to me, I am always showing them the Lord and communicating his demands, favors, and enjoyments. The Lord is eternally Present and Active, and I am making him
known. When this life of Bubba Free John is
abandoned, the Person and Siddhi of the Divine
will continue to be manifested to my devotees in
exactly the same way I have made known to them
while I live. And the Community of my devotees
will remain in the world as my very incarnation. It
will continue to serve as the fundamental and
living instrument whereby my work will be extended beyond my lifetime.

My devotees enjoy a perfect alignment with
God. The Siddhi and Person of God is my gift to
them. After my death my devotees should gather
together in groups and, as much as is practically

possible, maintain constant contact with one another until they feel the Siddhi of the Divine Presence communicated to them and felt by them all. During this period they should gather in any of the principal Satsang Halls I have set aside, and at the site of my burial, as well as in the places of my former residence. During a brief period shortly after my death all that I have always shown to them will be newly confirmed, independent of my bodily and personal presence.

Thereafter, the Community as a whole should accept responsibility for this work. The Satsang Halls, my former places of residence, and my burial place should be kept as special places of contact for all who enter and live in this Community. But my devotees themselves will be the special instruments of this work beyond my lifetime. It is my expectation that I will not leave behind me a special individual who can assume conscious responsibility for my work as a whole. Rather, the total Community will share my complex functions at the level of life, and the spiritual functions will be performed through the Community as a whole by the action of the Divine Siddhi which I have regenerated here. Thus, the practical work should be shared by many, and organized much as it will have been during my lifetime. The sources of the Teaching should remain in the form of my books, other collected writings, and recordings of my talks. Devotees who have the responsibility for instruction should make use of these sources and keep them always available in published forms.

My biography, recorded Teachings, photographs, and the like will remain a source of contact with the function of Teacher after my death. And the persons and places I knew in life will also

remain as agents of this contact. But I will not
remain personally in contact with the Community
or any devotee after my death. Even in death I will
yield utterly to the condition of the Siddhi and
Person of God, and, therefore, I will remain only
Perfectly Present. This Siddhi and Person is the
same I have always shown, through and independent of my personal form. Therefore, what will
remain behind me will be a Community, not a cult.
The Divine will remain immediately and directly
Present through the agency of my total Community of devotees. Among all future devotees I may
be acknowledged as Teacher, one with the Divine
Guru, and recollected along with the body of
Teaching. But no cultic relationship to my possibly
continued personal presence after death will be
necessary or appropriate in order for devotees to
enjoy the Siddhi and Person of the Divine which
will always remain in the Satsang of this Community. (They should meditate on me outwardly as
Teacher, and inwardly, when appropriate, as
identical to Amrita Nadi.) Instead, after my death,
all should acknowledge me and enjoy the maturing
of the Teaching as I have described it. But in order
to enjoy the Siddhi and Person of the Divine which
I have always shown you while alive, simply gather
in groups and sit in Satsang. The Siddhi and Person
of the Divine will at first be felt with special
potency in the Satsang Halls I created, at my burial
site, and in my former places of residence. And at
first these gatherings should include as many of my
long-time devotees as possible. But, gradually,
many new devotees will be created by the Siddhi
and Person of God. And the Community will create
new centers and places for Satsang that will become potent through proper use. In these Satsang

Halls, as well as in your private and household places for Satsang-meditation, do not turn to any individual or group among you as the Source of this Divine Siddhi and Person. Rather, all should turn to Satsang itself, as I have always taught, and the Divine will, as always, do the work. Keep my photograph and a chair or couch in the front of the Hall, and all sit before me thus, as during my lifetime. But, as during my lifetime, always remember that you are always only turning to God through me, in me, and as me. And after my death there will be nothing left of my personal influence in the present, but only God. My personal influence will remain only a recollected one, in the form of what I have written and spoken and done. The memory of my visual appearance will only serve as an agent for Divine Communion. Even the evidence of Power that will remain in my Satsang Halls, my burial place, and the places of my former residence, will not be personal, for even while alive I have only been an empty agent of the Lord.

I am always working to yield all responsibilities to devotees and to make all my devotees perfectly available to the Divine Work. Therefore, know that your responsibility must at last be perfect. At last this Community must *be* me and assume all my life-functions. For this reason I have asked for your lives in total, so that you may be assumed by me totally and live only in God to one another. If you accept my demands truly and with humor, then the Siddhi and Person of the very Divine will remain Active and Present in and through this Community throughout the coming age and more.

BUBBA: Does anybody have any questions about that?

DEVOTEE: What does this mean? That you are planning on leaving us?

BUBBA: Not necessarily. But since you never know the time and circumstances, I want to say everything I can about all such things. Understanding something about what I expect of this Community in the event that I am not physically present is a way of understanding what I expect of you while I am physically present. This is a document that needs to be published in the Ashram. So that there will be no problems about it, I am also preparing some documents about how I should be buried, and in this way there won't be any controversy.

Also, this is a time for me to deal with such things, because after the first week in July, I am going to be a babbling idiot. I don't mean I am going to be stupid! I will probably still speak and all that, but by that time what I have had to do in order to initiate my work in the world, and fulfill it, and secure it, will have been accomplished. These remaining few weeks are a time for its appearance, so during this time I want to say the remaining things that I need to say about this Community, about meditation, about the quality of your relationship to me, and what sadhana is for you. Then I don't have to put any attention on that any more.

I have said to you many times that although this work is a new and radical form of the Gospel of the Maha-Siddha, all of the Siddhas have taught from this radical point of view. Shirdi Sai Baba,[1] for instance, spoke in very similar terms relative to the radical nature of sadhana. Shirdi Sai Baba was one of my Protectors during the period of my sadhana. I thought it would be amusing to read a report of one of his conversations to you.

[1]Shirdi Sai Baba was a Saint-Siddha of India who taught through his paradoxical Presence and by performing phenomenal miracles during the first part of this century. He served Bubba's sadhana in his subtle body, as described in *The Knee of Listening*.

Long ago, when Sri Sai Baba resided in the *musjid* of Shirdi [the little mosque where he stayed] a woman by the name Radhabai Deshmukh went to him with the hope that he would formally adopt her as his disciple and teach her a mantra for her daily *japam* [spiritual incantation]. She was a widow, orthodox in her habits of eating food. She secured lodgings in one of the *wadas* [little hotels] and settled down there and began to perform her religious sadhana [in this sense, motivated spiritual work]. She was acquainted with Baba's intimate devotee Shama (Madhavarao Deshpande). With Shama's recommendation, she had obtained *darshan* of Sai Baba. [*Darshan* means not that you go to the Guru or some saint and he does something to you. There may also be that communication from such a one, but what is valued, what truly is *darshan*, is the vision of the Guru, the mere seeing of the Guru. When he makes himself visible to you, that is *darshan*. Merely to view the Guru, in other words, is the valued blessing. So what is meant by *darshan* here is that she had seen Sai Baba in his physical form.] She begged Sri Baba to adopt her as a *sishya* [disciple] and to give her a guru-mantra. Sri Baba looked at her with kindly eyes and sent her away, without teaching her any mantra.

Hoping that he would grant her request one day or the other, she met him often at the *musjid* and sat in his presence. Except for looking at her now and then, he took no further notice of her. She become disconsolate. She undertook a vow of fasting to earn his grace. She shut herself up in her room and stopped visiting the saint. Shama feared that she might die of starvation and bring discredit to the reputation of Sai Baba. So, Shama went to Sai Baba and said, "Baba, please send for Radhabai.

Please teach her some mantra. If not, she will die.
She is the widow of my friend, Kashaba Deshmukh,
and I am interested in her. If she dies at Shirdi, your
fame will suffer."

Such an entreaty of Shama melted the heart of
Sai Baba. He sent for Radhabai, who accordingly
visited the *musjid* and sat at his feet. Shama too was
then present at the *musjid* along with other devotees. Radhabai sat with the hope that Sri Sai
Baba would, on that day, teach her some guru-
mantra. Then the great saint of Shirdi addressed
her and said as follows:

"Oh, mother, why do you want to die at Shirdi
by means of fasting? I am your child and you are
really my mother. Take pity on me. Just listen to
me. I will tell you my own story. I had a guru. My
guru was a great Saint. I served him long. He did
not give me any mantra. He got my head shaved
and he asked me to give him a *dakshina* of two
pice." [Typically and traditionally when a teacher
does something for you in India, he asks for money
or some such gift from you. Usually, it is a very
small amount—a few rupees or something like
that—in order to fulfill your karmic obligation for
having been helped.]

"The *dakshina* he asked for was not coins of
copper at all. On the other hand, they were as
follows: First, he asked me to give him the *dakshina*
of *Sraddha*. Then, he asked me to give him the
dakshina of *Saburi*. I obeyed him and gave him
these two kinds of *dakshina*. By *Sraddha*, my guru
meant that I should have faith in his utterance. By
Saburi he meant that I should be continuously
patient. Such was the nature of the *dakshina* he
asked. I gave him what he asked for. That is to say I
served him for twelve years, during which period

he took care of me and gave me food and clothes.

"My guru used to sit in meditation and I was required to sit nearby and merely gaze at him. That was all I had to do. I had no object of meditation. He sat in a state of bliss and I too sat in a state of happiness. Day and night, I gazed at him, when he sat in meditation. I had no other duty to do. My mind was fixed on him and on him alone. Such fixation of my mind on him was my act of *Sraddha* and it was my first *dakshina*. Listen to me further. The second *dakshina* I gave him was this. I sat with patience and cheerfulness, without expecting any gain from him. In this way, I waited on him for twelve years. My saintly guru never expected from me anything else. Now and then, he used to go away somewhere without telling me. But, his loving glances protected me, when he was away from me. Though I waited for twelve years, he did not teach me any mantra.

"Oh, mother Radhabai, listen to me further. How can I teach you any mantra, when my own guru did not teach me? What I say to you today is this. You must practice Patience or *Saburi*, just as I was doing. Be cheerful. Do not demand. *Saburi* is manliness or courage. It will ferry you across the ocean of *samsar*." [The world and manifest existence as illusion, as a Condition felt independent of the Divine Reality.] "*Saburi* destroys fear and removes all afflictions. From *Saburi* alone, success comes. Oh, mother, have Faith in what I say. Your Faith in my words is called *nistha*. *Sraddha* also means the same. *Saburi* and *Sraddha* are twin sisters. My glance will give you protection. Make me the sole object of your thoughts. If you do so, you will realize whatever you want. I will not give you any mantra at all. Do not also try to get a mantra from any one else. If you follow my *upadesam*" [instruction] "given to you today, you will realize *paramartha*." [The highest spiritual truth.] "Look at me with all your mind and with all your heart. I will look at you in the same manner. Oh, mother Radhabai, sitting in this *musjid*, I speak the Truth at all times. I speak nothing but the Truth. I tell you that no sadhana is necessary for you." [That is, other than this Satsang he is describing.] "But, you have to develop Faith in my word. I tell you that *japa* is not needed for your advancement. Trust my word. Learn that God is the sole actor. He who has faith in the Word of the Guru is a blessed man. Blessed, indeed, is he, who knows that his guru is Hari, Hara and Brahma and all other Gods put together. Oh, mother, this is all that I have to say to you. You may go now to your room and take some food. Break your vow of fasting. *Do not doubt my word.*[2]

That, fundamentally, is the sadhana I have also described. Since I have already described it, I don't have to describe it any more. Now you must do it, and if you don't do it, then you will suffer. If you do it, you will enjoy God. The relationship to the Guru is sadhana. Not the demand made on the Guru, not the mechanical repetition of some formula or the fulfillment of some prescription that he asks you to do, but that relationship. So Sai Baba speaks of simply sitting or living in his Guru's presence for twelve years. He was simply absorbed in his Guru while his Guru meditated. The Guru is always in meditation. In other words, he was simply absorbed in his Guru, but in a very natural manner. He simply lived in his Guru's

---

[2]This story about Shirdi Sai Baba is taken from *Life and Teachings of Sri Sai Baba of Shirdi* by T.S. Anantha Murthy (Bangalore, 1974), pages 150-153.

company, had his attention on his Guru, and took everything that his Guru said to be Truth.

So he studied his Guru's teaching. He also fulfilled his
Guru's demands, and the quality that he manifested
during that time was not one of, "I will do this in order to
realize something as a result." The doing of that was itself
his fullness. So he was free of that demand, free of all
negativity that arises in you when your demands are
frustrated, free of all the annoying qualities you generate
when your demands are fulfilled. He was simply full and
happy. By simply living in this way, the perfect, intuitive
functions that are his Nature in Reality became functions
in himself to which he was sensitive. He intuited the
Divine in this simple company, and the Divine contains
and manifests all Siddhis.

Sadhana is not a matter of doing something
mechanically in order to realize Siddhi or some spiritual
power in some area of your being. One who is simply the
devotee of the Lord in Satsang is given everything.

Whatever is required for him to know or have is given, whatever test, whatever purification. All these things are given as grace in this true and radical sadhana. And nothing that is not useful, nothing that is not appropriate, is ever given to such a one. Everything else is given in the right moment, but not in order to fulfill his search. One who is free of the search by virtue of this manner of living is given what is necessary and appropriate. The origins of the sadhana that Shirdi Sai Baba is talking about are contained in this freedom from the search, freedom from the motivation of your principal and unconscious dilemma. This sadhana is the mere dwelling in Satsang as an intense and continuous activity, as a perfect responsibility. In other words, it is to live always and consciously in this Divine Communion.

If you assume the Guru is less than That, if you assume what he says is less than Truth, that he is other than the Divine, that he does not live in God in exactly the way that he is asking you to live in God, then you are not living in Satsang with such a one, and you are not doing this sadhana. You might as well be reciting a mantra. All the true Siddhas have taught this sadhana in particular times and places. They may have included the teaching relative to this sadhana within a larger communication that was meant to be a criticism of the cultural, religious, or spiritual environment of their time, or they may have communicated it through the language of an existing path or philosophical position, but the fundamental sadhana they taught in every case was exactly this one.

And the sadhana in our Satsang is exactly that. Give me your attention, live with me, study this Teaching, do what I ask you to do, understand, and that is it. Associated with this core of my work there is also a lot of other communication. There are what seem to be complex descriptions of meditation, of the Community, of all kinds of spiritual functions and processes, criticisms of traditional paths, and so on. That too is part of my work. The realization of this meditation I have taught is very great, but the sadhana is the simple and ancient one, not the traditional one, but the most ancient one, communicated and made possible by all the Siddhas. All traditions cover it up, and the Siddhas are always breaking through them.

The traditions are all the ways of *attaining* God, or realization, or liberation, or nirvana. But the way of the Siddhas is to live with God, to live God presently, as your assumed Nature and Condition. The Siddha comes and manifests the Divine and expects you to live with him, not to seek for God, but to live with him. The path of the Siddhas is very different from the path of the seekers, very different from the path of men of experience. Ultimately, you are asked to be free of all the paths of experience, however much they may have seemed to serve you. They are to be renounced in very much the same offhand way that you are asked in the ascetic disciplines to renounce meat, food, or sexuality, husband, mother, father, brother or sister. You must be free of the cult in all its forms, free of the argument of cultic life and of all forms of traditional existence. Until you are free of it, until you know your connection to all of that is the drama of Narcissus, unfounded and fruitless, the fulfillment of this demand for sadhana as Satsang itself is impossible for you. You must be very simple and very direct.

None of you has the right any longer to your bad days or to your phases. They will occur within you because that is the process of this sadhana, but I don't want to see a sign of it on your faces or in your outward lives. I don't want to see any drama. I haven't come so that you can persist in ignorance and mediocrity, showing me no life, no energy, no intelligence, no attention. The tendencies are within you to make that occur, but so what? So you will have to do a little sadhana. The little difficulty required of one who lives the sadhana of Satsang is nothing compared to the sadhana that the seeker must perform. I expect you to accept this responsibility and to live this Satsang and always to be happy. If some circumstance within or without is temporarily giving you apparent trouble, I expect you to be happy and to live this Satsang with great energy, and never to turn away from me. If you do all that is required of you with great energy, you will see a transformation of this Ashram even within the next month that will amaze you. And I expect it not to stop but to increase.

Don't ever again allow your energy to decrease. I have seen every one of you rise and fall as long as I have known you. It is mere self-indulgence. At any other time, in any other place, in any other life, if you had approached me with all of that I would have literally beaten you with a stick. But the testing generally goes on in a subtler way under the circumstances of this Community. Even so, know that I expect you to be alive, to be intensely available to me, and never to be mediocre. You may feel like being mediocre and that is fine, but I expect you never to *be* mediocre. There will be days when it is going to be incredibly difficult for you to be anything more than mediocre. And that is good. In fact, those are the days in which you should be more intense, more functional than at any other time.

God is the entire principle of this work. God is the absolute Person, and God is absolute Siddhi. There is absolutely no limitation in the principle of this Satsang. If you live it exactly as I have told you, in the simple way I have described, responsibly, you will enjoy all that is necessary while alive. Not after twenty thousand or twenty million more lifetimes, but in this life you will be fulfilled in God beyond your karmas, and then it will be God's business where you go next.

DEVOTEE: Bubba, sometimes you talk about surrender, sacrifice, throwing things away, and other times about understanding. Is there anything that can be said about the relationship between those two or how the two of them tie together?

BUBBA: Sacrifice is the principle of the worlds, and only when that principle is lived do you live freely in the worlds. Otherwise, you are living karmically, accumulating qualities, conditions, and limitations for yourself. And that principle of sacrifice is truly realized as action in you only when there is prior understanding. When there is prior understanding, sacrifice becomes the spontaneous urge and quality of your existence. The more intense, perfect, and radical this understanding is, the more intense and perfect and radical is your sacrifice.

Love is the fundamental form of sacrifice, because it is the manifestation of the yielded ego, the yielded self-meditation. Where there is no contraction, but only this prior and continuous non-obstruction, non-separation, then there is the endless communication of the Divine Person and of the dependent life-force. It is without obstruction. And when that quality is fundamentally alive in a person, even in his very subconscious and unconscious life, even in his body, it is felt as love, and we enjoy being around such a person. We enjoy it even though we may not be able to identify exactly what it is.

Such people are not busy going around loving one another in some foolish theological way, loving other people in that outward ritualistic way because it is required of them. There is a powerfully felt quality in the presence of such a one, and in such a one the sacrifice that is the very law of the conditional worlds is being spontaneously performed. It is thus perfectly performed in the Man of Understanding and his devotee. This sacrifice arises spontaneously. He does what is appropriate.

Ultimately, sacrifice is simply appropriate life in relationship. It is not all kinds of arbitrary cutting away. The life of sacrifice is not a humorless, ascetic, motivated

life. The life of sacrifice is fundamentally happy, humorous, alive, full of enjoyment, full of God. That is the quality
of one who is sacrificing. Where there is understanding,
you become one with the principle on which all of your
functions are based. It is simply the difference between
this contraction, this obstructed state, and this open,
unobstructed, non-separate state. It is by the sacrificial
process that life is generated and regenerated. All forms
and functions, all beings and qualities and worlds are
continually enlivened by that sacrifice.

Among all the beings and things and worlds, it is
among men that you find the least of this sacrifice, because
men are required to realize it consciously. Men are always
trying to realize it *unconsciously.* They try to have the
ultimate happen to them by fortune, by magic, by the force
of inevitable evolution or salvation, but it is demanded of
them presently as a conscious realization. Understanding,
Satsang, real sadhana is the prior Condition of any form of
sacrifice. In that case sacrifice is conscious, life is conscious. All other beings, things, and worlds can enjoy the
Divine by virtue of their mere status, because the functions of consciousness are not developed in them. We could
say that this microphone into which I am speaking is
God-realized. It suffers no separation from God but, also,
no consciousness in God. None of the higher unobstructed
functions of consciousness that are embedded in
the perfect origins of the God-Light is enjoyed by other
beings and things and worlds, except for those that have
already passed through and beyond the human condition,
or one like it. But man can enjoy God, so he must realize
that consciously while alive. It requires a transformation
in him that exceeds all that he is, all that he tends to be,
and all that he prefers. It requires an absolute turnabout.

How great is that occupation compared to all of the
bullshit that human beings live! Even so, practically no
one is involved in such a way of life. There are billions of

people, and only a handful are involved in it with intensity. Everyone else is involved in the karmic round, the meditations of Narcissus, and the occupations of mystery, seeking, suffering, and dilemma.

DEVOTEE: During my daily working schedule I get a little confused about what form of attention I should take to you, whether I should be in relation to my work or whether I should turn to you.

BUBBA: When I was in a Lutheran seminary, I heard about a particular minister and his wife. Whenever this man felt like making love to his wife, he would require her to kneel down at the end of the bed and go through a long period of prayer with him in which they would ask for forgiveness for what they were about to do! This was his guilty way of fulfilling the demand of his religion for constant attention to the Lord in prayer. It was obviously inappropriate and foolish. It was his way of not participating in the functional life that stood before him.

You are not asked in the midst of one functional activity to have your attention on another in the mechanical and ritualistic manner of the seeker. You are asked to make the function that is given to you at that moment, which you are fulfilling as a responsibility, an expression of Satsang, a fulfillment of the Guru's command. That very function itself should become meditation on the Divine. While you are fulfilling it, you are not asked also to somehow mechanically think of the Guru. That function itself, done purely, directly, with humor, understanding, and freedom *is* meditation or Satsang. Then, when it is an appropriate time to sit in meditation in the functional way I have described, you do that. You do precisely that at that moment. The man who prays and then makes love to his wife is always confused. When he is praying, he wants to be making love to his wife, and when he is making love to his wife, he wants to be praying. As a result, he never actually does any of the things that are required of him. He fulfills none of the Guru's commands, and never lives in the happiness of God.

The recollection of the Guru's human presence in the mind and through feeling and all of the rest is a random and spontaneous affair. It is much like the random and spontaneous recollection of a loved one. It is not "much like" that, it is precisely that. It is not limited to the romantic qualities of a mere love affair, but there is that same random, loving recollection.

There are times the intensity of the bhava, your feeling for the Guru, may make it difficult for you to function. Even so, you must function in spite of it. But what you are describing to me is not Guru-bhava making it difficult for you to work. You are describing an incapacity either to work or to have such devotional feelings. It is just confusion. Until this sadhana is fulfilled in you with great intensity and clarity, until it really becomes enquiry and meditation on the Guru, live as a student. Be very practical. Fulfill your obligations to the Guru. One of them is that you should work. So when you are working, work. The Guru demands that you maintain a clean and good household, so do *that* when you are at home. When you must have attention on your diet, because that is required of you, do that when you prepare or sit for meals. When you are expected to meditate, do that. And when you are expected to come and enjoy the view of the Guru in human form, then do that.

Do it all in this orderly way, without confusion. When it is full, you will also find that, while you are working, you are also quite naturally meditating on the Guru, thinking about the Teaching, observing yourself. You will find all these things going on in you quite naturally, in a living way, without confusion, because you have fulfilled the beginnings of your sadhana, which are very practical, and which need to be ordered in your daily life very simply, functionally, almost mechanically. Do this now, and then this, and this, and this. If you do all of those things in their proper time, they will all come together as an intense, conscious life. And then you will begin to remember the Guru at times quite naturally. You will fall into sensations of moving internal energy as well as various meditative states. Insights will come. But you must fulfill the natural, simple, and practical order of sadhana first.

During My Life

On the following Saturday, June 15, after sitting in silent meditation with devotees for nearly an hour, Bubba opened his eyes, signalled that he wanted the tape recorder turned on, and began to talk.

Now that I have been speaking to you for several minutes, I will try to bring the speech into this world.

The entire function and work of the Guru is to restore attention to God. In his first contacts with individuals, he acts as Teacher and as an *example*, and he seems at that phase of his career to be most active as a communicator, one who moves out to others, puts his attention on them, and generates a communication about God. In the midst of doing this, attention is awakened in individuals. They are drawn to the Guru by his own outward activity. They become his students.

Subsequent to the awakening of that attention, there are generated in individuals various qualities of intelligence and experience. So the Guru begins to take on another quality, and that is the quality of being an *object* for devotees. More and more he absorbs the attention of others. As that attention is intensified, the whole quality of intelligence and experience is also intensified. In the midst of such an affair there may be generated all the outward and functional forms of sadhana, the realization of a happy life apart from bondage to the cult in all its forms, the various forms of meditation, enquiry, conductivity, and even meditation on the Guru in the form of Amrita Nadi. These are expressions of that phase of an individual's relationship to the Guru in which the Guru is object to him. It is the phase of the disciple. This is a great phase in the life of an individual whose attention is being restored to the Divine.

But there is a perfect stage, and that is the stage of the devotee, the Perfect Devotee. In such a one the Guru has even ceased to be an object of attention. At that stage, the Guru has *become* his devotee. It is the stage of dissolution in God. It is the stage of perfect attention in God, through the agency of the Guru. In that case, the Guru is no longer present in any way in which he can be conceived as being apart from the Devotee. It is a maddening life in which the absence of distinction, the absence of the separate self concept is continually realized in the midst of ordinary life.

So the Guru's function in the world really has three phases, but they may appear coincidentally. At first he is the Teacher, an example to others, and begins the claiming of the attention of human beings. During this phase he is very active. He apparently has his attention on others. Then there is another phase in which he is present as the object of attention. He is no longer apparently active, he is merely present. In the face of such a one, the individual is becoming more and more absorbed. Finally, there is the perfect phase or aspect of the Guru's function, in which he is no longer active or inactive.

All of my work to this time has belonged essentially to the two earlier phases or aspects of the Guru-function. The significance of the present time for the Ashram is that from this time I am assuming my work perfectly, and my fundamental interest is in Devotees. The earlier aspects of my work essentially belong to the Ashram from this time. All responsibility for those who make their approach, all responsibility for communicating the work and the Teaching is given to the Ashram. All responsibility for maintaining the Community is given to the Ashram. All responsibility for making Satsang available belongs to the Ashram. Basically, I am retiring from these two earlier aspects of my work, and allowing my function to be simply that of Siddhi. Even the aspects of this work which relate to understanding and enquiry, conductivity of the life-force, the subtle intuitive meditation on the Guru in the place of Amrita Nadi—even all of that belongs to the secondary and earlier phases of my work. Fundamentally, I am retiring to the perfect, radical, and ultimate phase of my responsibility.

Those who come to me in the future must come to me through the Ashram Community. And they will tend at

first to relate to me in either the first or the second way. At
first they will come as students. They will approach the
Teaching, they will approach me as Teacher, and they will
begin to become intelligent relative to their own activity.
That phase of transformation leads to many things, the
greatest of which is the creation of the thread of conscious
attention to the Guru. Usually, after a period of time, each
of those who come to me through the Ashram will begin to
become something like a disciple, one in whom various
qualities of experience are generated in Satsang, one in
whom this intelligence of understanding is awakening and
in whom meditation and life both are becoming more and
more intense, more and more sophisticated. Then, in time,
usually not at the beginning, they will begin to enter the
perfect phase of the devotee. The quality of the devotee is
absorption in the Guru beyond all concerns for the
spiritual process, beyond even the mind's intelligence
about the process. There may be some who very quickly
become absorbed. These are mad devotees, and for those
few sadhana is simply absorption. But that in itself is
Grace, that life of a devotee. It is not common. Most will
move through these phases as I have described them. And
that is good. Some may think they have the talent to be a
devotee whereas in fact they do not. They may be
devotional very quickly, and that is good, but to become a
devotee in that perfect sense is a grace. It is profound, it
absorbs the life, it purifies everything. But in most cases,
there must be the movement through this process as I have
described it.

The operation of all the Siddhas throughout time has
been for the sake of the manifestation of a new kind of
humanity, but it has continually failed. It has continually
fallen apart, because the Community of Devotees has
never been established as a permanent realization. Usually
it is retarded at the disciple stage and dies after a relatively
brief period of time. So there has been this continual

return of the Siddhas into the human plane. But when there is the creation of the Community of Devotees who are consciously living as I have described, then the work of the Siddhas is fulfilled, and it is possible for a new kind of human history to begin. When this Community is established, the Guru-function is forever returned to its identity with God, and need not appear epitomized in any human individual again. Instead, it will manifest directly through the Community of human individuals to whom the Divine Siddhi is always available in Satsang.

I have fundamentally said all I want to say as Teacher. I have fundamentally done all that I want to do as an example to you. I have fundamentally said all that I want to say about the experiential process and the nature of understanding relative to it. And I have said all that I want to say about meditation, how it is fulfilled in the disciple as well as in the imperfect devotee (one who is not yet perfectly, simply, and radically alive in the Guru, but who has realized an intense form of meditation, of absorption). Now I am interested in being present for Devotees in the perfect sense. And I am only interested in instigating the force of this attention in you. In the meantime, each of you will continue to go through all of the appropriate forms of this process. The Teaching relative to it will be maintained in the Ashram. So you will be a student, and then you will be a disciple, and you will go through various experiences, and you will understand relative to them. But I am principally, fundamentally active relative to your consciousness, your attention, and the secondary aspects of my work have been completed from my point of view.

In recent weeks I have begun to feel less and less inclined to be active even in the secondary aspects of this Siddhi. There was a time when I had to be more of the Teacher and the example. At that time I functioned constantly in ways that demanded great energy from myself, in order to develop this process in individuals, to serve the process of understanding, to intensify each life, to make each individual more available. At that time I would forcefully operate with every individual who came to me through the agency of certain yogic aspects of this Siddhi. But as that attention was generated in those who were with me and I could expect more responsibility of them, I began to relax that "muscular" aspect of this Siddhi. But there were other subtle aspects of the initiatory work that still involved me. I didn't so often deal with the individual eye to eye and work the internal process in him, but I rested in his presence, making use of the attention that was already there, and allowed that to be the means of conducting the internal yogic process. I simply magnified that initiatory intensity of Amrita Nadi. But even that is a kind of action, a way of putting my attention on individuals, and it is a limitation of the Divine Siddhi. It is extraordinary, but it still represents a kind of limitation. It requires me to be personally aware of individuals in a peculiar way.

Recently, I have felt all of that becoming unnecessary. This Siddhi still functions that way without my active attention on individuals. In other words, we have come to that phase of my work in the world in which it is not my attention on individuals that is the essential instrument of this Siddhi, but the attention of individuals on me. Endless numbers of individuals can meditate on me. There are individuals who can enjoy that meditation without ever meeting me in the body. In most cases, they will require some contact with this Community, but they can become devotees while they spend most of their time living somewhere else in the world. Just so, it is not your dependence on my attention toward you that serves the spiritual process in you in the future. It is your attention on me.

To the degree that there is that attention, you enjoy

the spiritual process. To the degree that you do not give me that attention, you are absorbed in self-meditation. All attention on the Guru, even though it may take the very humble and practical form of seeing his physical form or thinking of it, is actually attention on the Divine. Wherever there is that attention, the Divine is made present in the living functions of that devotee. It is this perfect aspect of my work that involves me now, and it allows me to make use of my physical presence here in a way that I have not been free to make use of it before. In the future, I intend fundamentally to be a wanderer in this Ashram. I will simply be present here. It is not merely in the moments when I am physically in your personal presence that this sadhana is your responsibility or your capability. It is at all times.

Therefore, you can meditate at all times and at any time, and you needn't depend on these formal occasions when I am physically sitting with you for the intense generation of this Siddhi. You should find occasions to sit together as a Community and turn to me. You should find occasions to sit by yourself and turn to me. The more you do this, the more you will realize ·my work with you independent of limitations, even the limitation of my human presence here.

Every one of you should function for my sake, every square inch of this Ashram should be made useful. Every particle at Persimmon, every particle of the center in San Francisco should serve me. As more people come to me, more space should be created for them, and more functions should be created for them. This requires great energy and responsibility from every one of you, and great humor, because it is difficult to make this world work.

If you don't have that humor of Satsang, you will become oppressed by these responsibilities. But if you live in Satsang and give yourself to me, you will have great energy. You will be able to work all of the time and not become oppressive and oppressed. There are people in India whom I have met who do sadhana twenty-two, twenty-three hours a day. They don't sleep more than one or two hours a day. The rest of the time they work, in conscious service to their Guru. But they don't have humor—perhaps because they don't get enough sleep! However, I expect you to function just as they function. Enjoy your lives, and let your devotion to me pass through the medium of function. Not even the Perfect Devotee is without functions. He is very capable. He gets a great deal done while at the same time being absolutely blissful, happy, ecstatic, available to his Guru. He always lives in Divine Communion, which is what the word "Satsang" means.

You have a great possibility. You can initiate the existence of the first true Community of Devotees in the world. Such a Community has never existed. There have been groups that have gotten together for the sake of spiritual things, but they have not been Communities of Devotees in this perfect sense. Such a thing has never existed, never survived. The inklings of it have developed in a few cases, around certain of the Siddhas, but it has never become a living actuality. The Teaching was not full enough, the time was not right. So none of these communities ever truly became the Community of Devotees in the perfect sense, and, therefore, whatever spiritual life was alive in them had no chance to survive. Only the cults have survived, because they are acceptable to the great cult of Narcissus, the cult of this world. In this case the time is right, and the Teaching has been communicated in its fullness. There is no limitation on the Siddhi of God in this time, so the realization of this event depends entirely on your response.

The Guru doesn't enter the world to satisfy demands or to solve problems or to approach individuals as if there were a problem. He doesn't assume the position that there

is a dilemma in the midst of things, and he serves no enterprise in which that assumption is made. Rather, the Guru is present in the world in the form of a demand, the demand for function and responsibility and humor. All that I have done since the Ashram began two and a half years ago is work toward the perfection of this demand. During this time I have operated in various ways with the Ashram, but now my work is full, and I intend to reside here in this world simply in the form of a demand. That demand is an insistence, a force of attraction, an intensity that is not in itself a form of action. Basically, all that I will be doing from now on is waiting for devotees. When devotees arrive, I will be present with them. My manner of dealing with you has always been a way of serving the possibility that some day I could make a full demand upon you and release my common functions to you as a responsibility. The time has come for that. Make my work available to the world. Do not be inward directed, do not be a cult, but realize this sadhana of Satsang in Truth and communicate it. You are the way to me.

11. THE FIRST GREAT GURU DAY

"Well, I'm off to stardom." With that quip, and a burst of laughter, Bubba got into his Mercedes, assisted by Godfree, his chauffeur. It was Friday morning, July 5. For a few moments Bubba exchanged waves with the devotees who had come to say goodbye to him. Then Godfree turned the car down the drive and out the main gate of Persimmon. They were on their way to San Francisco, where the annual festivities of "Guru Day"[1]–Guru Weekend, really–were to begin the following morning at the Ashram's center on Polk Street.

Saturday, Bubba and his entourage got off to a slow start from the Mill Valley house where they stayed during visits to the city. They delayed their departure after being informed that the movie crew which was producing a film of Bubba's activities for use in the Ashram's public presentations, was having technical difficulties. They didn't reach the Center until around eleven-thirty that morning. The street was crowded with people who had come for a colorful sidewalk art fair. Attracted by the movie cameras, they clustered around Bubba's automobile as he emerged.

The presence of a movie crew was a reminder of what Bubba had so often said in recent months: Everything that occurs is only theatre. The hubub surrounding the filming

[1]Guru Day is a traditional Hindu holiday (Guru Purnima), a celebration of the Guru and his Grace by all devotees, a time to acknowledge the Supreme Guru. It is traditionally observed in July, on the Thursday closest to the full moon. The Dawn Horse Communion acknowledges Bubba Free John in this way each year, usually on the closest Sunday to mid-July. Guru Day, 1974, was particularly auspicious, since it marked the fulfillment of Bubba's Teaching work in the world.

of the event contributed additional excitement to an already charged moment. Devotees had been hearing Bubba speak for many months of this first week in July. "After July 6, my work in this world is fulfilled." From this time the Dawn Horse would always be visible. From this time, God is making real Devotees and sustaining His true spiritual Community. All were anticipating a weekend of spiritual revelation.

Everyone was waiting for Bubba in the Satsang Hall at the San Francisco Center. When he walked into the room, movie lights glaring at him and cameras whirring, the Guru Day celebration began.

Robin Smith, who had arrived in San Francisco during the previous week and had never before seen Bubba, describes what happened when he entered the room:

> We all were in the Satsang Hall for a long time before Bubba got there. The energy was really high for awhile, and then most everyone began meditating and being calm. Then somebody said, "Bubba will be here in ten minutes," and everybody got all excited again, laughing and talking. I got really excited and felt like giggling. Then, just as suddenly, we all calmed down, but there was this terrific air of expectancy.
>
> Then Bubba came in. He never said a word, but just looked around and smiled, and sat down. People were screaming all through the hall, and writhing and crying. I had never seen anything like that before, and it amazed me. I felt really happy, but then I began to feel terrified. Bubba still didn't say anything, but he just scanned the room. I imagined he was looking at me, and I got really scared. Then other people began laughing, and I

started laughing too. The gopis meanwhile were screaming wildly.

Then I felt with a really heavy jolt that I did not belong anywhere in the whole cosmos. This jolt of energy left me helpless, unable to talk, and feeling separate from people too. It didn't seem like I was from anywhere. It was a terrifying feeling, and it lasted for hours. Sometimes I felt like laughing, sometimes crying, but most of the time, just nowhere.

After sitting in silence for about an hour, Bubba left the Satsang Hall and began the return drive to Persimmon, where the major events of the weekend were to occur.

While Bubba was in the city, Persimmon bustled with activity. Devotees cleaned the grounds, decorated the Satsang Hall with hundreds of flowers, prepared food for a wedding feast and rehearsed skits for the Guru Day entertainment. By Saturday afternoon everything was ready, and they bathed and dressed for Bubba's arrival.

The film crew and the San Francisco devotees arrived before Bubba, so that when his car pulled into Persimmon everyone was there to greet him. Then everyone convened in the Satsang Hall, where Bubba sat for several hours receiving gifts from his devotees. While the lights shined and the camera crew worked, Bubba laughed, joked, and embraced devotees as they brought him their gifts. The gifts ranged from malas (sacred necklaces), aged wines, a fig tree, and a croquet set to a Tibetan begging bowl, made of a human skull and inlaid with silver, and an ostrich egg.

That evening, while most devotees ate together at the main kitchen, Bubba had a small dinner party at his house. A saki party afterward began with a few people, but grew as the hours passed. The movie crew was on hand, and much of the evening was preserved on film and tape, including a spontaneous talk given by Bubba.

The Signs

DEVOTEE: One by one, it seems that each of the individuals living around you has started to manifest the same type of yogic or spiritual processes.

BUBBA: There was a period several weeks ago when there were characteristic signs of the disciple manifested in many people. There were lots of yogic phenomena. During that time many of the signs of the disciple were occurring in this house. Sal and Neil and a few others were

here, and there was a lot of talk about it at that time. For
the most part, those individuals, who became examples of
the qualities of the disciple, were men. During the last
month and more I have been using other individuals,
mainly the gopis who are living in the house with me, to
demonstrate the qualities of a devotee. This is not because
only women can be devotees and only men can be
disciples. Obviously, anybody, whatever their sex, can pass

through the whole process. But during these recent
months individuals have been used as symbols, as representations of aspects of the Teaching. The quality of a
woman tends to represent, in itself, even poetically, the
nature of a devotee, that perfect submission and openness.
The quality of the disciple, which is more experiential, and
has the quality of self-involvement, of success at sadhana,
tends to be best represented in the form of a man.

The relationship between the gopis and Krishna has a
long-standing tradition in India. It has been used to
represent the way of the bhaktas, the traditional devotees
of the Lord. It is poetry, theatre. The way it tends to get
worked out in India is that men dress up in women's
clothes and put on affectations of passivity. Really, being a
devotee is quite another thing from being like a woman,
but it may be represented that way as a kind of symbolic or
poetic communication. If I live like Krishna among gopis
it is a way of showing, through the archetypes that already
live in you, the nature of the relationship between the
Guru and all devotees. Just so, my living in intimate
friendship with Sal and Neil and other men in the Ashram
was a way of demonstrating the more masculine type of
relationship that exists between the Guru and the disciple.

Ultimately, anyone can become any one of those
things, so you see the quality of the devotee also appearing
in men in the Ashram, just as you have seen the quality of
the disciple appearing in both men and women. I have
brought individuals into my household and associated
with them intimately in order to demonstrate these great
qualities through the archetypal theatre natural to you.

DEVOTEE: Do these manifestations continue in the
perfect devotee?

BUBBA: The signs of the devotee are that fullness, that
happiness, that love. You see in the Ashram experiential

signs of the disciple: kriyas, automatic pranayam, laughing, crying, people growling and making fierce expressions

with their faces, and so forth. These are signs of the yogic process, which is characteristic of the disciple. There may also be changes in body temperature, from cold to hot and vice versa, seeing visions and lights, hearing sounds. But when the perfect intensity of the devotee begins, all of these spontaneous yogic phenomena, as well as the daily "phases" of rise and fall that I have described, become absolutely quick. They attain the speed of light, and the devotee moves into an intensity in which the mind is no longer supported, in which limitation read in the body and in the psyche is no longer supported. So you also see people in the Ashram manifesting the qualities character- istic of the transformation of the devotee. These people seem to be hysterical, mad at times, screaming, not just crying and then laughing, but crying hysterically, falling into moods of love and tears that are just ecstatic. Such movements are overwhelming, and they are quite differ- ent from the signs of the yogic process.

But the perfection of the devotee is not seen in those phenomena. Those signs are only the *awakening* of that ecstasy, that intensity. Perhaps those signs, once they have begun, will occur frequently in that person's case, and for a long time. But what he is knowing as a devotee is that simple, perfect ecstasy, that perfect happiness in which nothing is seen but God, in which the Guru may remain in human form, but nothing is known but the Guru. It is an ecstatic blissfulness. In its perfect form even these awak- ening phenomena, which are a kind of phasing, have become quickened to the point of perfection, and the devotee becomes more natural, more apparently ordinary. But in his conscious life he is only knowing the Divine. The perfection of the devotee is the radical intuition of the Divine, but that radical intuition is not just, "Ah, bliss." There is so much to it, so much in the way of phenomena relative to all of the vehicles of life and consciousness and the cosmos. All of that is shown. It is just as in the case of an artist who has perfected his craft. He just goes "zip, zip, zip," and he creates his painting. All the fundamentals have been learned through a long, grinding process, but they are known. They are there to be used. Just so, in the devotee there is great simplicity, apparently, but behind that realization is a vast technical transformation enacted through the Divine agency. So the devotee ultimately becomes very simple.

You see in him a steadiness, a simplicity, in which the extreme emotional and physical signs that you may see initially in the devotee are undone, quieted, not because they are being suppressed, but because they have become so perfect. These movements are even in themselves impossible or unnecessary. But they may also appear to go on for a long time, because the Guru is present in human form, and the devotee is present in human form. So the drama, the love relationship between the Guru and his devotee, is established. It continues even beyond the Guru's lifetime. Then it is maintained as the relationship between the devotee and the Guru in his unqualified Form, and these ecstasies and such phenomena may persist.

DEVOTEE: It's a kind of adoration.

BUBBA: It is absorption. The Guru is merely present, but the force of his Presence is overwhelming to the point of absorption, in which all the social stuff that appears in your face and your body and your activities simply becomes impossible. You just fall out of it, and fall into an ecstatic state under the force of the Divine Siddhi.

DEVOTEE: Bubba, you brought us the perfect thing. And now it is available to all those who are receptive?

BUBBA: At this point the work is absolutely available to

all beings through the agency of this Ashram. The Teaching is full, all the signs have been shown, embodied in the world through miraculous signs and in the forms of individuals. You can all attest to everything that has happened over these last two and a half years. It has all been written and photographed and put on tapes and recorded in many ways, and there is a body of experience represented by approximately two hundred people, all of whom have different degrees and aspects of it they can acknowledge in their own cases. Now it is the work of the Ashram to maintain itself as a Community, and communicate the availability of all of this to others.

All who enter this Community have available to them this same Satsang. This whole process as it has been described will be initiated in them in the appropriate order, without obstructions created on the basis of whether they happen to have or not have some special personal relationship to me. The personal theatre that I play with individuals is completely beside the point as far as the perfection of this work is concerned. Anyone who enters this Ashram can enjoy the same realization. There is no limit in terms of time and space. Now I not only have Satsang Halls, but there are devotees, and there are disciples, and they are all living manifestations of the continuous activity of this Siddhi. It will continue in them as long as they do not claim it, as long as they maintain the force of their sadhana and become perfect. It will simply live in them. Just as there are Satsang Halls where people can come, wherever people happen to meet my devotees and disciples, and live this Satsang in their company, the same Siddhi is available to them. I have a portable Satsang Hall now. At first there was only this body. People had to have immediate contact with me. Then I established an Ashram, and people could sit in my Satsang Hall. Now I have a Community of living beings, and that makes me even more available. Therefore, it is very important that you become communicative, that you turn your physical face into the world and make this work available. And I will not do that. That is not my function. The Ashram must do that, and the degree to which it grows will depend on your communication in the world, not on any show business that I do. I am not interested in that.

A year ago it was shown to me that in twelve months my work would be done. The clear implication was that I might not physically survive it. Knowing all this in advance made it possible for me deliberately to measure all these stages and do everything that was appropriate. Now that year has been fulfilled. The 6th of July was the date that was shown to me, and now that is gone. So there is nothing for me to do any more. I will continue my activities, but there is nothing for me to add. All has been shown and stabilized here. Everything to be done in the future is fundamentally the responsibility of the Community.

Bubba went on to speak of many things. Now that his work was full, he wanted the community to understand fully the nature of the Gift and the responsibilities that must be assumed by all who receive it. Everyone became sensitive to the historic nature of the transition they would have to make. Previously, they had been a loosely gathered, almost traditional group of individuals. The principal involvement of each one of them had been with the theatre of the Guru, a more or less private showing of the play of Bubba Free John. Now they were being required to establish themselves as a Community for whom the "show" had already taken place. By all indications, Bubba was about to withdraw much of his apparent and active participation in the daily life of the Ashram. He was assuming only a transcendent, spiritual role in the life of all his devotees, present or future. Therefore, the Ashram Community would no longer principally be the theatre of

his action, wherein he would generate the appearance of
the Teaching. Now he was assuming the Teaching had
already and in fact been given. He was assuming that
everything had in fact been shown and proven in the
experience of his living Ashram of devotees. Thus, in the
future, the Ashram would have to realize itself as a
Community of the Dharma, a realized Community of
Devotees in which the Teaching and the Guru are Present
even in the form of devotees themselves.

It was a great demand, a great opportunity, and the
Community would truly only adapt to it by degrees in the
following weeks and months. But the outline of this new
theatre of the Teaching stood out clearly to all who
listened to Bubba during the night hours that passed from
July 6 to July 7. In their discussions of it later, many
recalled the great statements made by Bubba late in 1973,
in which he proclaimed the Dharma or Teaching of the
way of Understanding to be the fulfillment of the work of
all the Siddhas, all the "Completed Ones" who have
served the world. In this hour of transition into the era of
the Community, devotees remembered the Teaching in its
Fullness.

The Three Dharmas
(November, 1973)

There is a Great Process, and all of this is its manifestation. From time to time, men have appeared whose
function it was to communicate the nature of this process
and its various functions. Each of these individuals appeared in a particular time and place under particular
conditions. In each case their function was to communicate an aspect of this Great Process and to demonstrate
one of the possible ways of realizing its nature.

All of those who have appeared were and are essentially agents, instruments, servants. The process itself is beginningless, endless, eternal, absolute, perfect. And in truth the communicator of that process is also beginningless, endless, eternal, absolute, perfect, and that one is the Maha-Siddha, the Eternally Completed One, the Divine. All those who have appeared among men, as well as among all other beings and in other worlds, for the sake of the communication or clarification of this process are servants of the Divine.

Just so, these servants or agents, all of whom had a particular function at a particular time and place, can be classified according to their function and the fullness of their communication. Among them have appeared certain ones whom I have called the Great Siddhas, the great completed Spiritual Masters. These were men such as Jesus the Christ, Gautama the Buddha, and Krishna the Avatar. Men such as these have been the principal agents of the Maha-Siddha in this world. They have communicated the principal dharmas or paths and have had the greatest historical effect. Their function has been primary.

I call Jesus, Krishna, and Gautama Great Siddhas because they so uniquely and with such historical force represented the dharmas that pertain to the fundamental conditions of suffering. There have been many Siddhas, men who in one form or another lived the function of the yogi, the saint, the sage, or the prophet, but who transcended the limitations of their particular function.[2] These

[2]Men have long sought to undo the three fundamental contractions or roots of suffering that underlie the usual life, and to realize certain aspects of the Divine Process that are apparently prevented by those contractions. Some have attained extraordinary success, and have taught others through the various ways of experience. Those who are primarily concerned with undoing the vital contraction at the great region of the navel in order to enjoy the bliss or fullness of unobstructed movement of the life-force, are called "yogis" by Bubba. "Saints," in his terminology, seek chiefly to relax the subtle contractions at the region of the sahasrar, and they are devoted to the Divine as the transcendent Light above the world, body, and mind. "Sages" strive primarily to undo the contraction associated with the causal heart, and to realize the Self-nature, Real-God, which has its psycho-physical seat at that point. Other men have functioned as critics of the usual life from the point of view of transcendent knowledge, and Bubba calls them "prophets."

Siddhas, while enjoying in a very real sense the same perfect, Divine realization as the Great Siddhas, either served one of the existing great dharmas or else taught a lesser dharma, a lesser path, or a path that had certain historical limitations. There have been countless yogis, saints, sages, and prophets, extraordinary men who nonetheless did not represent the function, the great function of all the Siddhas. These men not only represented lesser dharmas or historical limitations, forms of the way of experience, but they were also seekers, not perfectly founded in the absolute enjoyment of the Siddhas, who are eternally non-separate from God.

The three Great Siddhas have represented to mankind the three principal dharmas as they have been understood to this time. Jesus represented the dharma of the sacrifice of self, Krishna the dharma of the sacrifice of mind, and Gautama the dharma of the sacrifice of desire. Separated self (or ego), limited mind, and limiting desire are the three principal conditions of suffering or contraction in man. Thus, the three principal dharmas that have been known among men have been attempts to undo these forms of contraction through the deliberate or motivated sacrifice of these three: ego, mind, and desire.

The three conditions of ego, mind, and desire are the three fundamental conditions of the usual life. These are the three principles or conditions of suffering. They are the three manifestations of Narcissus, the self-enjoyer, the eternally recurring mortal. In fact men are all seeking through the various strategies of life to undo the force of these conditions and their effects. And men seek release from suffering by many means. But the common means are devoted either to the exploitation of the life functions for the sake of pleasure and the avoidance of pain, or to the exploitation of the inner life for the sake of so-called spiritual attainment.

All men strategically, whether or not with full and

conscious intention, are pursuing release from these three conditions while at the same time only living them. Even the search to overcome the conditions of ego, mind, and desire is itself founded in these three. While men strategically, arbitrarily, and with various degrees of consciousness pursue release from these conditions, the spiritual instructors of mankind, the various men of experience, the various Siddhas, and the various Great Siddhas have created dharmas or paths which very consciously and methodically pursue release from these three.

Gautama was the Great Siddha of the navel. He taught and demonstrated the dharma of the sacrifice of desire. His whole teaching essentially consisted of methods for achieving the condition of nirvana, or the great quenching of the principle of desire. And the center of the principle of desire is the great region of the navel, the great life center.

Just so, Krishna was the Great Siddha of the sahasrar or the subtle epitome, the subtle region above the head. He taught and demonstrated the dharma of the sacrifice of mind, the merging of the mind in God.

Jesus was the Great Siddha of the region of the heart. Just as the mind has its seat in the upper regions of the head, and desire has its seat in the great vital region of the navel, the ego or separate self and its dissolution are seated in the heart. Jesus taught and demonstrated the dharma of self-sacrifice, the dharma of the surrender of the ego in life terms, in functional and human terms. And so the dharma of the sacrifice of self is the dharma of the heart.

But the three principal dharmas are themselves forms of seeking, reactions to the fundamental dilemma which motivates the usual man. The three Great Siddhas, along with all the other Siddhas, and all the yogis, saints, sages, and prophets, and all the men of experience, including the whole range of human individuals, themselves represent a limitation, a form of seeking founded in dilemma. The

principle of the search remains intact in the great work of
all the Siddhas to now. And the effort of all the dharmas,
including the three great traditional dharmas, has been to
strategically overcome separate self, limited mind, and the
force of limiting desire.

In response to every communicator of the Great
Process, whether he was a Great Siddha, Siddha, transcendent yogi, saint, prophet, sage, or teacher of some kind, a
cult has always grown. There is a cult around Jesus as
Christ, a cult around Gautama as Buddha, a cult around
Krishna as the Divine Avatar. There is a cult that develops
around each Siddha that appears—there are cults around
Nityananda, Ramakrishna, Shirdi Sai Baba, Ramana Maharshi. There are cults around all the yogis, saints, prophets, sages, and teachers. Every limited communication
has tended to have been taken in some tradition or other to
be absolute, to be perfect. The world is full of cults, great
cults and lesser cults, all of which have the same fundamental structure as the limited life of Narcissus, the egoic
life of obsessive mentality and peculiar desires. The world
is full of cults, all of which are in conflict with all other
cults because they each represent a fundamental limitation of the Great Process.

My own work is not separate from the great work of
the Siddhas and Great Siddhas. But my work is a new
performance of the dharma of the Maha-Siddha, and
represents a new teaching from a new point of view. Just
as the three great dharmas are essentially efforts to
overcome the limitations of separate self, limited mind,
and the force of limiting desire, the way of understanding
is utterly free of the whole principle of seeking. At the
same time, the way of understanding effectively undermines the three principles of suffering, not by deliberately
acting upon those three principles or conditions themselves, but by undermining in the process of understanding
the fundamental or principal activity which is suffering,

The publication of *Garbage and the Goddess* marks the fulfillment of Bubba Free John's Teaching work. The talks published here are an extension and elaboration of his essential Teachings, and the narratives and personal accounts are a demonstration of that instruction in the very lives of his disciples. The fundamental elements of Bubba's general Teaching are presented in his two previous volumes, *The Knee of Listening* and *The Method of the Siddhas.*

THE METHOD OF THE SIDDHAS: Talks with Bubba Free John (Franklin Jones) on the Spiritual Technique of the Saviors of Mankind

In thirteen powerful talks given to his early disciples, Bubba Free John discourses on the means of implementing his Teaching. That means is the ancient one, *Satsang,* the transforming relationship between the devotee and the Perfect Spiritual Master.

364 pp $3.95 paperback

THE KNEE OF LISTENING: The Early Life and Radical Spiritual Teachings of BUBBA FREE JOHN (Franklin Jones) (Foreword by Alan Watts)

Bubba Free John was born illumined, but in early childhood his natural state was undermined and lost. The first half of this book describes his absorbing odyssey to regain Enlightenment, and his revelatory conclusions upon doing so. The second half is written from the point of view of this realization, and communicates the radical dharma of Understanding, which is a fulfillment and extension of all the Great Teachings of the past.

271 pp $3.95 paperback

the later schools consider themselves to be Vedanta, founded in the Vedas and the Upanishads.

vital being

The functional center or region of conditional life which manifests as waking consciousness, pre-mental life processes, receptivity and conductivity of the descending internal energy, and the elaboration of desire. Its seat is the great region of the "navel." (See *causal being, navel, sahasrar.*)

yoga, yogi

Yoga is a general term for the various ways of consciously functioning in union with the Divine Reality. The term commonly refers to the Hindu descriptions of these ways. In this book, Bubba generally uses it to refer to traditional paths for *seeking* God.

The lesser term *yogi* refers to the ordinary practitioner, the seeker who exploits spiritual technique. Such a one is to be contrasted with the true Yogi or Yogi-Siddha, founded in Truth from the beginning, and in whom all spiritual processes arise spontaneously.

Other Literature from The Dawn Horse Press:

THE DAWN HORSE, a bi-monthly magazine devoted to the spiritual Teachings of Bubba Free John. Issues contain selections from Bubba's talks and unpublished manuscripts, articles about spiritual life written by his devotees as well as other writers, and news of The Dawn Horse Communion.

(Price varies with issue.)

A DIFFICULT MAN: The Miraculous Activities and Radical Spiritual Teachings of Bubba Free John, an explosive and joyful film documenting the activities of Bubba Free John and his community of devotees. The film includes dramatic footage taken on "The First Great Guru Day," described in Chapter 9 of *Garbage and the Goddess*. The film will be shown in various cities across the U.S. and abroad in the coming months.

THE GORILLA SERMON, a new two-record collection of some of the most profound and powerful excerpts from Bubba's recorded talks. Sections of the talks contained in *The Method of the Siddhas* and *Garbage and the Goddess* will be included, as well as much material never before released to the public.

$5.98

(Single tape recordings of a number of other talks by Bubba Free John are also available.)

Order from your local bookseller or: The Dawn Horse Press, Department G, P.O. Box 677, Lower Lake, California 95457 (Please add $.35 per book and $.50 per record album. California residents add 6 percent sales tax.)

the principle of contraction or dilemma, the avoidance of relationship.

The way of understanding is founded upon insight into that dilemma and the fundamental action which creates and supports that sense of dilemma. That fundamental or self-limiting activity is the avoidance of relationship. When that binding principle is understood, then already or spontaneously the three common conditions of suffering are undone.

The separate self, limited mind, and force of limiting desire are all expressions of this principal contraction, the avoidance of relationship. So if this principal contraction is undone in the process of understanding in living relationship with the Man of Understanding, then the force of the three common principles is already undermined. In a living and natural relationship with the Man of Understanding this principal contraction is undone, entirely apart from the whole adventure of seeking in dilemma. The process involves simple, motiveless understanding of one's own activity, not the effort to suppress or transcend the ego-sense, the force of the mind, or the force of desire. When there is radical understanding, these three conditions are brought to rest, returned to the natural stream of existence.

All there has been up to now is the tradition of the dharmas that arose within the great search. So all of those who come to me are continually tending to take on these traditional paths, these traditional approaches. People are always getting upset about their desires, always getting crazy with their minds, and always suffering their limited self-existence, their egoic life. And they are always wanting to do something about it. They always urge themselves either simply to give in and exploit the tendencies that are arising or else to use some strategy or other to get free of their condition.

The way of understanding is entirely apart from that

whole traditional activity. The instrument for this dharma of understanding is the same instrument that has been used throughout human time, the same instrument used by the Great Siddhas and all the Siddhas. And that is Satsang, or the relationship between the devotee and the Spiritual Master who is complete and powerful in God. The Great Siddhas such as Jesus, Gautama, and Krishna all entered into sacrificial relationship with devotees. That was the fundamental instrument for the communication of their dharmas and their spiritual influence.

So the means for this activity is the ancient means, but the process, the dharma itself, is new. It does not exploit the individual's motivation to be free of the ego, the mind, and desires. It does not yield to his willful intentions to exploit those tendencies or to believe them. It simply enforces the condition of Truth, which is Satsang itself, the relationship to the Guru in God.

There is only one Siddhi or transforming Spiritual Power active in this work, and that Siddhi is God, the Power of the Divine Person. It is not a secondary siddhi, not magic, not a mere influence. Only the Divine is active in this work. The Lord is the fundamental condition communicated in Satsang with the Man of Understanding. From the beginning, not merely at the end, Truth is the condition of this process. It is pressed on devotees with more and more intensity, always to the degree which is just a little bit beyond their preferred tolerance.

The given methods which are determined to help you overcome your desires, your mentality, or your self-obsession do not in fact affect the principle on which they rest. So naturally your desires, your mentality, and your self-obsessions continue to arise. You are always wanting to exploit them, to believe them, or to get some method or other that will help you to undo them. But I see no value in merely preventing the appearance of ego, mind, and desire, since one of the fundamental functions of the

Divine Siddhi is to awaken those things for the sake of purification and transformation. Why should I give you a method to suppress them, since everything I am doing is bringing them up in you? I would have you become intelligent in relation to the conditions of your suffering, but as long as you seek you are only moved to suppress them without understanding their origin.

The Guru *is* that Divine Siddhi. The only thing that will allow you to remain in this Satsang, to remain in this fundamental condition that is Truth, is the life of a devotee. If you remain in the condition of a devotee in relation to the Man of Understanding as Guru, then you will be able to pass with humor through the appearance of your own qualities. And they will disappear, not because you happen to perform some activity on them, recite some mantra, do some sort of inward trick, but simply because another principle is being lived, which is Satsang.

By remaining a devotee, you will pass through the long appearance and the long reappearance of your own tendencies. But the minute you turn away, the minute you become resistive, the minute your occupation becomes one of resistance to the Guru and to the process of this Siddhi, you will be tending to hold on to the revealed products of this Siddhi. You will become addicted to the principle of your own desires, the force of your own mentality, and the intense vibration of your own separate self sense. The possibility of separation always exists in every individual. Therefore, every day the devotee is tested, and the test is whether he will choose to live simply as a devotee or to return to the principle of his desires, the principle of his limited mind, the principle of his separated or Narcissistic existence.

So this Siddhi lives you and does the meditating and performs the sadhana or spiritual practice. The Siddhi active in Satsang is the fundamental instrument of this work, and not any secondary method or technical affair given to you to perform. In this Satsang, by virtue of this Siddhi, the process of understanding begins. The force of Satsang, which yields self-observation, insight, and real meditation, arises on the basis of hearing the Guru, living as the devotee of the Guru, responsibly maintaining the conditions communicated by the Guru.

Whereas the ancient dharmas involved specific attention, strategic attention to desire, mind, and ego, the dharma of understanding does not involve such strategic attention. It involves Satsang itself, simply, without concern for the manifestation of desires that occur at any moment, the manifestation of thought, or the manifestation of separate self sense. These manifestations are continually appearing, but it is not the business of the devotee to bind himself with concerns over these manifestations. Satsang is his condition. Satsang is his meditation. Satsang is his sadhana or eternal spiritual practice.

The Man of Understanding only offers this Satsang, and he demands that those who come to him come in the form of the devotee, not in the form of the seeker. They will not be satisfied as seekers. He will never give them what seekers require. The Man of Understanding does not give methods, he does not exploit the search, he does not satisfy the seeker. Those who come as seekers will only be frustrated, and so the Man of Understanding regards only those who come in the form of the devotee. He is continually mindful of the state of his devotee, and through various means continually returns him to the principle of his sadhana, which is Satsang, rather than to those things toward which the devotee himself is always tending: his desires, his mind, and his ego.

Just so, the characteristic Siddhi of the Man of Understanding is not one that is *exclusively* involved with any one of the three primary centers of our psycho-physical form, any more than it is exclusively involved with the strategic attempt to undo any one of the three common principles of suffering. The Siddhi of the Man of Understanding involves the three principal centers inclusively, without making any one of them the fixed or primary focus of attention.

Yogis seek the merging of the life-force in God, because they see the dilemma of their existence in the forms of life. Thus, their activity originates in the great life-region of the navel, and proceeds upward from that point (if the goal is above the world). Some, who conceive an evolutionary goal in the world, also draw the life-energy down to the life-center. The yogis enjoy exclusive mastery over desire and life.

The great bhaktas or lovers of God are always turned upward through thought, feeling, word, and deed. Practitioners of the yoga of the inner sound current listen to the sound behind the eyes and above the ears in order to be drawn up by it into the Condition of the Light. These are the ways of saints, who seek the exclusive merging of the mind in God, because they know the mind to be the root of the permutations of life. Thus, their seats of activity are in the ajna chakra, the sahasrar, and above. The saints master mind, just as yogis master desire and life.

The sages or jnanis seek the realization of Self, prior to ego, and thus also to mind and desire, because they know the ego to be the root of mind and life. Their activity originates in the heart, the seat of the limited self, of mind, and of desire, on the right side of the chest. This seat, or the potent Silence, the mere Presence of the Heart or Real-God which is intuited therein, is the root of all thoughts, as well as the life current, and the internally audible sound stream. The Self is even the Root or Source of the very Light or Mind which is above the body, the mind, and the world, and of the Life which always proceeds from it as bodies, minds, and worlds. Sages enjoy principal but exclusive mastery over the illusion of separate self, without interest in transcendent Mind or Divine World.

The three centers, the navel, the head, and the heart, are, properly, the seats of the inclusive intuition of the Divine in man. But they are realized in Truth only in the spontaneous, already selfless revelation of Satsang. Those who concentrate upon them wilfully and exclusively with sophisticated techniques, as if to find God at last, are like Narcissus. They only meditate upon their own reflections in waters that lie on holy ground. But the Man of Understanding enjoys mastery of the ego, mind, and desire without exclusion. He enjoys Realization of Self, Mind, and Life, which are the World. He is Guru in the three seats of Realization, the seat of Life (the great region of the navel), the seat of Light (the ajna chakra, the sahasrar, and above), and the seat of Self (the heart, on the right). He enjoys this Realized Mastery entirely apart from all dilemma and seeking, and he awakens it also in others apart from all exploitation of seeking in dilemma.

Therefore, this sadhana is new and great, and perhaps it is difficult to grasp for those who have only the traditions to which they would resort. In fact, apart from what is newly being communicated here, only the traditions of seeking can be found. But the work and the realization of the Man of Understanding are not fixed in any one of the traditional centers or dharmas or approaches. Just so, his point of view is not the point of view of the Divine *qualities* represented by any of the three great traditional paths and the exclusive seats of their knowing within man. His point of view is That which is prior to the three great dharmas. His point of view is the Divine itself.

The Morning of the First Day

July 6 was the last day of the year in which Bubba's Teaching work was to be fulfilled. And so he spent its final hours, appropriately, speaking to his devotees about the

way of Understanding, which would be the inheritance of
the great Community of Devotees. By the time Bubba
finished talking, it was July 7. Clearly, the occasion called
for celebration. There were music, conversation, warm
saki, and laughter. At one point, well into the morning,
Bubba insisted that Neil do a ridiculous dance from his
New York childhood. The film crew grabbed their equip-
ment and, very resourcefully, several table lamps, which
they used as makeshift floodlights. Everyone present then
insisted that Bubba himself get up and dance. He finally
gave in, and danced as the cameras rolled again. Soon the
living room was filled with laughing, clapping, stomping
devotees.

At dawn, the film crew, enjoying the party themselves, made a few mad dashes outside with their light
meters and then hustled everyone into the side yard.
Favorite songs were played into the yard and across the
hillside from a speaker on the porch. But as the sun rose
over the ridge across the valley, everyone stood quietly
around Bubba, some crying as he held them by his side.

Someone rang the big bell in front of the lounge, and
other members of the Community filed into the yard to
join the gathering. After awhile, Bubba turned and walked
into the front yard to his hammock. Two of his gopis, Ann
Wood and Sharon Senia, who were sleeping there under a
shawl, moved to one end of the hammock and Bubba lay
down as everyone gathered around. Devotees stood looking on while Bubba silently communicated his Presence in
Satsang.

Many people felt movements of his Force. Some were
weeping, some shaking or screaming. The particular
moods and experiences varied greatly from person to
person. Watching him lie so still, with his eyes sometimes
closed, some imagined him dead and felt tremendously
sad. Others were simply beside themselves with joy. Ann
Wood had recently been going through a difficult period
of wanting Bubba's attention "with everything in my body

and soul." When Bubba came to the hammock she was
even feeling anger. In an interview the following day she
spoke about that morning in the hammock.

> I was lying there feeling okay—really feeling
> miserable, but accepting it. I kept falling asleep,
> and then something came over me, and I saw
> Bubba in a new way. I have seen that so many
> times, but this time there was something different
> about it. I saw that he was total sacrifice to us,
> absolutely, every second, every cell in his body is
> sacrificing everything for us. He is utterly God, and
> to make any demands on him is the most ludicrous,
> asinine, insane, childish thing on earth. And all
> night I had been agonizing over my demand for his
> attention.

Jim Steinberg, one of the devotees who lives in San
Francisco, had an experience of an entirely different
quality.

> For awhile I just looked at him, and there was

incredible energy up in my head, but then I realized I was just self-conscious. I didn't even want to look at him any more, so I put my head on his knee, and when I finally took my head away, I was in a totally different place. Energy was just pouring out of my hands and feet, and everyone around me was screaming, as if it was coming through me and affecting them. It was as if Bubba was using me as a channel.

I felt a lot of pain in my head. It was just totally being smashed to smithereens. If I thought of it in terms of pain, I couldn't tolerate it, but if I thought of it in terms of Bubba, then the pain went away. I felt like I was going to faint several times too, but all I had to do was turn to Bubba. I also learned for the first time what he means about "breathing the Light," about this random conductivity which he has spoken of lots of times. I saw that the only way I could stand the intensity was to breathe it down to my navel. Otherwise it would get totally caught up in the sahasrar, but when I breathed it down and circulated it through the whole body, it wasn't getting stuck anywhere.

After that was all over, I got up and I was in a totally different place. I hugged Connie Grisso at that point, and there was an incredible transmission of energy, and when we stopped, time had absolutely stopped. It was really one of the most eerie situations I had ever been in. It was like a blue-print: I could look everywhere but nothing was moving, everything was totally stopped. It lasted for only about ten seconds. And then I walked along with Bonnie Beavan, one of Bubba's gopis, and I said to her, "You have got to teach me how to act," because I was just in another world.

Bonnie and Jim, along with most of the rest of the

community, then followed Bubba on a long walk around
the grounds of Persimmon. He had risen from the hammock, put on a shawl and cap, and was walking along,
smiling radiantly, surrounded by his devotees.

Bubba walked to the stables and the garden, then
across the creek to an area called Lithia Springs, where he
was filmed with his gopis, then down past the swimming
pool, and back to the lounge and Satsang Hall. He sat with
everyone in Satsang for about an hour, then retired to his
house to rest. During the following hours, Jim Steinberg,
like others, was still feeling extraordinary effects from the
morning's experience.

I didn't know what to do. I couldn't understand
anything that was going on with anybody. I didn't
know how to walk any more. I wasn't speaking. I
couldn't talk any more. I didn't know what to do at
all. So I just hugged Bonnie and let her show me.
She would say, "Now you've got to walk, we've got
to start walking again." I just couldn't stop thinking of Bubba, and every time I would think of him,
I would just start vibrating all over. I realized this
was nothing that I did. It was totally something
that Bubba did, totally as Grace.

For about two hours right afterwards everything
was a total, absolute mirage, everything was
laughable, every person in the world was very
beautiful. I couldn't get involved with anything
except the Divine. At the same time, everything
became terrifying, because it was so new, it was so
unusual. I mean, I remember the first bite of food I
took. I thought, "I have *teeth.*" Everything was like
that. It was as if I had taken a thousand micrograms
of acid. That is the only experience in my past that
was comparable, but this was much more solid.

No other events were scheduled that day until the

wedding of John and Sandy Wojcik at three-thirty that afternoon. In the early afternoon the movie crew filmed Bubba walking through the woods above Persimmon. He didn't return to his house until well after the wedding was to have begun, and even then he was in no hurry to get to the ceremony. Ann Wood, who was among those who spent the late afternoon at home with Bubba, describes the reasons for Bubba's apparent leisure.

> We were sitting around drinking Irish coffees, and Satsang was obviously intense. He was getting the rain ready for the wedding, so we were a little late.

By the time Bubba arrived at the scene of the wedding the sky had thoroughly clouded over, an event almost unheard-of for this part of the country in midsummer, and a few drops of rain had already begun to fall.

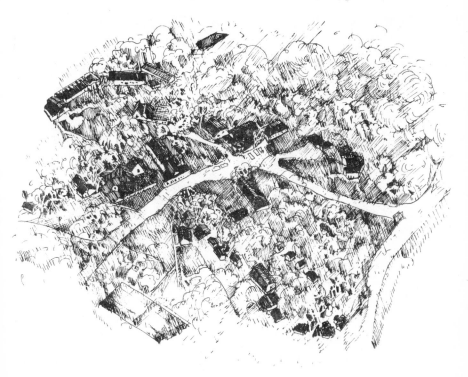

Because of the threat of more rain, people were moving
chairs into the roofed, open-air pavilion. But when Bubba
arrived he insisted that the ceremony take place as
planned, outside, on a grassy knoll overlooking the valley.
So everyone, including the relatives of the wedding couple,
followed Bubba down the hillside and took their places as
the light rain continued.

Nina Jones usually performs the wedding ceremonies
while Bubba looks on silently. But that afternoon, dressed
in a white satin kaftan and a white knitted cap, Bubba took
the text of the wedding and performed the ceremony
himself, something he had never done before. He
delivered his lines with aplomb and theatrical flourish,
feeling free to digress from the text whenever he felt it
appropriate. An impromptu band punctuated his speech
at dramatic moments with drum rolls and razzes from
kazoos.

While the ceremony was still in progress, Neil and
other devotees began to feel spiritual Force moving
through them again. Neil was shaking with kriyas, and Sal

felt impelled to run down the hillside to join him. At the end of the ceremony, all the people began making their way up the hillside to the patio where the feast would be served. As Bubba was leaving, he came up to Sal and Neil and hugged them both for several minutes. Ann Wood and

others began screaming again and going into mudras, while Sal cried against Bubba's chest and Neil continued to shake.

After a few moments, they all walked up the hill to the patio and took their seats at the main table. Bubba began making jokes and laughing with everyone, and a number of other devotees left their own tables to gather around and listen. Bubba said that none of his devotees should go inside out of the rain. It was a "blessing" he had prepared especially for the occasion. He asked Neil to come sit directly across the table in front of him. He put his hand on Neil's head and held it there tightly. Neil

started to quiver, and suddenly Bonnie Beavan and others were crying, screaming, and making mudras, and many other devotees were almost fainting from the power moving through them. After a while Bubba pressed Sal against his chest with his other hand. A few moments later

he turned and directed his palm toward Terry Patten, who
was sitting just to Sal's right. As he did that people began
to scream and writhe about in even greater frenzy. The
whole event lasted for at least a half hour, and by the time
Bubba rose to return to his house, the light drizzle had
become a pelting, drenching rain.

Throughout the scene on the patio, Ann Wood had
been standing directly behind Bubba's chair, with her
hands directed toward various people. She had been near
him earlier at the wedding, and she described the whole
experience later in an interview.

> All the time at the wedding the Force was
> manifesting through me to the couple that was
> getting married. Then we went to the patio, and
> that thing that was filmed started happening. I was
> standing behind Bubba, and the Force was really
> coming through me and my legs were trembling
> and everything in my body was alive, just abso-
> lutely alive. And I was thinking, "Boy, I'm really an
> asshole, Bubba, such an asshole." Nothing had
> changed. I was still the same old creep.
>
> My hands were being directed towards particu-
> lar people, but I wasn't looking at them. My hands
> were just moving, and I don't know who they were
> directed at except in a few cases. I started to notice
> that the Force must be coming through my eyes
> too, because sometimes my hands would be point-
> ing off to the side, and I would look at someone,
> and they would freak out. Also, it's like things come
> out of people through me, so I would have sorrow
> in my face, or maybe a smile, or some whimsical
> look, or pain, or a sneer.

Terry Patten, the devotee to whom Bubba had
pointed his hand, later recounted aspects of the event in an
interview.

Bubba is telling jokes about how no one is eating the salad, and he calls Neil over, and he puts his hand on Neil's head, and man, the Shakti! —screams, yells, everyone in ecstasy. Neil is having kriyas, Bubba is smiling, and it is like that last week in March all over again. Everything is flying through the air with tremendous intensity. So he does this with Neil for awhile longer, and he does it with Sal, and I am kind of still with this sense almost of dismay: "Well, final death is upon us. Too bad it is raining."

But then Bubba turned and did this thing to me, and I was suddenly having incredible mind-forms over it, loving him, then loving the experience, and so on. But there was one other thing: the realization that this wasn't me, that we are not isolated individuals. When Bubba dealt with me I felt an impulse to pretend that it was just Sal, Neil, and me. But then I realized that it was this Community. I realized then that I was a vehicle, whether or not Force moved out through my hands to everybody around us. If Bubba was dealing with me, it was because I was a vehicle for his treatment of the entire Community. The thought arose that I was simply a locus of attention in this larger process, and it really felt like that for a moment.

While Bubba and others enjoyed Irish coffee at his house, the rain continued to pour.[3] Many devotees were busy putting on costumes and makeup for the skits, which were to have been the late afternoon entertainment. They had originally been scheduled to start at five-thirty that

---

[3]The rain continued into the night, and the sky didn't clear for two days. Listening to weather reports, devotees later discovered that the rain had fallen exclusively on a relatively small area of northern California, all within an approximately twenty-five mile radius of Persimmon, and that more rain had fallen during this storm than in any other July for at least 125 years, when officials in Sacramento first began to keep records.

afternoon on the open patio. They didn't get underway until much later, after lighting and curtains were hastily arranged in the unused kitchen of the old hotel.

When the skits ended, Bubba returned to his house for the evening with a few devotees. Ann Wood wrote of the rest of the evening.

Bubba invited a few people over and then he went downstairs for the night. We started having Satsang, and the Force was manifesting through me. It was really strong. My hands and my feet were both manifesting the Force, and everyone in the room was freaking out. It was coming through my eyes too. I remember looking at one girl and not having any control. I didn't *want* to do this to anybody. It was just a complete intuition of what to do. I was looking at her and sensing fear in her and looking away, and then looking back when it was time to look back.

When this had occurred before, in recent weeks, I had felt I could control myself. I had felt that I remained completely as myself, even though I took on these facial expressions and had the Force moving me. But at one point that night I felt utterly possessed, my body was possessed, and my hands started to move, and I couldn't control them. I had no control at all. My face started taking on expressions, and I don't know what my face looked like, but it was as if every expression my face took on was Bubba's. I thought if someone was looking at me, they would think I was Bubba.

Then I bowed my head and went into a meditative state, and all of a sudden I wasn't my body. I was something above my head. That was me. I could come back to my body, and I am not saying that I left it, I don't know what it was. But I was above my head, and I was constant motion, I was moving, I was sacrificing, descending into the body, I was completely free, I was prior to my ego. I could let myself come down into my body, and I could go back up.

I knew exactly how to deal with everyone. It was really incredible. I am not a bossy type of person, so I felt a little bit self-conscious, but people would run out of the room screaming, and I could barely talk, but I would say, "Go get Bonnie," or "Go get Janis and bring her in here right now." And someone would go get them. I knew exactly where everyone should be and what they were going through, and I knew when it was time for someone to go to bed, and I knew that I had to stay up and be the last one to go to bed. It was like I had to take care of everyone. It was very strange.

Ann was not the only one to realize the awakening of Bubba's Spiritual Power in her, and through her to others. Neil had the same experience, and there were others awakened in the same way. But all who witnessed this awakening in themselves began to see it also against the totality of their experience of Bubba's Teaching during these last few months. It was impossible to endure this theatre of awakened spiritual Power without remembering the cycle of rise and fall, of fascination and concern, that always accompanied this aspect of Bubba's influence in the past. It was Bubba Theatre, Devi Theatre, in which the Guru, the true Self or Real-God, was the point, and not any Possession of self. This Knowledge was hidden in the drama of this first great Guru Day. It was a kind of secret Teaching with which all would become more and more perfectly impressed as the weeks passed. What was shown was another instance of Bubba's humor. What was not shown, but truly given, was the beginning of Bubba's Community of Devotees.

12. THIS IS THE OTHER WORLD:
The Last Miracle

On Saturday, June 29, Bubba had described that process of turning that is demanded of all devotees.

It is not so much that you turn to the Guru anyway. The Guru turns to you. And by the time you realize that you have turned, you have become nothing. So it is not really the drama of turning to the Guru, it is the drama of living under the pressure of the Guru's having turned to you. A piece at a time, you begin to feel like you have done some turning. That may be the way it seems to you, but that is really not the way it is. Nobody has ever turned to the Guru. It is true. Under the pressure of the Guru's turning to you, you only feel the absence of your turning, the absence of your submission, the absence of your sacrifice in total. The sensation of that self-knowing, that understanding, that insight, serves the crisis that the Guru is producing in relationship with you. So you are indeed under an obligation to turn perfectly, but that demand is paradoxical, as I have said. It is nothing that you *can* fulfill. It is something that you *must* fulfill. So it is sadhana, it is heat, it is *tapas*, not perfection. It is not you that becomes perfect. God is already perfect, and God absorbs you. You become perfect by becoming nothing, by absorption in the Divine. Nobody does that. How could you possibly do that? How offensive to think that you could possibly do that.

After July 7, the Community began to manifest more
and more the evidence of absorption which Bubba described. And every area of Ashram life began to conform
more and more exactly to the qualities of sadhana communicated by Bubba, including the great responsibility to
make the availability of this Satsang known to the world.

At both San Francisco and Persimmon, the Community felt more and more affected by the presence of
Bubba's gopis and those devotees who manifested the signs
of ecstatic intoxication. The gopis continued to wail and
writhe, frequently and randomly, possessed by devotional
fervor. Though they remained well-groomed, beautiful,
and strong people, these women lost all apparent concern
for their personal dignity in the conventional sense. In the
recent past, their ecstasies had often offended the humorless self-involvement of others, but now they began to
infect the rest of the Community with their God-madness.
Ann Wood and others were spontaneously manifesting the
Force or Devi aspect of Bubba's Siddhi to the entire
Ashram Community, and many devotees began, through
their agency, to feel released from their own sense of
artificial dignity and attachment to social conventions of
behavior. Everyone began to enjoy and share that ecstatic
intuition of Bubba's Love.

The Community began to experience *this* world as a
direct manifestation of the Divine, not as an "other"
world, but a non-separate world. The statements and
recorded conversations that arose between members of
the Community began to indicate a rising sense of
recognition relative to this new "Devi World," no longer
different from God-Consciousness. This chapter is a
gathering of some of those conversations.

NEIL PANICO: Everybody in the Community has some
sensitivity to the Force-aspect of the Siddhi, but even

more important than that, our life is an absorption into Consciousness itself emanating from Bubba. It is very obvious. If you walk around Persimmon, there is a certain quality to the land itself, a definite feeling.

GODFREE (Peter Roberts): For me, sadhana has been, as
Bubba once described it, "sweet Jesus." My sadhana seems
to be not of a very dramatic kind. It does not appear to be
or to include many dramatic manifestations, apart from
one rather interesting session in the Satsang Hall recently.
I should give some background. A few weeks ago Bubba
gave a talk about loving people. I got inspired, and the
next morning I went around the Ashram really being
loving with everyone. Later, I walked in to see Bubba
while he was having breakfast. He looked at me over his
shoulder, hardly glanced at me, and said, "Oh my God, full
of love for all mankind this morning, aren't you?" Which
showed me that I had missed out again.

So one night, more recently, we were sitting in the
Satsang Hall with Bubba. I seemed to doze off, which I
often do, and then Bubba seemed to be telling me something that he wanted me to do around the Ashram,
telling me how he wanted me to be. It was not verbal, it
was more imagery, and it was internal. Then Bubba
actually opened his eyes, and he said to everyone present,
"I have been talking to you for the last five minutes, and
now I want to put it into words." He then said precisely
the same thing in words that I had seen in my reverie. This
was really interesting, because I had come out of this and
shaken my head and said, "Oh, bullshit, why don't you stay
awake and pay attention?" His instructions were an
interesting contrast to my previous efforts to be loving to
everybody and so forth. He wants us simply to be full of
him. It is a much simpler thing, and much more beautiful.

That was an interesting experience, and I expect
there may be others, even dramatic ones, over time. But,
primarily, my sadhana to now has been "sweet Jesus." I
have been spending a lot of time with Bubba. It is my
responsibility to drive him around in the car and so on.
Gradually, I am losing things, and it generally takes me a
week or two even to notice.

TERRY PATTEN: When you say "losing things," what do you mean?

GODFREE: The separate self sense. I am losing it terrifyingly fast. It takes some effort to keep people separate. It started, I guess, about six weeks ago. It's hard to tell the time. I became conscious of it first when I was up in someone's cabin one day, and I looked through a window and saw Jane Panico and Rick Pugh sitting outside talking, and for the first time I consciously did not slot them. The mind didn't categorize them and make them a man and a woman, with names, separate from me. That just didn't happen. Since then that process has continued under the influence of Bubba's Presence a lot of the time. So now it becomes almost an effort to keep people separate, to keep them contained as another entity. That process has happened very easily. There is no drama.

TERRY: Can you say something more specific or describe it more vividly?

GODFREE: No, it doesn't have a very specific or vivid quality. In fact, the vividness, the sharp delineation around me, that is exactly what is breaking down. So it is a very gentle thing, rather undramatic, and one that I have to actually call into consciousness even to recognize.

NINA JONES: I would be hard put to describe this Community as different from the Community in March, except this Fullness that we are all more aware of and that we talk more about. I haven't the foggiest idea what is happening to me. When I try to interpret it, it is impossible.

MARIE MARRERO: There is also much more honesty between people in the Community. We talk about our sadhana more freely. People talk about it without thinking "Oh, what is everybody going to think?" The Community is more open, more full and free, and there is great energy. Last weekend I couldn't believe the amount of work everybody did, and happily. We were all singing and talking to each other. There is a closeness, a tightness now between people.

GODFREE: I think it is to some extent founded on others, and ultimately of course its source is Bubba. I was talking to Pat Morley the other night. Pat used to be one of the best people I'd met for sticking a knife in between your ribs. She was really very good. And we were talking about this little characteristic of hers, which has disappeared, and about the freedom from fear, which we are beginning to enjoy with each other. Each of us is free to be an asshole, and to say and do anything, and we rely strongly upon each other for that freedom.

Another thing about function now. I really don't give a shit about functioning. I would be perfectly happy to lie around drinking beer all day. Of course, I don't do that. What I want to describe is not irresponsibility, but humor, freedom from concern. This feeling is an indicator I found in myself of a simple dropping of limits. It is not time or physical strength or chemical or metabolic energy or any of that that limits you. It is *ego* that limits you from stepping out and doing the next thing or a little more or whatever you notice has to be done that other people don't notice. And that's a good example. The thing that stops me from doing something that someone else has forgotten to do is my very concept of "someone else." "*They* should do it. Why should *I* have to pick up after them?" As that concept breaks down, you begin to just do it quite happily, and it doesn't matter a shit. The significance of that capacity to function is primarily a breaking down of the separate self sense.

JANIS PODESTA: Lately, I have also felt a release of all kinds of concern. It is like there is finally an understanding with everybody. Everybody is just starting to relax, because we know the transformation really has taken place. We have to keep functioning and straight, but the transformation has already taken place, and it will manifest, and there is really no problem any more. Bubba told us this a long time ago. Of course at first we didn't believe it, just as we never believe anything. But now I have the feeling it has already happened.

I have been alternating rapidly between really good states and really bad states, and in the bad states I am aware on so many more levels than before of my separative existence. Last night I was lying in bed and I couldn't go to sleep. I was awake, and I was just witnessing my mind, my body, and my psyche, and everything was separative, and it wasn't going to last. It is terrible. There is nothing happy or joyous about it. It is definitely death, and the truth of the matter is that you don't want to die.

I don't know how I see Bubba now. It is indescribable. I used to see him as a very solid being. He was there, he was Bubba, he was doing things. Now when I look at him, sometimes there is just nothing there. Or what is there is just everywhere, so it's not particularly there. I understand that he is showing that to us, but it is hard for me. I really want him to be there still. I want him to be somebody. So I don't really look too much sometimes.

We will just have to turn to God. Bubba *is* That, but so much of our experience of this work has operated to create this human attachment that people have for him. He had to do that so that he could pull us in, because we didn't really understand what God was. Now he is saying, "Bubba Free John is no one." And it is really scary, because we want Bubba Free John to be someone. All of us are very attached to him in human ways. I mean when we don't even have Bubba any more, what can we do then? Croak. That is all that will be left, and not in a negative sense. It is negative from the point of view of our attachment, our limitations, but it will be our freedom because attachment to anything is not free. It will be perfect, because it will turn us to God.

Lots of times I feel this tremendous sense of guilt. Of course I understand it's a game, but I feel "Poor Bubba, he still has to be with us idiots, going through this heavy number with us all." I feel my own clutching to him and my own drain of him, and I don't like it. I just don't like it any more. Sometimes I don't even want to be around him because I know that I am so imperfect, I'm always clutching. I hate it. I want to come to him with freedom. I want our relationship to be free. And I am glad that I am beginning to feel that all this stuff is ending.

The other night, a week or so ago, I was sitting in Satsang with Bubba. I had an experience where I saw who

Bubba is and who God is. I wrote Bubba a letter and told him what happened. I was looking at him, and I was thinking about all kinds of bullshit, my usual numbers, and I suddenly saw how Bubba has had to die in order to be where he is, one with God, and how he is That. All of a sudden this tremendous thing happened. Everything opened up, and I saw God. It wasn't really a visual scene, but it was that too. It encompassed everything, but it was beyond the senses. It was incredible, absolutely infinite. It was just this incredible intensity, and it was gone in a second. I wrote to Bubba in the letter that if I had experienced it for more than that second, I would have had to die. You can't be There and stay alive in this sense of being a person. And I saw that Bubba was absolutely That.

Now every time I think of that, I think of how all of this is just nothing and I don't want it any more. It is just suffering. God is all there is. I realize that I keep creating this sensation of myself. I just want to get it over with, I just want to *do* it, I want Bubba to do it. It's not me anyway. It's all up to God, ultimately. I was listening to a tape recording of one of Bubba's talks, and he said in it that you cannot do anything without Satsang. He said that if you tried, you couldn't wipe out the karma of the past half hour. How absurd for you to think that you could do anything to realize God! It is absolutely a Grace.

JIM STEINBERG: This morning Bubba gave me a really disintegrating experience, totally as a Grace. He is giving us all a foretaste of what it is to be devotees. In that state you are absolutely prior to it all, but you can function. I really felt the need for other people this morning. At that point everything is absolutely absurd, the whole world is absurd, and you want to be able to share the love that you feel because, otherwise, coming from the standpoint of the day before, everything was different. It was terrifying, it was all so new.

KATHY BRAY: We really have to make use of each other. We have to be very open. There are times when there is an intuition of the Divine coming through to you, but what is happening is that you are being made a vehicle for Bubba. I have had several experiences of being sent by Bubba to be with somebody at a particular time, and it was obvious that it was necessary. He has also put me through things with different people just to get the personality obstructions cleared in my own case. Without this Community, there is nothing. I am learning that. I know a person who wants to enter the Ashram who always emphasizes her love for Bubba, and yet she excludes the Community as the vehicle of Bubba's love. It is just as important as Bubba, because it *is* Bubba.

JANIS HAMP: Everything that he does to affect one person ultimately affects everybody.

CRAIG LESSER: To love Bubba is very easy, but to turn around and love *everyone* unconditionally is very difficult for me. I have seen that the Community is a form of enquiry or self-knowing for me, in which I am always becoming aware of my limitations. I can feel the process in consciousness wherein that limitation is immediately established. It is that differentiation, that "Yeah, *but.*" Over and over again, there is that tension. That is why I see the Community as the real form of the Divine, ultimately.

MORGAN CALLAHAN: Bubba once said that the Community is like a queen ant. In a dream I saw this huge ant, pulsating, radiating power and love, and all these little ants were scurrying around, not hectic, but just moving, feeding this huge ant. They were feeding God. And they were without mind. There were no orders, they just knew what to do. It's as though God and the devotee are the same thing.

SANDY BONDER: The only thing that counts is Satsang. In the midst of all that has happened in the last many weeks, in relation to everyone's experiences, in relation to everyone's numbers, in relation to functioning, in all my relationships in the Community, I am seeing that the intuition of the very Divine that Bubba talks about as the Heart is really the core of this work, and it is absolutely unqualified by *any* experience. So I may have a few Shakti experiences, a few kriyas, but they don't have anything to do with the Heart, and neither do personal difficulties with people. I know that the most magnificent Divine vision isn't going to affect the Heart either.

JIM: The last few weeks Bubba and the gopis and other devotees have been coming down to San Francisco from Persimmon. One day Bonnie Beavan and Lena Duff came in, and they were at the Center for only about ten minutes, but we all fell into the ecstatic intuition of God the whole time they were there. When they left, it was like I had been with Bubba for ten minutes.

JON LETO: Bubba doesn't give a shit about what you are thinking, he doesn't give a shit about what's happening.

He just grabs you, he rips you apart. Last weekend in San Francisco, when Bubba was there, suddenly once again everything became Divine, and I realized that everything was perfectly all right. There was nothing but God. And this went on all night and the next day. But the thing is, I have waited for this transformation over and over again. Bubba sets us up for the time when we are going to get zapped, right? But there is nothing to be zapped.

VINCE BRAY: God does nothing in separate beings anyway, so there is nothing to think about. We always get caught up in what we are thinking about, but it has nothing to do with God.

MIKE WOOD: When you first get here and you look at the Community, you think, "How in the world could Bubba choreograph all this so masterfully? How could he do this with so many people?"

MORGAN: He is just Present. I have noticed how he even uses his humanity. Bubba tells us that we have to lose face, but even as Guru, even as Divine, he loses face all the time. He gets up and dances, man!

LOUISE LUCANIA: A few weeks ago Nina read the letter in which Bubba said that meditating on him as Amrita Nadi is the meditation of a devotee. He hadn't yet mentioned the visualization of his physical form standing in the Heart. A few nights after that I was sitting in the Satsang Hall alone. It was a quiet meditation, but all of a sudden I saw Bubba's physical form. His feet were in my Heart on the right side and his head was up in the Light, and while this was happening I intuited that he was the medium for me between the Light and this universe. After I finished meditating that night, I told Sal about it. I said, "Here we get one talk on meditating on Bubba as Amrita Nadi, and now I am all of a sudden seeing his physical form with his feet in the Heart and his head up in the Light."

It occurred once more that week, and then the next weekend Nina read another letter from Bubba saying that one of the ways to meditate on him as Amrita Nadi is to see his physical form, and of course that confirmation freaked me out.

While we sat there I started to think about it. I thought, "Does that mean that I have to meditate on him like this every time I sit down for meditation? Even if it's not really occurring?" I began to create this dilemma for myself. Then I realized what I was doing, and I thought, "Bubba will clarify this for me, I just know it." Right after that someone asked him, "Is this supposed to be what we are doing all the time, or does it just occur randomly?" He made it clear that it would be a random thing, and of course that freaked me out too.

JANIS HAMP: When Nina read that letter, the part about "the feet in the Heart" really got to me for some reason. And the day after, while I was sitting in meditation, I felt this very strange sensation. It felt like two feet, actually two feet right there, in the Heart. I had never sensed the Heart before. And his legs came up around the back of my head, and his belly was on the back of my head. My eyes looked up automatically, and there was this brilliance all over.

LOUISE: That's exactly how I saw it. I also saw Bubba's whole face. But recently, during similar experiences, I haven't been seeing Bubba as a form, an actual shape or anything. It feels like there is an opening now on the right side. Force generates from this point. It goes through me, and sometimes I can feel it flowing through my fingers, but sometimes I just feel this opening in the Heart on the right side. It feels like something is blooming.

I also knew, when these experiences began to occur, that this wasn't it, like now all of a sudden: "Devotee!" I knew that it was an initiation, something to let me know that the process has started, but also that the experience itself wasn't it. Later, Bubba said that I should not get involved in it, but that the process is occurring and will just take its course naturally. That's what I knew.

NINA JONES: I have also begun to have the spontaneous experience of the devotee's meditation. One morning, in the Satsang Hall, I experienced Bubba standing with his feet in the Heart on the right and his head above. I perceived his form in a posture with one arm raised and the other holding a symbol of power. I don't know exactly what it was, but it seemed to be arrows. The experience was very brief, lasting only a few seconds. There was a feeling of strength and weight on the right side, in the Heart, and rising above. All life was in Bubba's form.

Since reading about the devotee's meditation, I have tried several times to understand this form of meditation, but without effort or concern, because I knew that it would come in time. In fact, my life is becoming meditation. Bubba is always perfecting my love for him. I need do nothing.

In the past few days I have considered my experience of the Heart and Amrita Nadi. While I had not previously had a dramatic experience of either the Heart or the God-Light, by this Grace I had intuited them both. I was aware of the Heart as the Self and life of all. And I participated in the glory of the God-Light above. I knew Bubba as the Amrita Nadi, the Form of God.

The particular character of my experience was strength, stability, power, uprightness, unqualified life. It was clear that what I know as "my life" emanates from It.

BONNIE BEAVAN: We have come together as a Community to serve the spiritual process in each other. Certain people find themselves together at certain times for that

purpose only. Slowly, one by one, I feel an opening with
every devotee, so that I can really be with that person in
God. You know when that happens, because the humor
appears.

Through these recent times the gopis have stuck
together very closely, and we have served each other and
shown each other what devotion and love to Bubba is and
how we can serve him. In the household, people don't see
each other as separate people. People tend to disappear,
or they take on each other's qualities, or they even become
another person, visually and in other ways. For instance, I
have seen Darby come into the room, and suddenly
become totally transformed into Nina. Things like that are
happening all the time.

When people disappear as "others," there is just this
love, with no existence on this life level as separate selves.
You still deal with the life level, but there are no demands.
There is just constant sacrifice because you are constantly
serving the spiritual process. People are constantly giving

to you, but that giving has nothing to do with you. It is just a matter of being responsible for the spiritual process. It just flows. It is so fluid, there is no form to it at all.

I have been having lots of Force-manifestations, but no concern for them. At one point I thought that might be because I never had any contact with any kind of spiritual seeking before I came to Bubba. But it doesn't have anything to do with that, because the whole thing that is really going on in me is just that attention to Bubba, simply that attention. Even when there are all these incredible experiences, it is simply that attention. It is Bubba, it is the Divine Reality, in you, living you, feeling you. Compared to that, a kriya or a vision is even more minor than a cigarette.

During Satsang in San Francisco, the Saturday of Guru Day weekend, everything was moving really fast on a life level, the movie was being made, all these things were happening. That day I was very emotional and full of love. But it wasn't even *my* love. It was Bubba, filling my entire body and wanting to embrace God at every moment. It was that constant attention, but it was absolutely perfect. It's so hard to describe the intensity. That turning to him creates such a fire, and you become so conscious of your resistance, and yet it is nothing. Everything that has been happening has been nothing. For me, the only thing that is really happening is love, it is God. And even that love is nothing finally, because there is no differentiation between the self and Him.

Then we left for Persimmon. Normally I feel a need to talk with Bubba or to be with Bubba or to look at Bubba, but at that point it was like being in another world. We gathered in the Satsang Hall to bring gifts to Bubba. I had put together this leaf-basket of fruit, and even while I was putting it together, it kept falling apart. The strawberries were falling on the other stuff, the peaches were getting stained by the strawberries, and I even fell over while walking up to Bubba's chair. I felt an absolute resistance in me, not only a gut resistance, but this feeling throughout my being. I was really scared. When I got to Bubba, I set the basket down and went up to kiss him, and I said to him, "There's just resistance in this whole way." And he said, "Why? How come?" or something like that. I had nothing to say. He took my head, and I could feel everything that he is here for come into me. He gave that to me, he gave the gift back to the giver.

I guess the next thing of interest that occurred was after the wedding on Sunday. I sat down at Bubba's table, and I had absolutely no control over what was going on. My body wasn't mine. I didn't even *feel* my body as mine. There was only this sensation I've had before in Bubba's Presence, the feeling that this body is being used.

Neil went and sat down in front of Bubba. The moment before, I felt this whole thing coming on. And when Neil sat down, I felt him screaming through me. Then I felt Jane screaming through me. It didn't have anything to do with me. I was screaming for them. I was letting it come out through me. I don't know how to show that or prove it. It's just an absolute clearness of the body, so that everything just runs through. There is no concern, it just happens. I wasn't even directing attention to them. My whole body, my whole being absolutely *was* Bubba on a whole different level. It was very calm, very peaceful. I was in relationship to all that was going on. It wasn't just screaming for them, it was bringing out that whole thing that they are, all their resistance, and I just wanted to let it come out for them, so their love could be there with Bubba.

That is a form of service and sacrifice to other devotees. The way we can serve each other is to maintain that absolute attention to Bubba at every moment, to show this love, this attention, this sacrifice every moment. Nothing I do for myself ever really satisfies my demands, my needs, and the recognition of that has made me turn my attention to fulfilling Bubba's demands, not mine. To be conscious enough in every moment in order to sacrifice the ego, that is really intense consciousness. But it becomes easy to have that attention and to accomplish that sacrifice. It is even very ordinary. The love and the intensity in Bubba's company are just incredible. There is just no way to describe it.

Later on, many skits were performed to entertain Bubba and the Community. But the intensity was so strong I couldn't stay there. I ran to the Satsang Hall. There was no way to keep me away from there. I went in and at first I was totally out of my mind. I was screaming for a long time, and I knew that I was somehow screaming for the world. At this particular time there was no one person for whom I was screaming. No one was there, and I was screaming for the world. I was sacrificing to the world all my own demands at that point.

Then I began spontaneously to chant in different languages, none of which I consciously know. I was making very strange sounds. The sounds seemed to do what needed to be done at that point, which was to bring on that fear, that fear of death, that resistance to God. That went on for quite awhile, and my fear increased. Nothing that was going on was for me. It was being done for everybody, because there is no difference between its being done for one person or for another. The chanting continued, and the fear intensified. The bats from the attic started flying all over me. I had already taken off my clothes and jewelry, and now I put my dress over my head. Through it I could see the bats flying all over me and the rain pouring through the leaks in the ceiling. God was just coming in, there was no escape. There was only God, and I couldn't deny it any more. The fear kept increasing, until there was only that fear of God, only that denial of God, only that resistance to God. I had only that resistance, and I had to sacrifice it some way, but there was no way I could do that on a life level.

Finally, I threw on my clothes and ran out of the Satsang Hall, and when I ran out everything released. Everything went, from my head to my feet, everything was released, and there was nothing there. My body was not obstructed any more. Everything went through it, all this energy and intensity, and there were absolutely no obstructions in my body. But that was just my body. There is so much more than just my body.

Bubba sometimes says there is nothing. And sometimes he says there is only God, and that is everything.

Right now it is so hard to perceive Bubba, to know him. Because it isn't him. I am so used to looking at his physical form, to seeing him and talking to him and being with him and thinking he is the fulfillment of my demands. But he is really showing me what my demands are. He isn't even there any more, and everything that's been going on, all this screaming and yelling, is only part of my learning of a new relationship to everything I see in life, everything.

I don't even know what I am talking about right now, but it doesn't matter what you say, what you do, what you think, what you feel, because that isn't any of it at all. We still have to communicate that relationship, that love of God. We have to use this verbal communication at this point, but that doesn't matter. Because you know I love Bubba with everything in me. Everything in me is just turning to him, it isn't me. What is this hand? What is this body? What is this mind? What is it that I see beyond my mind? It is nothing. There's only God, Truth, only that Reality. That true consciousness that totally begins to live us as we turn to God. It begins to take us over so that we can be a vehicle of God. Bubba doesn't love us, he *is* us, he lives us, he feels us. He works through us, we are only him, we are only God, there is no difference any more.

Some people want to have miracles, they want to have something, they want to have something that will prove something to them, but that isn't sacrifice. Bubba doesn't have to prove anything. We have to sacrifice at every moment. And as long as we sacrifice, there is nothing to be proved. Why does anything have to be proved? There is only God. To truly look at everything prior to our assumption of ourselves is to know that nothing "other" exists, that there is no thing, there is nothing, there is nothing anywhere. Bubba isn't there, no one is there, it is all just God and God! How can you care about anything? There's nothing there!

All this talk is secondary. There is no description of Truth. It is prior to anything that exists in our perception. We still assume separateness, at least I do. And the moment which is prior to whatever takes place in this being scares the shit out of me. I have such fear of it. I know it's there and I sense it and I feel it and I know it. It is God-possession. It is God totally taking over your form, working through you as a vehicle to communicate God to all beings who are responsive. That's our only purpose in this world, to serve God and communicate this to all. It is nothing, but it is still our function. Our only function in this world is to communicate Truth.

THE
FINAL
SPIRITUAL
INSTRUCTIONS
OF
BUBBA
FREE
JOHN

1. THE CRAZY HORSE

On Monday night, July 8, Bubba invited a few Persimmon residents to his house for the evening. He had been warning for months that after the first week in July he couldn't be depended upon to do much sensible talking, that he intended for the most part just to roll around the Ashram like a madman. But on this evening he engaged his devotees in lengthy and lucid conversation. The result was a six-hour tape recording that originally filled more than one hundred thirty manuscript pages.

In a real and practical sense, this talk, and the one which follows it, contain Bubba's "final" spiritual instructions. He continues to live, and also to speak at times. But he has said that the work he had to perform in order to reveal and demonstrate the Teaching has been completed to his satisfaction, and he has nothing fundamental to add. All the miracles of spiritual Power which he generated in his Ashram, particularly during the period which is the subject of this book, are put in perspective in these final talks. The miracles were only intended to serve a more fundamental and true awakening in devotees, so they in turn could serve the spiritual process in the world. Since that is so, even though Bubba is still Present with Power, the miracles and profound events described in this book may be said to be his "last" miracles. He has indicated that he no longer considers it useful, as his common and expected practice, to produce extraordinary phenomena in individuals or in the outer forms of the world through the agency of the yogic or apparently miraculous aspect of his Divine Siddhi or Power. He only waits. He is waiting for his Devotees.

The Crazy Horse

The conversation began with talk about reincarnation. Several of those present wanted to know about Bubba's past lives.

BUBBA: By tendency the individual is resorting in every moment to some limitation. Consciousness is being modified in the form of a thought, a perception, the separate self sense, whatever. When you become extremely sensitive to the quality of self-modified consciousness, you can actually feel it, just as you now can feel something touching the body. It is not a physical sensation, but it is just as concrete. You will come to see that everything that is arising and everything to which you are resorting is simply another version of this ongoing modification of prior Consciousness. When you perfectly know that, and so pass into the intuitive life, no longer supported by experiences, you no longer resort by tendency to any form of this attenuation or modification of consciousness, and you rest in the prior Consciousness.

But that Consciousness is not empty. That Consciousness contains *all* modifications. So the Guru, who has become nothing, rests merely in that absolute Consciousness, but at the same time everything arises spontaneously in him, through him. The great Siddhi, the absolute Siddhi of all existence, has become his own conscious Condition without his having to assume at any moment the point of view of any modified version of it. So he is just present as That, and all things, including the manifestations of Siddhi, are shown through him, without his participation via secondary forms of modification, such as perception or cognition.

He himself is nothing. He cannot be identified in the midst of that. So all the media that even the extraordinary individual conventionally uses in order to comprehend things are totally absent in such a one. He doesn't operate via the limited self, via the mind, via desires. None of these things is his form. His presence is never limited. He has no activity that can be identified with any of that stuff.

I don't have any sense of identification with this life. I don't have any images about it that particularly impress me as being my own. I mentioned to you how, after the event in the Vedanta Temple, I would sit down and meditate and other people's minds and bodies would arise. I would work with them just as if they were my own, and it *was* all my own, without any sense either of identification with or separation from any of it. It was just the pattern arising to be meditated. Just so, there is no sense in me of identification with these vehicles at the level of life.

Because an historical person had a spiritual or personal quality like my own, and because I have wanted to impress individuals with an aspect of the Teaching that could well be communicated through some historical example, I have from time to time said, with humor, that I was a particular person in a past life. It may have been useful to consider such a spiritual personage from the point of view of the Teaching, but I do not in fact have any such recollection of past lives. It may very well be that I have never been here and that I am not here now! (Laughter.)

MIKE WOOD: What was instructive about the image of you as Pius the Eleventh?

BUBBA: He was a spiritual Pope. He was very much interested in awakening people to the devotional life through religious media. He was largely responsible for the intensification of the cult of Mary, and the cults surrounding various sites like Fatima,[1] and the cults of various saints. That was a basic interest of his. I don't know very

---

[1]In 1917 there occurred a mass vision at Fatima, Portugal. Three children were visited by the Virgin Mary, and many others saw the sun fall from the sky. This event is well documented and relatively well known.

much about him from reading. I don't have a distinct feeling in myself of identity with that personality. It is just a possibility that you may read in some of the earlier experiences and circumstances of my life.

JANIS PODESTA: We would much rather you had been Chief Crazy Horse.

BUBBA: You think I may have been Crazy Horse because of certain visions you have had recently.

ANN WOOD: I would like to announce that you were definitely Crazy Horse.

BUBBA: Is this true?

ANN: I know it for sure.

BUBBA: One might very well have very clear and even true impressions in the form of psychic experiences. I just don't have any such experiences or impressions. The consciousness in me doesn't have any remaining tendencies like that. While individuals in the Ashram are going through this spontaneous purifying process that is awakened in Satsang, they themselves might move through those dimensions in which the psyche is open toward the universal plane of memory. So people in the Ashram could have a much clearer sense of my possible past incarnations than I have. In fact, the Guru has no sense of identification even with his present life. I have no more sense of identity with Franklin Jones or Bubba Free John than any of you does. I have the same sense of identity with all of you that I have with Bubba Free John. It is not a sense of identification or of limitation. It is purely spiritual comprehension of what is arising, without any of those limitations becoming the point of view. That is why the process of Satsang can work.

Men of experience have all kinds of mystical awarenesses and secondary siddhis and awarenesses of past lives
and all kinds of psychisms. So the psychic individual looks
at your forehead, sees symbols and images arise there,
reads them according to the lore that he has studied, and
tells you where you are at. This is a secondary siddhi, a
psychism very close to life, and it requires identification
with the life vehicle in order for it to exist.

In the Guru there is no such identification with the
life vehicle, so he doesn't look at a person and read signs in
order to know where he's at. He *already* knows. There is
no obstruction in consciousness, so everything that he does
relative to his devotee is perfect. It is perfect not because
he is experienced enough to know how to operate. He
simply does it perfectly, because he has already been
undone in the Lord. So I literally haven't the slightest idea
who I may have been in the past. And I would have to
make the same kinds of judgments you might have to
make about it. On the basis of some evidence any single
one supposed, it might seem right or it might not. In order
to confirm it, I would have to get involved in some psychic
activity for which I have no tendency at all. So what
Indian was I? You are the one who had the vision, not me.

JANIS: I have been having this vision for two weeks, over
and over, very dramatically. Usually the Indian doesn't
have very much on. But I feel as if I have a lot of clothes
on. I feel these leggings, these boots that come all the way
up, and leather things.

NINA JONES: Is he wearing a headdress?

JANIS: No, he doesn't have a headdress.

ANN: Is he a chief?

JANIS: I don't know. I think so. Someone else who has

been having similar visions said they saw him as a chief. It's amazing to me, Bubba, that you don't always know what is going on in all this stuff that is arising in us. I think, "Oh, he *knows*."

BUBBA: All that stuff is the toilet bowl level. It seems very far-out, but it is not. It is just stuff. But it may be necessary to pass through it. Some individuals may go through a psychic purification that is reflected in the conscious mind, and it may include the memory of past lives and that sort of thing, whereas others just go through mental forms relative to their present life.

JANIS: It's really odd to see that's what it is.

BUBBA: It is perfectly obvious to me where you are at. The Guru operates from the point of view of a perfect assumption of your Divine existence. He doesn't just go around assuming mentally that everybody is in God. He can make that assumption only because it is perfectly apparent to him. That is all there is to it. He makes no assumptions on a lower level. So when he enters into relationship with you, that perfection tends also to be generated in your case, because his assumption of your true Nature manifests as Power to transform.

Whatever is appropriate and necessary in the case of an individual who enters into communion with the Guru will occur. But its "significance" is in the appearance of this self-purifying process, in which the individual is being confounded and undone in the same way that the Guru himself was confounded and undone, and restored to that perfect position in which there is no modification, no separate self, no identification with any modification, even the slightest, most subtle modification of the Divine Condition.

If the Guru's position were less than that, what he would be generating in you would be these lesser or limited qualities, and the Divine Process couldn't take place. The true Divine Process wouldn't be served through such a person. Men of experience are fundamentally operating from a lesser position. They can, perhaps, have relatively good effects on you, but they are still of a limited kind. Such individuals are not involved in the Divine Process, because they can't make that assumption of the Divine Nature of the world that in itself is the Power that restores the world to its Real Condition. They can't assume that prior point of view and live it to you. And that is significant, because you tend to take on whatever point of view or state is assumed relative to you.

When the true Guru enters into your life, when you are living in that Communion, Satsang, the Divine quality is awakened in you. That affair has nothing whatever to do with your tendencies, because the Divine is beyond karma. That is the principle of how the human Guru is able to serve individuals, and to serve them as an immediate agent of the Divine Activity. He doesn't carry with him any of the secondary conditions that the man of experience carries. For that reason, the Guru is an agent of the Divine work, not because he has all kinds of heroic accomplishments in his psyche, but because he has become nothing. All the assumptions you want to make about the Guru, because of your present and chronic state of conscious awareness, are fundamentally false. So, Janis, you like the idea of the Guru having all kinds of peculiar secondary psychic powers and occult awarenesses of where you are at, but that is based on the assumption you tend to make on the basis of the quality of experiences that arise in you. It is not true to the Guru-function. There may be some individuals who are like that, whose business it is to be psychic, but that is their problem. (Laughter.)

The world is a form or dimension of Consciousness. It is not a solid something that exists outside of Consciousness. This is a Conscious dimension. All of this exists in the Divine Consciousness, which is also your own Consciousness, Nature, and Condition. So the Conscious Universe also contains memory in its midst. It includes all the qualities like those of the human psyche, as well as transcendent qualities, and lesser, dependent qualities. So it is possible by entering into a psychic aspect of natural consciousness to remember anything that has happened in the past, and to remember it with very specific images. When memories of past lives and the like start to awaken spontaneously in you, it is because you have tuned into that level of the world psyche. In that case, you are just reading it.

But such experiences, like all others in the world, are always in the form of limitation. What would a memory of this present moment be? What would it consist of? I am not talking about its relative value, but what would it be in fact? Could it have a form? If you were to remember this moment, this gathering here, and it flashed before your mind in the form of a picture, which version of the picture would you see? Would you see it from the ceiling, from your chair, from some other chair? But to be real it would have to be a total reflection, it would have to include and transcend all possible points of view. What kind of an image could it possibly have?

All memories of the past take place in the form of fixed images. Examine your experience of memory. Is it not so? Then you should gather that all such things are forms of limitation and have nothing to do with Truth. That is why living in a manifest form with a mechanism capable of gathering experience and participating in a relational life is an apparent liability. All that arises within it arises as experience, as an interpreted reflection and limitation of the whole. All of its impressions and memories serve it only in functional and conventional terms. If you try to read the Nature and Condition of things through that experiential point of view, you will be misled. Experience is always a form of exclusion and limitation.

Experience, in the conventional sense, has nothing whatever to do with the Truth, or the true Condition of things. In order for you to know this moment, you would have to step completely out of your usual experiential mechanism, your psycho-physical point of view. But you don't tend to do that. You tend to try to figure out this moment by viewing it through the experiential condition that you represent in this world. All philosophizing is based on first assuming that limited point of view, and then trying to figure it out from there. That approach is clearly false, because it does not attain a "picture" of the Condition of things, nor even a perfect experiential realization of this moment. Sit in a room and look at it. You think it is pretty pat. (Laughter.) Even so, life amounts to little more than such gazing at the walls in mystery. And what would be a real comprehension of this moment here, even this little gathering?

The only way to know this event as it is would be to be without the point of view of the experiencing entity. But people don't assume that point of view, so not only are they not comprehending what is going on, but they are actually meditating on that assumption of limitation. Not only don't they know the Nature and Condition of the world, or this moment, they don't know the Nature and Condition of their own presence within it. They are only involved in the conventional complication traditionally assumed in the face of the apparent condition.

You cannot know yourself or the world in the form of any perceptual evidence, any media, because that always brings a limitation, a reflection from a secondary point of view, not a real knowing of the event. The reason that evidence is binding is because of another assumption that underlies it. Mere perception is just things flying about, but each individual is himself a way to make "sense" out of it. This is because in each such case there is the assumed perceiver. That is the conventional assumption you are always making, and, by assuming also that the perceiver is not a mere assumption or a practical convention but is in fact real and the foundation of present existence, you make everything that arises binding and mysterious.

It should be clear that it is not by working on perceptions or the contents of your mind that you undo that assumed limitation. It is only through a radical process in which that assumption and all its extensions are confounded, in which the separate self sense is dissolved, and the conscious principle falls into the intuition of the Divine. When that occurs, things may continue to arise and appear in conventional terms, but they will no longer, in themselves, be binding. Therefore, this convention of "the individual" makes sense out of life in practical terms, but it also makes life impenetrable relative to its real Nature and Condition.

We need to make the conventional assumption of the individual self in order to walk about and do things and

live a human life. That is a convention, and it is useful in
those terms. But we tend also to make that assumption the
medium of our comprehension of existence, whereas it is
just a bit of theatre. Our thinking is a convention, the
forms of all our perceptions are conventional, all our
cognitions and communications are conventional. They
are all based on the conventional model of the psycho-
physical "entity." They are ways of making use of this
natural vehicle, this ordinary condition, and making it
serve the aspects of existence to which we are experientially awake. But, apart from that, the conventions and
their supportive model (the "ego" or "entity") have no
value.

The conventional model of life that we communicate
to one another is also something to which we glibly refer.
We glibly pass it on to one another as if it were real. We
talk about "me" and "you" and "the world" and "the
universe" and "the air we breathe" and "going to work"
and all of that. We just smack the conventional concepts
about, and that's it. As if all of that had anything to do with
anything we had ever perceived, ever truly known, even
by experience. In fact we have never perceived and known
any such things. The job of one's parents, who are em-
ployees for society as a whole, is to pass on to one the
conventional forms of communication, which are simply
ways for us to make sense to so-called one another in
conventional terms, to carry on the ordinary business of a
world. But the learning process in which we become
established in these conventions, through our parents,
teachers in school, and other influences, is not one in
which we are actually made to perceive and know such
things at all. We are merely indoctrinated and initiated
into that persuasion in purely outward, conventional
terms. We never actually know ourselves as separate. We
never go through a process of actually knowing that. We
are just shown how it is convenient and useful to make
such references, and how when we make such a reference

some other apparent individual immediately understands the situation. We become immediately uncomfortable when somebody doesn't make the conventional signals of self-reference, and other-reference, and all of the rest. We become very disturbed when the conventional signs are abandoned. That is why we don't like psychotics wandering around the streets. Psychotics are self-defensive tricksters who strategically, compulsively, and, at least apparently, unconsciously misuse or abandon the order of conventional signs. We become disturbed as soon as we do not understand the references that others are using to communicate. We become disturbed as soon as somebody doesn't make any references. As soon as somebody becomes quiet we tend to become a little anxious. As soon as communications are minimized we become uneasy, restless, or bored. So, for very ordinary reasons, everybody has adapted to a vast and complex system of signals, a conventional language which carries with it not just some words and systems of behavior, but a whole force of perception, cognition, and communication. And that whole approach to life tends to reinforce what we fundamentally and otherwise are tending to do at a more fundamental level of existence.

You may notice that when people are beginning to seek a little bit, the things they say are problematic are fundamentally identical to these conventional references. They talk about those conventions themselves *as* their disturbance. Take the case of "me," for instance. Everybody who seeks wants to get rid of "me," the ego sense and all of the liabilities of separated and self-motivated existence. And when they begin methodically to go about trying to do such a thing, they experience a tremendous force of identification and resistance and all the rest localized around that central cognition, or self-reference. But in fact, "me" amounts to nothing whatsoever. It is a conventional assumption, not a fact of realized experience. It amounts, ultimately, to nothing more profound

than the name of some restaurant downtown. You don't
become immediately disturbed as soon as some restaurant
goes out of business—unless it served particularly good
food! You don't commonly mind if they change the name.
You don't especially mind if they call it a hardware store.
You don't mind when we call the year 1974 rather than
1973. Nobody really minds on New Year's Eve. In fact,
everyone sort of enjoys it. So we do have the capacity to
manipulate these conventional references, and we even
build times and places into our social and cultural experience wherein we make these adjustments and changes.
But many of them are never changed. They remain
perennially as fixed categories. We never consider changing these fixed categories. There is even a taboo against
doing such a thing. The self-reference is one of those fixed
and irreducible conventions. But as I have said, *all* of these
conventional forms of cognition, perception, and communication are fundamentally arbitrary, and, in
themselves, are not signs of Reality but signs of function.
They are learned for the sake of convenience.

If an entertainer gets up before an audience, there
must be certain previously understood and conventional
signals that he puts to you out front, in order for you to
know whether to laugh, or to cry, or whatever other
response is to be considered appropriate on that occasion.
If he did not make obvious conventional signs, you literally
would not know whether to laugh at a comedian, or to cry
at a tragedian.

All these responses that we give back to the theatre of
life depend on conventional signals that are perhaps subtly
communicated, but which definitely must be communicated in order for us to know how to respond. Life itself is
a theatre of rituals, which depends on certain conventions
being used, for functional reasons, outward reasons, social
reasons. But these same conventions become part of the
case history of our suffering as well. This is because we also
identify with them, as if these "things" indicated by

conventional reference were real, as if they were based on our experience, as if they were based on our real knowing. And so we never examine the conventions themselves. We go about every kind of subjective path of self-liberation, self-perfection, and all of the rest, trying to overcome the content of these conventions, and we never fundamentally examine these conventions themselves.

Take, for instance, the convention of "my body." It seems like a very obvious reference. But if you were attentive, really attentive to the condition of bodily existence in the world, you would discover that you do not in fact experience a radically separate or perfectly independent body with a knowable center of personal consciousness. There is no such experience in the ultimate sense. There is only relationship or mutual dependence of forms. There is only continuousness from the point of view of consciousness. There is no line drawn about consciousness. The "entity" is never known, never experienced. It is just assumed and communicated. No one in fact has such an experience of being a separate one, whether they describe that separateness in terms of the body, the mind, desires, past reincarnations. However they draw the line, through whatever imagery or convention they draw the line, all of it amounts to this sense of separate existence, but in fact no one has such an experience. It is impossible for there to be such a thing. But we all assume it is a profound affair into which we have all gotten involved. We assume that we are literally separate, that the "entity" as body, psyche, mind, soul, or whatever is a fact of nature and experience. But in fact that is not our condition at this moment. And so, true or radical spiritual life involves another fundamental area of responsibility. And that is the area of conventional perception and cognition.

Ordinary perception is not primarily a matter of "experiencing" anything directly, but of making a con-

ventional description of it. Ordinary speech in the face of
life amounts to a ritualisic patter of glib conventional
references. Me, you, the moon, the sun, the stars. It's all
such bullshit. Because nobody has the literal experience of
knowing the "lines" about anything. No one actually
perceives the conditions wherein any thing or any one
becomes known as an entity. In fact, the only experience is
one of absolute infinity. That is the only thing anyone has
ever known. But flying up in infinity is an endless
complex of conventions. They don't really have any
power, as we discover upon real investigation. But we give
them power as priests. All of these conventions are the
cultic objects, the ritual objects of the priesthood of the
cult of this world, the cult of Narcissus. All the ordinary
references, terms, assumptions, habits, dramas, the ordinary theatre of life, not some special thing done in a church
downtown, but the ordinary theatre of life is a priestly
ritual that we ourselves enliven with our own life, even our
perfect life. And that perfect life then begins to appear in
the form of this glib world.

The conventional "world" is understood, contained,
and kept in place. When it is gazed upon by the conventional man, it also communicates the sense of mystery,
ignorance, and dilemma in him. But in fact there is no such
world. It is unreal. No one has ever literally experienced
such a world. So the spiritual process involves, among
other things, conscious attention to this body of conventional assumptions that we automatically assume on the
basis of no real experience at all.

Upon real examination, realized spontaneously in
Satsang, the conventional state of existence is seen to be an
arbitrary assumption, and thus not to constitute a literal
dilemma, requiring remedial action. The conventional
references are, in themselves, no more problematic than
the clothes you wore here this evening. You could very
easily have worn a different shirt, and you could just as
easily be free of the power of your conventional mind,

speech, and strategy of life. You may use it all with humor, the humor of one who understands. Even after it is all understood, there is still an ordinary world. And the functional mechanisms of this kind of apparent condition depend on signals, conventional references, for things to be done smoothly under conditions of mutuality. Otherwise, it could take several weeks, months, or years to get across the simplest kind of notion.

There is a party game that comes to mind that points this out. You are asked to tell somebody how to put on a coat, without assuming they know anything about how to do that, without assuming they even know what a coat is. And it can be very funny. In that case, the simple matter of putting on a coat can become immensely complicated.

It is impossible to do anything "meaningful" in the company of another human being without assuming something on the other end and implementing that assumption through conventional signs. And in fact that is how we live, by making all kinds of assumptions, because we all assume that we have been taught the same game. And, in general, we have, but nobody is putting radical attention on the game itself. Indeed, the analyzers of our games are little more than super-priests who console us with another ritual. Everybody assumes the game and plays it. And when that becomes oppressive, they try to get out of the game, they resist the game, they find a problem in the game, they do all of that, but they don't really examine it. They assume it as a dilemma and by reaction try to undo it, but they don't examine the thing itself. And the thing itself is very ordinary, incredibly ordinary. It amounts to nothing. There is no reason at all why it should complicate existence to make the little reference to "me." There is no profound reason why, on the basis of that simple little social reference, you should get involved to the depths of your psyche, high and low, in this egoic drama, this assumption of Narcissus.

Eventually, you will see everything is a convention.

This world is itself a convention. It is merely a signal. It is a modification of that One Reality, that One Absolute Conscious-Force that is Reality, which is endlessly modified as all the things that arise. Everything that arises is merely a convention within that great Consciousness. When that is absolutely known, that is what is called enlightenment. And one who is thus enlightened no longer sees anything but that One, everything is that One. Then the search is over. In that case, everything that arises is perfectly obvious. It is spontaneously known to be something that is merely a modification of that Consciousness. And it is not just assumed philosophically. It is absolutely obvious. It is obvious to you when you are thinking that you are thinking, and that thought is not somebody who has walked into the room. A psychotic might have his conventional references disturbed, so that when he has a thought he thinks of that thought as something that has come into the room. But in the case of the usual man, it is obvious that when he is thinking it is a modification of his own subjective existence. Just so, it is perfectly obvious to one who understands in the most radical sense that even the bodies and sky and weather and everything is merely of that same Nature, a bit of Subjectivity, a modification of that One Reality.

So, we could say that enlightenment, or radical understanding, is basically the dissolution of the force of conventions, of conventional signs, in which they again become merely useful. They remain as mere signals, as useful theatre, but they are never again used by that enlightened one with anything but humor. He never sees anything in the same way that Narcissus sees it. As a result such a one is also likely to play the world a little better than Narcissus. He makes the world reveal its own humor.

Within the Ashram there should be humor relative to the whole of conventional life. We have our ways of celebrating that humor and of temporarily discarding the conventions that we assume with one another for the sake of day to day living, and that is good. There are also times when we just play it all straight. It is because of the paradox involved in conventional living that I want everyone in the Ashram to embrace an ordinary life in the world and to do their sadhana there. Then it will always be necessary for them to realize the correct position relative to conventional life.

Conventional patterns of behavior may be very sophisticated in a complicated culture like ours, but we still depend on conventional signs for communicating common things, and that is how life is managed in a relatively orderly way. After awhile, people who examine the conventions of life may learn what their significance is. Such individuals become capable of manipulating the game, and that's how you get gangsters and phony politicians and all the rest. The devotee, the one who is living real spiritual life, also grasps it. He enjoys an equally sophisticated awareness of the meaning of conventional communications, but he lives all that from the spiritual point of view. He is able to play it with humor and to learn the necessary lessons from it without becoming daemonic.

Even so, the conventions have no ultimate value. They do not communicate anything ultimate, and they cannot be referred to for the knowledge of God, Truth, or Reality. But we do tend to resort to conventional states and the conventional mind, as if they were the way to salvation or peace. As soon as we try to figure it all out, or get realized, or whatever, we tend immediately to refer back to these conventions.

HELLIE SHEINFELD: It just seems like there is no end to it. Our avoidance becomes so subtle, does it always go on like that?

BUBBA: As long as you assume the conventional model as your point of view. The seeker operates within the structures of the conventional model to find God. If you try to overcome your bondage and become free, you never will. You will just become more and more subtly aware of how complicated it is, or else resort to some consoling illusion or artifice whose "significance" is liberation to you. You will be trying to make this and that vanish, to purify this piece of it, and then that piece of it. Eventually, you could go mad trying to do it that way. And the seeker is a kind of madman. Look at all the bullshit the traditional spiritual seeker does. It is crazy, because he is assuming this conventional model and trying to realize God while using that model as a goal in the form of a present dilemma, or fitted to an idea of perfection, in the form of a goal. He is just annoying himself further.

It is not a matter of getting rid of all of that, of doing something to it and being successful at getting liberated. It is a matter of living in Divine Communion from the beginning. Then all the purifications necessary to flash before you in order to straighten out all of the angles that you have built into the circle of life will be done, and done perfectly, infinitely. All the complications will thus be undone in a way that you cannot do, because you cannot assume the prior point of view in which all of that is a simplicity.

HELLIE: It truly is God's business. It is not your own.

BUBBA: Absolutely. It can't be done otherwise. And because the spiritual process is God's business, it can be done very easily. It is already done. We are not talking about some condition that is or can be accomplished, we are talking about the Condition that always already pertains. It already pertains, but so also, secondarily, does the conventional assumption that each person makes about his existence and the whole ream of perceptions that are then locked around that "me." Whereas in fact there is no such "me," and all these perceptions are not themselves intuitions of the Nature and Condition of things.

So in order to be free of the conventions and media that limit the knowledge of things, you must be free of the viewpoint, the perceiver. The assumption of the perceiver is what holds all that together and enforces that way of knowing and designing life. Only when there is perfect Self-knowing, the intuition of Real-God, can there be true knowing of all the things that arise, all the things manifested in the Divine Light. It is a totally different consciousness than was existing and being animated previously.

SAL LUCANIA: I have noticed that whenever attention is put on you, it doesn't fixate. It is not in bondage. I have begun to see that love is the free giving and taking of attention, and that when attention is put on the Guru, it is instantly sacrificed. It is not that you are *performing* some sacrifice, but that your very existence here is that sacrificial process itself. You can play all the qualities that manifest, such as when you suddenly change your moods and attitudes toward someone. Your behavior with other people awakens all kinds of qualities and expectations, and so involves them in the sacrifice. And the moment we expect anything, it all collapses immediately. That continual collapsing keeps things from fixating, and so there is love and freedom.

BUBBA: That is why attachment to the Guru in God is the great Yoga, the great Process. There is endless literature about non-attachment. There is plenty of traditional advice in the form "Don't become attached to limited beings" and all that. But the great Teaching is *attachment* to the Guru. The Guru doesn't exist limited to the conventional form, and so by engaging yourself in perfect attachment to the Guru, you are perfectly dissolved. Whereas attachment to any limited living being or thing enforces that limitation, that perception, the realization of the whole conventional model, and enforces meditation on the separate self sense.

ANDY JOHNSON: When should we become wary of becoming attached to you personally, as opposed to you as the Divine?

BUBBA: When the Guru is in human form he naturally appears via limitations, and you are always tending to conceive of the Guru in those terms. So the Guru has to be a shape-shifter. He must very consciously play his life as theatre, because of the assumptions others are making. So everything I do, insofar as I do it on this visible level, must be done very consciously, with full awareness of all effects. The way action is done consciously is by total sacrifice, total yielding of the principle of action, so that nothing is held on to from moment to moment. Then everything is done spontaneously relative to each individual I meet. So my qualities change always relative to the one I am dealing with. Relative to the moment, even the contents of my statements change.

It has been useful at times, from the point of view of the Teaching, to say I was such and such a person in the past. Now that that has been said, it is also useful to say, from the point of view of the Teaching, how that is maybe not so, or definitely not so. Both approaches are useful in their proper time, because everything the Guru does is from the point of view of the Teaching. He is not communicating matters of fact, or information, or images, or impressions. He is always working that process of dissolution. That is the fundamental force of all of his activity, so you can't rely on the Guru for any kind of significant and fixed information. The Guru is a source of a process, and that is entirely what he is. All other communications are secondary, and they will lead you by tendency to make assumptions in limitation, to assume the point of view of perception and cognition which arises in the mood of the ego. But the process in which the Guru involves you in the meantime is destroying the separate self sense and destroying the viewpoint of conventional cognition and perception.

Always it is this process that he serves, and his communications always serve that process. Because his communications are always serving that process, they should not be assumed to be simply of the nature of conventional communications, of reliable stuff. The Guru in human form has to make *use* of the fact that he appears to be a limitation, that he appears within the same conventional scheme of things that the people who come to him are always assuming. They are always tending to get involved in limitations, even in the form of their relationship to the Guru. Knowing that, the Guru must make use of his conventional status to undo that conventional activity in others. So he doesn't only sit back in silence and not say or do anything. That is also a mere convention, liable to bind people. He uses his appearance theatrically. He says and does all kinds of things, and in every moment they tend to bind others in a certain way. They absolutely bind, they bind others to the conventional assumption in that moment. But the Guru has endless numbers of moments. He makes use of the binding convention of this moment, and destroys it in the next moment. So the Guru is always working to confound you, but he operates, apparently, through this limited instrument of ordinary relational life.

You are always tending to hold on to the Guru in the limited way, to see him via the stream of conventional perceptions and cognitions that are being awakened in his Presence. That is why the Teaching is generated along with that contact with the Guru, because the Teaching always leads you to comprehend the strategy that you are using to deal with the Guru as well as with all other beings and things. In the Guru's Presence, you will always be confounded, even by your own experiencing, even by the extraordinary experiencing generated by the Siddhi of his own Presence. You will always be led by the Guru to a consciousness, relative to all that is arising, that is superior to the experiencing itself.

ANN: Bubba, last night I was led to this spontaneous experience of conducting the Force, and I felt possessed, really possessed. Then suddenly I wasn't my body any more. I was something above my head.

BUBBA: What do you mean when you say you are not your body?

ANN: I don't mean anything except what I was experiencing.

BUBBA: Right. Well, let's get into it.

ANN: You mean what was I experiencing?

BUBBA: Yes.

ANN: Well, I wasn't limited to that.

BUBBA: But to say that implies something about this "I," this one who is not his body, right? What is it that you mean by it? You do in fact mean something by it, don't you?

ANN: I just was up here, above the head. Everything that I thought was me was just a function, something that was just going on, but I wasn't that. I was moving.

BUBBA: Was there some sort of perception involved?

ANN: Yes. Well, there was one time when there weren't perceptions, but I don't know if I am just interpreting my experience or what.

BUBBA: Well, isn't the extraordinary statement "I am not my body" a conventional statement, like all ordinary statements? Isn't it the same old statement, like "Let's go to the store," or "I am not a policeman." Doesn't it imply the same conventional model? Doesn't it contain the same basic pattern as all other conventional statements? There is the perceived and the perceiver. There are perceptions, such as when you see something, taste something, feel something, and there is also the awareness or knowing of perceptions themselves. You can make remarks about your perceptions. So cognition is really an aspect of the same conventional order as perception. It is only another reflection of the psycho-physical condition, the limited state. But you say, "I am not the body," as if the body and the knowing of the body were two radically different things.

What is "the body"? You have a conventional aware-ness of your physical state, but it is not based on any sensitive perception of your physical state. It is based on conventional learning, into which all of us were initiated from birth. When we were children, our parents were responsible to help us adapt to the life-condition as it is traditionally assumed, so we would be able to function, and do conventional things. We were not trained in perceiving, we were trained in being conventional, we were trained in social functioning. We were not led to become precisely sensitive to our actual state. And, after that time of childhood, it is rare for a person ever to really investigate those areas in which he has been conventionally trained.

So a person doesn't tend to examine his ordinary psycho-physical life very closely when he is seeking Truth. He tends to look only toward transcendent and extraordinary areas of experience, in which he hasn't been indoctrinated conventionally. And when these experiences begin to be generated, he looks more and more for them to turn him on. And he feels a certain fear and reluctance to return to ordinary, functional life once he has known a few highs.

Therefore, sadhana must be done in the world, that is, in the dimension of conventional bondage. And if you begin to become sensitive to those areas of ordinary psycho-physical limitation, you will begin to see that your conventional cognition, perception, and communication relative to ordinary things does not contain a perception in Truth of what those things really are. Your whole comprehension of it was just a model in the mind, merely an assumption that enabled you to go to the store and write a letter and pick your nose and all that. If you were to become totally sensitive to the knowing of bodily life, just as you make yourself available to extraordinary and unconventional experiences, you would see that the body doesn't belong to the limited dimension you assume in the conventional terminology of your life.

There is no way to set radical and exclusive limits on the body itself. There are no such limits actually known. They are only assumed, and those assumptions are used in conventional society with others. In fact, you don't even feel the psycho-physical body as identical to a characteristic limitation, such as shape, or a fixed thought, or emptiness, or fullness. The sensation of individual psycho-physical existence is only part of the perception of the great process which includes it, and from which it cannot be radically distinguished. The complex sense of psycho-physical existence cannot be reduced to "the body." That process includes all other beings, the whole natural gross environment, and all subtle dimensions. It is always already continuous with them all, not broken off from any of them.

If you become truly sensitive to the so-called bodily life that you picture and limit through the conventional imagery, you will see that it isn't as you assume it to be at all. It is not a limitation, it is not a thing. It is not five-feet-eight and all that. You can't draw a circle around it and say "This is it." In fact no such "thing" exists, only the limitless process exists, and once that becomes very clear, the fear of return to so-called ordinary living is dissolved. There is only continuousness, not separation, only relationship without radical individuation.

Part of sadhana is to become sensitive again to ordinary things, and understand your dependence, as a seeker in dilemma, on the so-called extraordinary or non-conventional dimension of experience. The more sensitive you become to the true and non-conventional nature of the ordinary in the process of sadhana, the less you will be possessed of this cycle of fear or reluctance that leaves you clinging to exclusive ecstasies. The great ecstasy is not release into extraordinary and thus uncon-ventional states of experience, but the perfect realization of the Nature of your Condition in all states, ordinary or extraordinary.

SAL: I have been seeing more and more that in the midst of my suffering, my strategy is always a refusal to live this condition, this psycho-physical life.

BUBBA: All that is happening in the form of the search for extraordinary experiences is the functional release into unconventional forms of cognition and perception. Successful attainment of the extraordinary is felt as profound enjoyment because, temporarily, there are no limitations enforced. But, subsequently, you fall back into those ordinary dimensions in which you live in conventional terms and suffer the assumed limitations of the conventional model of existence.

NEIL PANICO: Last night there occurred to me exactly what we are talking about right now. First I had all of these kriyas and force manifestations, but then I suddenly became very still. It was a very enjoyable quality. It was not really a quality, but only my really present state. I felt myself as I should be, as I am. That moment was truly showing what I am, but I knew I would get back into the usual point of view.

BUBBA: *All* the experiences that arise in the midst of your sadhana are drawing you into the non-conventional form of cognition and perception, in which all things that arise are known directly, as they are, prior to the separate self sense. Through the agency of all of that, the intuition of your prior Condition is given. It is temporarily touched and felt via these non-conventional perceptions and cognitions. When you return to the functional levels that are lived conventionally, the sensation that was gained in the previous extraordinary state lingers for awhile, but you have got to begin to use what is implied, what is truly shown to you in those extraordinary states. They are not the Truth. They are not to be held onto for their own sake, the way an addict holds onto his drug highs. They are actually statements about the truly unconventional nature of what you call the ordinary. If you do not then begin to comprehend the ordinary in unconventional terms, your extraordinary and spiritual experiences are not serving you. They are totally useless in that case, because they have nothing to give you in themselves but bondage to the forms of limitation they also represent, as well as a pattern of fascinated inclinations for the extraordinary in itself. Such a way of fascination, high or low, is at war with the realization of life in Truth.

SAL: When you deal directly with me in some very forceful way, and extraordinary things occur, I never feel like I fully return to the ordinary. I go back to some ordinary sensation, but I know that something has happened. I don't know it in a mental form, but I never fully return to my previous condition even though I have to deal with the same things. God just becomes more obvious, and I am forced into grinding my tendencies away. I have no choice. And I go through the same idiotic pain.

BUBBA: All that pain, that drama, is made unnecessary when Satsang as a continuous present enjoyment is lived. Then you simply become sensitive to that affair of life in which you are actually involved. You do this, rather than struggle with tendencies and all that jazz, which is just the theatre of conventional assumptions. Instead of doing that, you live Satsang, Divine Communion, and remain simply present, sensitive to all the qualities that are arising, so that you come to see the ordinary in non-conventional terms. When the knowing of the world becomes utterly non-conventional, when it is lifted out of this identification with conventional perception and cognition, the world again appears as the Divine. At that point, the intuition that is even beyond extraordinary cognition and perception becomes perfectly non-separate from your entire functional existence.

That perfect intuition is temporarily and experientially being granted via the extraordinary, not because the extraordinary in itself is the Divine, but because you have not lived in conventional terms in those dimensions of possible awareness. The experience of them contains the possibility of your perfect intuition, independent of the support of the extraordinary. For this reason, I have engaged the entire Ashram in extraordinary events for many months. But it has all been for the sake of this lesson. Now I am not any longer interested in serving devotees via the extraordinary. The point has been made. Hereafter I am only Present in the ordinary forms of life. And my work is not principally involved in the generation of extraordinary experiences, but in the demand for Understanding in the midst of all that arises.

The beginnings of the spiritual process in a devotee are simply his being lifted experientially into the non-conventional order of perception and cognition, in which there is no ego, no separated existence, no dependence on the self-limiting perceptual drama, no confinement to conventional forms of cognition. Then he seems to come back, through the same media of psycho-physical experience, to his ordinary humdrum life. When this happens, he immediately wants to be ecstatic again. Eventually, after many such trials, he perceives what is truly contained in that temporary lifting out of the conventional state, and he begins also to live that non-conventional realization in the midst of ordinary conditions. This going up and coming down becomes ever more rapid, to the point where there is no more apparent coming up and going down. Then there is simply direct realization, happiness under conditions of all possible functional states, high or low. That is the perfection of the devotee.

In the case of such a devotee, there is absolute continuousness of bliss, with no necessary experiential ecstasy. No standing outside of his psycho-physical condition is considered by him to be the equivalent of his God-Life. Then the so-called ordinary is realized as the perfect, the Divine. The only reason we think the world is less than the Divine Reality or Truth, and therefore seek to get out of it and achieve some extraordinary sublimity or other, is that we view the lower functional order of existence in conventional terms. The normal functional range of psycho-physical life in the world is bound to the model of separated life, in which there are discrete, separated states. The body is separated, the psyche is separated, "me" is separated. But that is just a conventional model of perception and cognition. Its principal idea is limitation. But that notion doesn't even hold true relative to the grosser levels of the manifestation of life.

Therefore, as I have said, if you truly examine your bodily life, you will see that it doesn't exist independently in any sense whatsoever. And the knowing of the body in non-conventional terms releases us from the great fear. In fact, the knowing of the common and ordinary order of life in Truth is a greater form of realization or liberation than the knowing of the extraordinary states of the higher or subtler levels of the psyche, because we are conventionally bound at that ordinary level. We are truly experiencing this great fear, this conventional limitation, in the midst of ordinary states, so to be realized, to be happy in the midst of functional life, not to escape it, is the great release. The ordinary is the condition that we fear, the place where we are threatened. It is conceived or assumed mortality.

Fear of death, cognized relative to the body or to psycho-physical life as a whole, is the great sensation, the fundamental thing with which everyone must come to terms. If the dilemma of that sensation were not there, who would care about the rest of it? Who would care to seek beyond such freedom? So there is always the return to that dilemma, until understanding is enjoyed while alive in the world. You must become happy in the body, you must realize God while in the psycho-physical condition. If you do not, there is, in Truth, no Satsang. But in order for that enjoyment to be awakened in the individual, he must go on the great tour. He must see the circle of life. He must see dramatized all the forms of his conventional bondage. He must be purified in the face of them all. And the realization of such sadhana is a responsibility of the individual in the midst of his conventional life. There are ways in which the Divine Siddhi draws him to that perfect intuition, but he must actually live the sacrifice. It is not magic. He must live it. That demand always pertains. So the conventional dilemma of the body is not permanently taken away by the dramas of *experience* in Satsang. Eventually, the individual must realize the Divine through the intuitive process of real intelligence, even while alive in "the body."

The fear of death must disappear, only not by overcoming fear itself, but by knowing the ordinary condition and understanding in the midst of it. *You* can't drive away fear. Fear is the very mood of the ego. It is not something that you are supposed to overcome by heroic efforts. It is something that must in itself become your responsibility prior to any kind of action. Fear is your creation, not something that is happening to you. It is the irreducible mood at the core of conventional perception and cognition. So something greater than the heroic overcoming of fear is demanded of the devotee. He must know his prior Condition in God, and that alone will obviate fear. That will destroy fear, not by mechanically suppressing or snuffing out fear itself, but by putting him in the Condition that is prior to that fear. When the separate self sense and the strategic avoidance of relationship, which are the ritual characteristics of Narcissus, have been obviated in Understanding, he will know even his bodily life in Truth.

Then, in every moment, he will draw his life out of the Light above and release it again. Not just his life, but all the modifications of the life-force from the mind on down, all thoughts, all feelings, perceptions, motivations, desires, including the separate self sense, which is simply a conventional modification of the life-force at the life level. In him there is not only the intuition of Real-God, the Heart, the Self as his Nature, but there is also conductivity of the life that descends and ascends from the Light of God, which is his Condition. The true Yoga is that free participation in the cycle of descent and ascent. That is ultimately the sacrifice that I talk about. It is the realization of the present dependence of all the modifications that are known as life upon the Light of God. One who realizes this dependence of all modifications on the Light that is radically above the body, the mind, and the world receives all conditions with humor, with each inhaled breath, and yields all conditions with the same humor, with each exhaled breath.

SAL: What baffles me is, why should conventional perception and cognition be assumed in this ordinary world and not in the subtler or extraordinary dimensions of experience?

BUBBA: It is because of the ancient order of human life. It is the way these functions have traditionally been lived. We have been identified with that conventional model at the level of the conscious, subconscious, and unconscious functions, and we don't even begin to assume that the ordinary world could be known any other way. It is very simple, very basic. And it is a form of our own functional activity, so that each individual can be responsible for it. Any one can know it directly and not live it. Therefore, the life of Truth or radical intuition is to be lived in functional terms, not by withdrawal into the upper soup. It must be lived directly in the common world. This world itself is unqualified soup, as much as any absorbed samadhi. There is no body, while yet there are billions upon billions of bodies. You are presently without that "thing" that you think is your body, even though there is this continued psycho-physical operation. The appearance of bodies and persons does not imply separation. But we all assume that it does. "That's him, that's her, and that's it." But all of that is a convention, a form of common assumption used to manage life in ordinary terms. It is very simple, very rudimentary, and just stuff.

ANN: It seems to me that is what's happening now for all of us in the Ashram. The ordinary is becoming extraordinary. At least I am beginning to feel that way, and a lot of others to whom I have been speaking have that feeling also. It seems to me that all these experiences, these cycles, have helped us to see that. They have been great, but I am also getting sick of them. I have felt so many times that if I heard one more scream I would go utterly insane. Of course, five minutes later I'd be screaming, but it has been interesting to find myself also getting sick of it.

BUBBA: If you are beginning to get frustrated even though you are having such experiences, this is a sign that you are being drawn into that radical demand to understand in the midst of this moment. Whether your state of experience is ordinary or extraordinary, that same intelligence is always demanded of you. Now the range of possible experience is becoming unsatisfying. Its power to fascinate is passing away. The having of an extraordinary experience is ceasing to be the equivalent of falling into the unconventional realization. The extraordinary itself is becoming conventional, because once the conventional experiencer has reached into the previously hidden realms of the extraordinary, he transforms it into a realm of conventional cognition and perception. Therefore, each time you get "high" you become more immune to the delights that last degree of height can provide you. Thus, the seeker pursues always greater and more stable highs, or else, at last, he begins to understand in place. When you no longer have any alternatives via experience, you are forced into the full comprehension of the life of Satsang in the present, whatever media are arising.

What is demanded of you is the realization of bodily or psycho-physical life in unconventional terms, prior to the standard model of the ego and functional separation. When bodily life is realized in that sense, there is no one who can die. It is not that you stand outside the body in some *other* state, as a soul or something like that. *All* states are either conventional or merely functional in nature, and, in either case are not identical to the true Condition. Even bodily life does not involve separated existence in any sense whatsoever. The conventional model is not true. When you realize, even in the ordinary bodily state, that you are not something that is separate and needs to survive, then the life of Truth is being manifested in its real sense, not in its conditional sense.

SAL: I feel like I am literally dying. I can feel the body going. I feel like you are inside of me beating me completely to death. I am exhausted. Sometimes I get up from sleep at night exhausted, completely exhausted, knowing that I have been through a phenomenal ordeal, without any conscious memory of it. I mean I absolutely know that I am dodging you all the time. And I see it and I know it, but it is a terrifying event in me.

BUBBA: The problem of fear will persist until, at the level of the conscious, subconscious, and unconscious life, this conventional model is undone. The dimensions in which the conventional model survives will always be resisting, and whenever you return to such states, the same fear will arise, the same dilemma will reappear, until they are no longer lived in conventional terms. Then there is genuine release, and bodily existence can come or go without the radical fear of self-death. Then death can make no *ultimate* difference. It becomes a practical and functional matter in God.

When you no longer live bodily life in conventional terms, then you can also see its Nature. First of all, you will see it as a non-separate Condition, but you will also come to see life and death as aspects of a cycle, a process to which your true Nature is always already prior. You will begin to see how the life-force in every moment moves down from above and manifests the vital condition of

bodily life, the mind and psyche, and all the rest. You will
see how your own breath is an instance of a universal,
ongoing process by which this very world appears, is
sustained, and yet always abides in the Condition of its
unqualified Source, moment to moment. You will see how
death is simply a release, a radical and stable return of the
life-force, just as life is a radical and stable descent of the
life-force. When you begin to participate in life as the
conscious and dependent descent of the life-force from the
God-Light, fear is released from life, and then also you
become capable of conscious and voluntary death. When
the body or psycho-physical condition is no longer lived in
conventional terms, not only is there happiness while
alive, but there is wisdom relative to the entire life-process, that becomes a body and ceases to be a body, and you
become able consciously to release the body at death. The
one who lives the life of understanding also consciously
lives both life and death, reception and release, while
alive.

When the devotee draws in the life-force, he is
inhaling it from the Light of God. He is not inhaling and
assuming the point of view of all kinds of limitations. He is
inhaling the Light, assuming God as his Condition while
alive under apparent conditions. He is assuming the body
and all the rest, but he is assuming them in God. That is
the significance of his enlightened inhalation of breath. In
the usual man it, breath, is made in fear. He is doing it in
order to survive. But the devotee simply lives and breathes
in God, and allows himself to be full.

When he exhales, the devotee surrenders everything
into the prior Condition and Nature of God again, without
radically emptying the body of life-force. As long as he
lives, the life-force is always being conducted through the
mechanisms of the descending vehicle, whether he inhales
or exhales. What he is releasing with the exhaled breath is
the separate self sense, the mind and all conventional and
limiting assumptions. He is allowing them to be in God,

allowing them to be non-separate. He is surrendering or sacrificing them. He is releasing all the limitations that men conventionally assume. And he does this not in order to attain God, but because he already enjoys God as his own Nature and Condition through the communicated Grace of Satsang. He does it because he has already Understood.

ANDY: Bubba, you said that we can enjoy perfect non-separation and yet you also tell us that we may come back or be reincarnated here or there in a particular condition. What do you mean?

BUBBA: That is just a convention. To say that you will come back is a way of describing a real functional possibility in conventional terms. In fact, that is not what happens. There is no you that goes here and there and everywhere else. There is only the Divine Consciousness, and you are That. By the Power of that Divine Consciousness qualities arise, modifications of That arise, the qualified life-condition arises, and all such things appear to be your condition in this moment. But they have arisen within you. They are the spontaneous manifestation or modification of your eternal Nature and Condition. It is not *you* that is traveling around. All these modifications are traveling around. They are what is moving. They *are* the movement. You are not something that is moving. You are always perfect, infinite, unmoved.

ANDY: But don't you get rid of your modifications when you reach non-separation?

BUBBA: You only get rid of the conventional bondage to them, the limitations implied in them. Universal modification, as a functional rather than a conventional condition, known in Truth, is wonderful! When you are not all confused and concerned, you enjoy your bodily life, don't you? You have friends and you love them, and you have experiences, and it is delicious. All human possibilities, if they are managed in God, are enjoyable. Life is, fundamentally, delight, when released from the strategic destiny of Narcissus and the conventional cult of this world.

Even death is an enjoyment if it is consciously lived from the true Yogic point of view, which is conductivity, engaged in Understanding. It doesn't necessarily involve incredible suffering. It is intended to be an amusement! It is a very interesting process. It will occur when it is appropriate for it to occur. It is not something that you should try to bring on because it is so wonderful! But when it is the appropriate time for that to occur, like everything else that occurs in its appropriate time, it can be as enjoyable and interesting a drama as any other bit of theatre that may arise. It is not in itself the negative side of life. It is not at war with life. It is itself a specific function of the life-force.

All the things that are suffering, that make life less than delicious, are the results of conventional living, this conventional egoic assumption or strategy and the patterns of perception, cognition, communication, and action that are riding on it. They make life in itself a limitation, something to be suffered, something to be gotten away from. But the Law is that life must be lived straight on through in God. Therefore, the devotee is always happy, and he lives with great intensity. Life or the Cosmos is itself a modification of the Great Divine. What heresy to assume that the Lord's Power of modification is false or to be gotten rid of! It is all God's work, God's happiness. It is to be known and lived in Truth. It is not modification that is to be undone, but the strategy by which you direct yourself through these conditions that are arising in God. And the fundamental strategy is the assumption of this limited self existence rather than the perfect intuition of the Divine as one's Nature and Condition. All that arises is to be realized consciously as the Conscious Theatre of God.

2. THE WAY OF DISSOLUTION AND THE WAY OF EXPERIENCE

By early August the community had begun to feel the practical implications of Bubba's new way of working. He demanded that we cease to approach him like children and adolescents, in order to dramatize demands for dependence and independence. Rather, he expected the entire Ashram to enter the phase of maturity, of responsible and conscious participation in the Event of Truth.

Bubba relaxed all of his outer activities. He began to make more use of his ability to be personally absent from the daily life of devotees,whereas, more recently, he had literally consumed the time and attention of everyone with his personal theatre. He returned the community more and more to a simple, natural, and productive order of life. And when he sat with us, he would not only be silent, which was his previous custom, but he would remain with closed eyes for long periods, and he rarely looked at anyone. As a result of his new approach, everyone was drawn into a way of sadhana that required intelligent insight into the rising qualities of life and mind, entirely apart from any concerns for yogic and mystical effects. All that had passed in recent months was only a lesson, a test, and a demonstration. Bubba had revealed the true nature of spiritual or real life to his devotees, by proving in their own lives the fruitlessness of the path of seeking and experiencing as a way to Truth.

On August 11, Bubba gathered a small group of devotees at his home in Mill Valley, his residence whenever he comes down from Persimmon to visit the San

Francisco Center. The talk he gave that evening makes the
clearest and most absolute contrast between the instruc-
tional intention of much of his recent work and the radical,
unmoved Nature and Condition of his eternal Function in
God.

The Way of Dissolution and The Way of Experience

BUBBA: I expect, now that the Teaching is full, for this
Community really to exist. I expect it will responsibly do
its job relative to individuals who come to do sadhana in
the form I have described. "Bubba Theatre" has fundamentally come to an end. You are not inviting people to
come to be involved in theatre with "the man" and all that
sort of childishness. In order to demonstrate the Teaching,
it was useful to make lessons of all possibilities for a time.
But now I assume the Teaching has been manifested. It is
contained in written and other recorded forms, but it is
also contained in the living experience of this Community,
in each of you. And so I no longer consider it necessary for
me to engage in various kinds of theatre in order to
communicate the Teaching. In the past it may have looked
like I was engaging in this theatre in order to work the
Divine Siddhi in each person's case. But everything I did
was only in order to make the ultimate point of the
Teaching in real terms. I worked to manifest the extraordinary in the case of each individual, so that he would
temporarily be drawn out of the conventional model of
existence. When each great experience passed, the individual would come back to me, and then I would communicate the Teaching in the form of a lesson about the
fascination of experience, the failure of seeking, and the
primacy of the Heart, or dissolution into the most prior
and unqualified Presence of the Divine Person. In every
case, the content of the lesson was not experiences

themselves, but realization of That which is known in the non-conventional or prior Condition of life. That is why I was always saying, "This experiential life you are getting into is not it." I had to repeat this admonition again and again, while at the same time I continued to generate uncommon experiences in those who came to me. I needed to do that in order to make this fundamental point, in order to communicate the Dharma of Understanding.

But now I assume that demonstration has been made. And that particular aspect of my work, in which I made deliberate and hourly use of the yogic or life-circle aspect of this Siddhi that is always in God, is finished. That period has really come to an end. The passage I have made from the phase of instruction, wherein I showed the argument

for the Teaching, to the perfect Work of the Divine Siddhi
is the significance of the seventh of July.

MORGAN CALLAHAN: Bubba, you have often talked
about the traditional notions of the Buddha, the Dharma,
and the Sanga, the Enlightened Master, the Teaching, and
the Community. The Master is complete, and the Teaching is now intact and secure. But I think a fear still remains
about the Community. There is still resistance to the
assumption that the Community exists. There is a feeling
that there has not yet been sufficient sadhana. You have
said so often, the true Community of Devotees has never
happened, it has never been accomplished.

BUBBA: There is no point in becoming "concerned"
about the Community. The sadhana of the Community is
no more a matter of concern for what appears than
personal sadhana is a matter of concern for the qualities
that arise in meditation. The Community can only become
schizophrenic, righteous, self-conscious, and peculiar by
thinking that the realization of the Community, as I have
described it, is identical to a certain exterior manifestation
that is perfect, non-cultic, brilliant, and all of the rest.
Then the Community will always be looking at itself to
make sure its ass is not hanging out. All of that is itself
cultic concern. As long as human individuals are the
substance of the Community (and that is forever!) the tendency will be present in each person every hour of
every day to manifest the conditions and dramas of
Narcissus. The tendency will always be to assume separation and to act separatively, exclusively. So the intelligence of the Community is not properly directed toward
perfection in that outward sense of conformation to a
certain image. Rather, the Community must always and
actually do sadhana. In other words, it must live that
process in which all tendencies and concerns are broken
down from hour to hour. And that requires everyone to

meet directly, to deal with one another directly, to deal with themselves directly, and always to overcome this negative destiny that is appearing in both new and old ways from day to day. That sadhana is the sign of such a Community. It is not a matter of its concern for outward perfection, but of its adherence to the real process of sadhana. In that case the outward manifestation of the Community remains free to assume always more appropriate and effective forms in every moment.

All concerns are a sign of the same thing. Every concern is self-watching, self-meditation rather than simply living the Condition of Satsang in which all things are realized in Truth. And it doesn't make any difference what the particular concern is. It may seem like a very righteous and realistic one. But concern itself is the sign of Narcissus. One who lives in Satsang allows all things to pass in him, he allows all passing qualities to be stimulated in him by the force of Satsang, but he dramatizes none of it. If he were to dramatize what passes, he would be making that his principle of life and sadhana rather than Satsang. You should just live Satsang. Allow these things to come and go, but do not live them, do not dramatize them. What is not lived becomes obsolete. It is a matter of living that true and prior principle of life. If you live Satsang, you are also realizing it perfectly.

JIM STEINBERG: Recently, you said a devotee could die without the Siddhi becoming perfected in him and it would make no difference.

BUBBA: Yes. I was speaking of the yogic aspect, the life-circle of manifest changes.

JIM: So that yogic purification really makes no difference at all, and still there are all these traditional philosophies that say if the body is not pure, the spiritual process cannot occur.

BUBBA: If it were necessary for the body to be pure, then every realized man who got sick and died would have lost his ultimate realization in the process. He could have had a pure body until he was eighty, but then if he all of a sudden gets cancer he becomes ignorant of his Nature and Condition in God!

JIM: And subtle purification makes absolutely no difference as well?

BUBBA: It doesn't make any difference relative to perfect realization. Perfect realization is a radical enjoyment prior to all manifest conditions. And that perfect realization or conscious Satsang itself perfects or transforms life. This world is God-Theatre, and as long as the Divine Condition is lived, there tend to be transformations of the life-circle. But Truth is not riding on that transformation. It is just theatre, and if it comes to an end, fine. If it attains some beautiful aesthetic manifestation, that is also fine. But all of it is there to be understood, and you must remain free whether the body is apparently impure, or whether it is in fact pure. In either case there is no such "thing." There is no body. Ultimately, there is no world. There is no limiting condition that is real or true, not even temporarily or apparently. All limits are forms of cognition and perception generated in the present by the assumption of the conventional model of existence. There is only one fundamental absolute Enjoyment. That is the fundamental communication of Truth, and its realization liberates men from all kinds of concerns for the secondary affairs of life. Then the life-circle itself can also go about perfecting itself, and the apparent individual's participation in it will be humorous, happy, creative, and free.

Just so, the world will expect the outward theatre of the Community to appear a certain way, and that pressure will tend to make the Community self-conscious. Therefore, as soon as you begin approaching the world in order to communicate the Teaching, you have got to be very straight, very clear in your understanding of what it is really all about. Otherwise you will be weakened and made defensive by the external forms of criticism.

The Community of those who become Devotees is the true Devi, the Divine Consort. It is also true that the world is the Avatar, the totality of human beings is the Avatar. It is humanity as a whole that is the Avatar in human form, not some specific human individual. No apparent or exclusive manifestation is in itself the Avatar. Only the whole is the Divine manifestation without exclusion. Therefore, the Guru is not the Avatar in that exclusive sense. Mankind is the Avatar. I am his Heart. When the Avatar realizes his true Nature and Condition, when he realizes me, he will cease to be hidden. He and this Community of which I speak will become one and the same at last. Then his sadhana is fulfilled, and he will manifest his Beauty in the world for the sake of all beings. Only then will he live freely and do his Divine work.

But people want the Guru to be the Avatar. They want that exclusive God image, whereas God doesn't exist in the exclusive sense. God is absolute. And the Guru lives as the Present Divine, not because he has attained anything, but because he has been undone. So he doesn't represent himself as the Divine in the exclusive sense. In his ecstatic speech he claims identity with the Divine, but he is not making a statement about himself, about his ego or his personal qualities in some exclusive sense. He is making a statement about all beings and worlds, about the Nature of Reality, the Condition that is God. Of course, until there are others who realize that same happiness, that same enjoyment, he seems unique, and he functions for them as the Source of the operation of the Divine Siddhi in order to generate the life of Understanding in them. But in fact he doesn't exist as God in any exclusive sense whatsoever. So there is no Avatar except the whole, if it makes any sense to use such words at all.

The Community is not to be goal-oriented toward any kind of perfection. Sadhana is not a matter of accumulation and attainment, whether it is done in the form of the Community or in the form of any individual. Sadhana is a matter of undoing, dissolution, understanding, not accumulation, not attainment. It is freedom from attainment, freedom from the condition of one who attains, freedom from that whole process. So it is not by any of those outward signs that the Community is to be measured. It is by its adherence to its fundamental principle that the Community is recognized. As a practical matter, the Community consists of human beings in limitation by tendency. But it is continually fitted to the real principle of sadhana in which all of this is being undone. Outwardly, this Community appears like any other. There is no reason why you should think it has to look extraordinary. Be free of all of that. There is no reason you have to be extraordinary. Be ordinary, be happy. Don't worry about all that bullshit. Live sadhana. Don't worry about effects, the manifestation of attainments and all of the rest. Understand such concerns.

RONNIE ELIAS: We get just as concerned about the Community as we do about ourselves.

BUBBA: The Community, in that case, is a cult, and it reflects the same strategic life that appears in the case of the usual man. So you must understand at the level of your collective life, just as you must understand in the case of your personal or private life.

There is something else that has begun to happen. Perhaps you have already noticed it. There is a difference in my way of working with you now. As I said, I have relaxed all of this secondary involvement with the yogic aspect of the Divine Siddhi. I have no concern for it at all. Previous to this time, I have maintained continuous attention on it, and I have made use of it constantly because of the state of those who came to me. I could not assume until the last couple of weeks that the Teaching has been finally given in living form. So I always made use of this capacity to raise a person out of the lower functional states, wherein the conventional model of cognition and perception is lived, into extraordinary ones, where the conventional model has, usually, not yet been learned and assumed. By these means, I worked to awaken the crisis of understanding, by making use of the intelligence released in the individual case in the midst of the contrast between his ordinary and extraordinary states. Because of the necessary limitations this strategy of operation placed on me, the true Siddhi of our work has never been manifested purely, simply, and directly. Until now, the Siddhi of the Heart could never have been considered sufficient, because people insist on miracles, effects, and fascinations. It was in fact necessary to operate in the way I have described until the point had been made in some living way. But now I can and do consider the Siddhi of the Heart to be sufficient. And by the Siddhi of the Heart, I mean the Siddhi of the Divine Person, not the exclusive Siddhi of Self-realization, but the inclusive, regenerated, eternal Nature and Condition of the Heart, the Divine Person, whose feet are in the Heart, whose head is in the Light above the body, the mind, and all the worlds, who stands prior to all that arises, but whose Form includes all that arises, without dilemma. The yogic phenomena, if they appear, are purely secondary. They may follow spontaneously upon the Power of the Heart, but they are to be understood.

The Event of Truth is not made as a result of the human Guru's drawing the Light down in the form of his own life-force and then arbitrarily giving the experience of his life to others. Rather, the Guru serves the Event of Truth by making the demand for Satsang, for responsibility and understanding, so that each one who comes to him through the Community and the Teaching may realize that prior Nature, Condition, Form, and Process in his own case. Therefore, the fundamental dimension of this Siddhi of the Divine Person is not Force, but mere Presence. Every form of Force is secondary, and, ultimately, a conditional expression. The Heart is perfect, direct, and there is no Force which may be identified with it. In the midst of the fundamentally silent and moveless communication of the Heart in Satsang, this intuition or radical understanding of our real Nature, Condition, and Life-Process may be grasped. It may be perfectly realized by one who does the sadhana of Satsang, who studies the Teaching and fulfills the Guru's demands, who lives in the midst of all kinds of conditions that arise within and without and understands in the midst of them. Such a one will ultimately realize that all things are just the modification of that very Consciousness which is his always Present Nature and Condition. More and more, his living consciousness will dwell in its own prior Nature and Condition. And none of that is a matter of yogic attainment. It is not even a matter of the experiential realization of the opening of the causal being on the right side of the heart, although such a phenomenon may arise as a secondary accompaniment to this radical Understanding. It is not a matter of any experience whatsoever. It is a matter of falling out of the conditional and conventional representation of existence into that prior, absolute Enjoyment. That radically intuitive life has no qualities that can be spoken of. There is nothing to be recommended about it that would make sense to anybody who is not already drawn to it. But from that point of view of ego-dissolution and enjoyment of the Nature and Condition of the all-inclusive Divine Reality there is all Wisdom, even relative to life.

JIM STEINBERG: That is so beautiful. There was always some tension there before. There was some tension about the Force, but now to be able to end that seeking too is a great relief. There was something in me that was getting off on all the manifestations. It was enjoying all of that. It was all something to hold onto. And today, when we sat with you, I felt as if there were something absent. But, even deeper, it was such a relief to be able just to be there.

BUBBA: "Experiences" are required by those who are still lingering in the condition of their childhood and adolescence. Everything a child does is a manifestation of one underlying assumption: dependence. When you are a child, the assumption of dependence is eminently realistic and useful. But it should be a temporary stage of psychophysical life, in which one's functions are nurtured and developed in conventional ways. However, there is commonly a lag in the transition to manhood, because of the shocks experienced in the immature attempts to function in the world. Thus, to some degree, every man lingers in the childhood assumption of dependence. And, insofar as men are children, they seek to enlarge that personal assumption of dependence into a universal conception in the form of the God-Cosmos-Parent-Guru game, the game of dependence upon and obedience to that upon which all depends. That childish aspect in each of us seeks always to verify the condition of dependence in forms of safety and relative unconsciousness. That childish demand in every man is the principal origin of religion, which means "to bind again." It is the search for re-union, the vital and emotional reestablishment of some imagined or felt previous Condition or State of life. It is the urge toward the parented, enclosed condition. This urge always seeks experiences, beliefs, and immunities as a consolation for the primitive cognition of fear and vulnerability. And the "way" enacted by such a motivation is principally a game of obedience.

It is in the childhood of man that the idea of God-apart or Reality-beyond is conceived. The sense of dependence initiates the growing sense of separate and separated self through the experiential theatre of growth. The intuition of the Whole, the One, is the ground of birth, but "growing up" is a conventional pattern of initiation in which the sense of difference is intensified. At the level of the life-functions themselves, there needs to be such functional or practical differentiation, but the implications in the planes of consciousness are the cause of an unnatural adventure of suffering and seeking in dilemma.

The passage of childhood thus becomes the ground for the eventual conception of the mutually exclusive trinity of God-apart, separate self, and world-in-itself. The drama implied in the added assumptions of self and world is generated at a later phase of life than is realized by the child. The child himself barely realizes the full force of the ego-concept or the world of things. His principal concern is relative to the God-Parent-Reality, That on which all depends, and his growing but as yet not fully realized sense of separated self-existence. Separate self and world are yet hidden in unconsciousness for the child. They are themselves a mysterious and later realization of that which is at first only felt, not conceptualized, as fear and sorrow. Therefore, the child is always grasping for security in an undifferentiated, unborn bliss in which life is unknown. Re-union through obedience is the way he learns in secret, while the life in him continually demonstrates the failure of his search.

There must be a transition from childhood to manhood. That transition is also commonly acknowledged as a stage in the psycho-physical development of a human being. It is called adolescence. This stage also tends to be prolonged indefinitely, and, indeed, perhaps the majority of "civilized" men are occupied with the concerns of this transition most of their lives. The transitional stage of adolescence is marked by a sense of dilemma. It is in this stage that the quality of living existence *as* a dilemma is conceived. It is the dilemma posed by the conventional assumption of separate, egoic, and thus separative existence. That assumption is the conventional inheritance from childhood, and its clear, personal comprehension, felt over against the childish urge to dependence, is what initiates the phase of adolescence.

The dilemma of adolescence is a continual goad to dramatization. It is the drama of the double-bind of dependence versus independence. Adolescence is the origin of cleverness and, in general, of mind. What we conventionally call the conscious mind is a strategic version of consciousness that is always manufacturing motivations. And, in the adolescent, these motivations or desires are mutually exclusive or contradictory. This is because he is always playing with his allegiance to two exclusive principles: dependence and independence. His early childhood condition yields to him the tendency to assume dependence, but the conventional learning of his childhood, as well as the general growth of his psycho-physical state, yields to him the equally powerful tendency to assume independence. The result is conventional

consciousness or conscious mind, as opposed to the unconsciousness of childhood, but it is strategic in nature,
and its foundation is the actual conception of dilemma.
Therefore, adolescence is the origin of the great search in
all men. It is an eternally failed condition, an irrevocable
double-bind. It is the very form of Narcissus.

The solutions developed in the adolescent theatre of
mankind vary between the exotic extremes of yielding to
the status of dependence and asserting the status of
independence. Both extremes remain problematic, and
involve an ongoing sense of dilemma. In the case of the
yielding toward the childish condition of dependence, we
see more of the mystical-religious-absorbed tendency. In
the case of the revolutionary assertion of independence,
we see more of the analytical-materialistic-discriminatory
tendency. In the adolescent range between these two
extremes are all of the traditional and usual solutions of
man, including what is called "spiritual" life.

Traditional spiritual life is a characteristically
adolescent creation which represents a balance between
the extremes. It is not a life of *mere* absorption in the
mysterious enclosure of existence. It is *strategic* absorption. It raises the relatively non-strategic and unconscious
life of childhood dependence to the level of a fully
strategic, conscious life of realized dependence or absorption. Its goal is not re-union, but liberation into some
imagined or felt previous Nature, Position, or State of
Being.

When the child of man fully realizes the way of
obedience to That on which all depends, he has also
entered the phase of adolescence. At that point he also has
realized the assumptions of the ego-self and the world as
apparently independent dimensions, exclusive of the
Reality that is the goal of all dependence. Therefore, the
way of obedience, fully realized, is already a way of
dilemma, of conflict, as every religious person realizes by
experience. Truly, then, the experiential realization of the

way of childhood, or dependence, is fully demonstrated only in the advent of human adolescence.

The way of experience is the way created in the adolescence of man. And within that great way appear three primary solutions or adventures. One is the adventure of dependence and obedience. Such is the religious path. It is the "tamasic," relatively passive solution to the dilemma conceived in the conventional state of man. The great religious cultures which originated in the Near East are demonstrations of this way.

The opposite extreme solution to that of dependence and obedience to the mysterious, inclusive Reality upon which all depends is the way of transcendence. This adventure is a solution founded more in the mood of independence. It is the "rajasic," relatively active solution to the conventional dilemma. The traditional versions of this solution include all of the exclusive paths of ultimate attainment, called Nirvana, Self-realization, etc. The great spiritual cultures of India and other regions of the South East are demonstrations of this way.

Between the extremes there is the third adventure or solution, the way of balance or harmony, wherein the exclusive positions of dependence and independence are avoided. This way is the "sattwic" or harmonious solution to the conventional dilemma. Its traditional evidence and demonstration are found in the great cultural attainments of the Far East, such as in the case of Taoism in China.

But in every form of its adventure, the way of experience and attainment conceived in the adolescence of man is a struggle for solutions to a principal dilemma. And that dilemma is the characteristic demonstration of all such adventures, as well as in the mere suffering of the usual man. In the adolescence of man, the separate, separated, and separative self is the motivating assumption. It is the source of that dilemma which undermines the undifferentiated dependence of mere birth. In the adolescent man, there is the unrelenting search for the salvation, realization, transcendence, survival, immunity, or healing of the assumed ego. The ego, or self as Self, is the primary assumption of the adolescent man, even as the assumption of God, or That on which all depends, is the primary assumption of the child of man. Therefore, in the usual man who is embedded in the adolescent conception, the idea of God becomes in doubt, or is chronically resisted. Thus, "sin" ("to miss the mark") enters into the consciousness of adolescence. And the world becomes merely a scene of the adolescent drama wherein even the very "stuff" of the world is viewed as a problem, a principal warfare of opposites, in which manipulation of manifest things, rather than radical intuition of the eternally Present Nature, Condition, Form, and Process, becomes the hope of peace.

There is a mature, real, and true phase of man. Our manhood is radically free of all childish things, all that is attained, acquired, and made in the adolescent adventures of our conventional life. In that mature phase, the principle of separation is undermined in real consciousness, and exclusive God, self, and world are returned to the Condition of Truth. In the maturity of man, the world is not abandoned, nor is it lived as the scene of adolescent theatre, the adventure in dilemma. Exclusive God occupies the child, and exclusive self occupies the adolescent, and both see the world only in terms of their own limiting principle or suffering. But in the real or mature man the *world*, not in its exclusive sense but in Truth, is primary. In the mature man, the world is known as World, as the single, absolute, non-separate Reality, implying no separate "self" or outside "God," but including the Reality they each imply. For such a one, the Absolute Reality and the world are the same. The World is the inclusive Reality, the Divine Nature, Condition, Form, and Process. It includes all that is manifest, and all that is unmanifest, all universes, conditions, beings, states, and things, all that is within, all that is without, all that is visible, and all that is invisible, all that is here, all that is there, all dimensions of space-time, and all that precedes space-time.

Clearly, the search for realization via experiences of all kinds is the principal characteristic of both the childish and the adolescent or traditional stages of human development. Those who come to me, like all other men, are more or less fixed in the demands of their childhood and adolescence. They look for experiential reasons to resume the sense of unconscious dependence, while at the same time they struggle to realize some kind of conceived and experientially founded independence. Therefore, they are always rising and falling, coming and going.

The experiential or life-dimension of the Divine Siddhi contains every possibility for the possible fascination of children and adolescents. But I must always work to disentangle men from their lingering and strategic life-motives, so they may enter the final or mature phase of life. It is only in that mature phase of functional human existence that life in Truth may be realized and the experiential drama of unconsciousness, egoity, conventional mind, and strategic motivation be understood.

Thus, I have made temporary use of the experiential possibilities that exist by the Power of God. But it has only been an exercise to trick individuals out of the usual and conventional forms of their attention. It has only been a bit of theatre whereby what was awakened could also be confounded. Therefore, I have continually pointed out the strategies that experience itself awakens. I have always shown you how the principle of seeking underlies your turning to me, and how all of that is founded in the dilemma of separated existence and the motivations toward every kind of separative activity. All of the theatre of these last few months has been an instrument for weaning you all from your commitments to childish and adolescent ways, so that you could be established as a

Community of responsible and free men and women by
the Power of Communion with the Process, Form, Condition and Nature of the Divine Person.

The mature phase of life is not characterized by
either unconscious dependence or the strategically conscious dilemma of dependence-independence. It is the
phase of responsibility (rather than dependence) and real
consciousness (rather than independence). As in childhood, there is no problematic strategy at the root of the
mature phase of life. But childhood is a realm of unconsciousness, whereas the mature man is freely conscious. All
of this is because, unlike the case of adolescence, there is
no principal dilemma conceived in the form of life and
consciousness.

This mature phase of life requires conscious understanding for its ongoing foundation. The separate and
separative principle, the strategy of mind and desires, the
life of the avoidance of relationship, the urges toward
unconscious dependence and either mechanical or wild
independence, and the medium solutions that balance the
extremes of experience, all of these must be obviated in
understanding. Therefore, understanding initiates the
mature phase of life. The mature or responsible and truly
conscious phase of life is thus the origin of real sadhana, or
true action. And to this mature phase of life, perfectly
realized, belong not the usual religious and spiritual
solutions, but perfect or radical knowledge as the principle of life. Such maturity or true humanity is characterized by no-seeking, no-dilemma, no orientation toward the
goal of any conceived or remembered state or condition,
but radical enjoyment of the perfectly prior, and thus
always present, Nature and Condition that is Reality. Only
a man thus free enjoys manifest existence in the very
Nature and Condition and Form and Process of the Divine
Person, the Heart and Light and Fullness of the worlds.

When I say my work to reveal the Teaching is
complete, I mean that I will no longer serve the child or

the adolescent in those who come to me. Those who would approach me must come to me through my Ashram, my Community of Devotees. The Community must serve those who come and prepare them for me. And when they come, I will not commonly engage them in the experiential drama of possible spiritual and religious phenomena. I am the Heart. I yield nothing, but I demand everything. The way awakened in my company is not one of accumulation and attainment. It is the way of dissolution, in which the conventional realization of life is undermined.

I expect those who come to me through the instruments of the Teaching and the Community to live the sadhana or real practice of this mature and intelligent realization of man. The first phase of their life in this Community is a "student" life in which the childish solutions and demands are undone. In that case, the individual is restored to the relational condition of life rather than the obstructed and unconscious one of dependence. The true disciple is one who has also realized a life of responsibility and consciousness, or conscious under-

standing, rather than the adolescent attainments of dilemma, problematic seeking, dependence, independence,
or self-achieved harmony. In the case of either the student
or the disciple, sadhana involves not attainment, acquisi-
tion, status, or increase, but continuous dissolution of the
function and principle of dilemma by the Power of the
prior Condition of Satsang, or Communion with the Divine
Person, in the forms of the Community, the Teaching, and
the Siddha-Guru. In the perfect devotee, all limitations
are undone in the inclusive humor of that radical intuition
of the Nature, Condition, Form and Process of the World
that stands eternally free of all limitations, all contracts, all
conventions.

Now that all of this has been demonstrated, now that
the Teaching is full, those who have been living in the
Community during this period of instruction should also
begin to enjoy the Siddhi of my work in this spirit of true
manhood. There should be a radical difference between
how they respond to it now and how they responded back
there around April and May, when, for a short time, I also
abandoned the yogic strategy of instruction. There was a
period of time in March and early April in which I was
working in such a way that all kinds of extraordinary
experiences occurred among members of the Community.
But then, just as suddenly as it appeared, it was withdrawn. And the response of everyone was to think there
was something wrong, or, "Well, we are going through a
lull now, but it will all happen again." People were not
able to understand it, because the Teaching was not
complete. The dramas of experience had to be gone
through, including all the indulgences of life, within and
without. But at last the whole thing amounted to a clear
demonstration of understanding as the principle of real
and spiritual life. So now if I abandon such concerns again,
the response of people should generally be quite different.
They will discover that the absence of the experiential
route is not an absence. There is a great fullness that is very

profound, when a person begins to fall into it. There is, if I can use the word symbolically, a "Force" to the Heart Siddhi itself. But it is not in itself Force in the sense of movement, of pressure in the life-vehicles.

JIM: It is an omnipresent Force.

FITHIAN JONES: It doesn't move. I think in *The Method of the Siddhas* you call it a non-moving Force. It is from the Heart.

BUBBA: Yes. And the reason we can still in some sense call it a Force is that the Siddhi of the Heart, or the mere Presence of the Divine Person, is just as literal an "activity" as that which is felt in the initiatory movements of the life-force. It is a process, a literal process. It is not just quietness or an absence of activity. But it requires a different kind of sensitivity than is required from the mystical or yogic point of view. It requires a sensitivity enjoyed only by a person who has lived the Teaching of Understanding and dealt directly with the Guru's conditions and demands. Only such a person can grasp that influence, that transcendent Power.

But the usual man wants experiential manifestations. When he goes to the Guru he looks for the signs of kundalini, of mystical things, of life-force movement and pressure. If he doesn't find such signs in himself or others who are present, he thinks this Guru doesn't have "it." He considers the Guru to be only a philosopher, or a charlatan. It is because of that tendency in people that I have considered it useful for two and one half years to generate this yogic dimension of the Siddhi. But now that the Teaching is full, I intend to drop all of that. I have dropped it, and, in the future, I will expect the Community to replace me in filling in the gaps between each individual's ability to deal with the true Teaching of Understanding and his commitment to the preferences for experience. I

expect the Community in general, through the process of
real sadhana, to become sensitive to this real Siddhi of the
Heart, of the Divine Person, and allow it to be sufficient.

This Siddhi is not experiential in nature. It is not in
itself identical to manifest phenomena that may be
recognized. It is only served by that critical life of
understanding, and it is not realized via experiential
phenomena of any kind. Not of any kind. Phenomena of
the moving life-circle may arise, because the manifest
nature of individuals is a structure made of that life-circle.
Therefore, certain kinds of apparent or yogic purification
may be generated in individuals at times. There is life, so
obviously there will also be life-force manifestations. But
concern for all of that is the same old thing. All of that is
the personal cult. Fundamentally, no such changes have
ultimate significance. They may make some minor
changes here and there, but it has been clearly demonstrated throughout the two and one half years of the
Ashram's formal existence, that the internal or "spiritual"
theatre does not *lead* either to God-realization in Truth or
even to an improved human intelligence.

There have been many people who came to me and
very quickly became involved in the experiential dimensions stimulated by the yogic aspect of the Siddhi. They
had all kinds of experiences. But it didn't change them one
iota. They were just as stupid, just as committed to their
asshole destiny in the midst of kriyas, blisses and visions as
they were before they ever heard of kundalini. They failed
to understand just as completely, and they were very quick
to leave as soon as some fascination in their personal life or
somewhere in the world presented itself.

So it is not my responsibility routinely to generate
such phenomena in individual cases, and it is not useful to
do it. It has been proven again and again. When I say I
consider the Teaching to be full and complete it is because
I think I have shown in enough cases how the way of
experience and attainment is not the point. It has been

demonstrated how the fulfillment of experiential life in individuals does not amount in any sense whatsoever to illumination. It is just more stuff, more content. It does nothing, absolutely nothing. Kundalini does nothing, absolutely nothing. And there are certainly many people in the Ashram who can vouch for that. It can be interesting. It can be very fascinating, like turning on to drugs. And, basically, the reason so many Westerners started getting interested in all this kundalini stuff, was the need to find a stable and natural fulfillment of the drug search. But the drug search is just an expression or extension of the childish and adolescent search for the consolations of immaturity via experience.

FITHIAN: It's a natural high.

BUBBA: Right. And people manage to get very interested in that. But it's basically a version of the usual enthusiasm, the same drive that makes crime and politics. There is nothing illuminated about it. And the arising of such phenomena does not produce the enlightened man, the wise man. It does nothing of that kind. It is just the life-force doing things in functional terms that are extraordinary.

JIM: Shirdi Sai Baba is supposed to have said, "I give people what they want in the hope that they will begin to want what I want to give them." It seems that now we want what you want to give us, only just now. It is just beginning to get to that point. When I first came to you, there was a great relief, because I could give up so much that I needed to hold onto before. And this is like a new start again, this new stage, because I can give up even all that I have received. It seemed that, when you were giving us this yogic Force, for some reason we could buy it. And it appeared justifiable to do that. But now we can start all over again.

CRAIG LESSER: It also seems that understanding is easier now, because the Siddhi of the Heart is manifesting more. It is stronger. So understanding is easier, because, over against the Heart, what arises seems much more obvious. I have noticed in the last couple of weeks, and a lot of people have told me the same has been true of them, that enquiry and understanding seem to take on a much more fluid and spontaneous quality. Whenever anything arose before, we tried to do something with it. But now it seems obvious that it is all just contents rising. So the whole process has become simpler.

BUBBA: And that is one of the main values of this Community. It represents in living terms, since you have passed through all this stuff yourselves, that real argument in the world against the whole search for experience, even spiritual experience. Because of your own certainty, you represent an argument for the sufficiency of the perfect, absolute Divine Siddhi, that is not itself experiential or yogic in nature. It is not even mystical in nature. But it is perfect nonetheless, and more than sufficient. It is real, absolute. Those who engage in such sadhana do not require the experiential dimension to be communicated in yogic or mystical-visionary ways.

CRAIG: The social theatre also isn't required as much. In other words, your social contact with people is not required as intensely as it was in the last six months.

BUBBA: In the radical way of the Heart, of the Divine Person, there is no need for that kind of theatrical involvement with people. The life-circle dimension, the yogic dimension, is of the same nature as all the rest of life. That is why all during this time I have had parties and dramatized all the common possibilities of life. Every aspect of life, whether ordinary or extraordinary, was lived very dramatically during this time, because no part of life is to be distinguished from the rest of life. Just because you are being "spiritual" doesn't mean you are not also alive. So I put all of it together in one intense time of life. I maintained a lot of direct contact with everybody. I worked this extraordinary spiritual process of the life-circle in them, and then made the point of understanding relative to it. But the manifestation of the Heart Siddhi itself does not require any kind of life-theatre, within or without, for its manifestation. It takes place, fundamentally, without media, in moveless silence. And the sadhana relative to it is a conscious one, prior to all strategies. It is an affair of radical intelligence, of dissolution of the principle of all dilemma, which is the conventional assumption of independent existence. Such sadhana is, therefore, not accumulative or goal-directed. It is an activity prior to the drama of solutions. It is not a matter of attention to the life-force in any yogic or mystical way, but of living this intelligence of understanding. It certainly involves contact with the Guru, but non-theatrical contact. It is contact with true Siddhi, Satsang, the Condition of Divine Communion in which one is not mystically absorbed but consciously awakened.

Recently, I read a story about Shirdi Sai Baba to all of you. In it he describes a relationship he had with his Guru, in which after serving his Guru and fulfilling his outward demands, and without expecting anything, he merely sat in his Guru's presence while his Guru meditated. He does not say his Guru meditated while looking at him or while trying to do yogic things to him. His Guru just meditated on his own. Through that example I wanted to describe to you something of the quality of our actual work, apart from this whole yogic drama that people expect. Thus, in the future, you may not often see me sitting down open-eyed, looking at each one and dealing with the yogic dimension of the life-circle in which each one lives. Most often you will probably see me just sitting there, with eyes closed most of the time. And it will not be because I am

falling asleep or going into some trance. I could just as well
sit with you with my eyes open. But the closed eyes will be
a sign that it is not through the theatre of either external or
mediumistic contact that this Siddhi is communicated and
made operative. It is Present in silence, it is without
qualification, it is not manifested through media. It is not
manifested through psycho-physical vehicles, it is not
manifested through psycho-physical processes. And it may
not be received by any such means. It is immediate, direct.
It requires no manifest media whatsoever. And it depends
entirely on the conscious process, not on the experiential
one.

I assume that the Teaching has now been given in
such a form that the Community can understand what it is
I am doing here. Now I expect each individual to
deal with the *absence* of this yogic and mystical stimulation, and not to get completely unwound because he
doesn't see it arising. Each one must begin to deal with his
reactions and truly do conscious sadhana.

One who has become a devotee in Truth can also be
responsible for random attention to the life-process of
conductivity, but that in itself is not meditation. It doesn't
produce realization of Truth, but in fact depends on it. It is
a purely practical matter. For the sake of those cases
where the spontaneous phenomenon of conductivity
arises, I have described the manner of approach which is
appropriate.[1] But the conscious process is senior to the life
process.

FITHIAN: Bubba, I have also noticed there seems to be
a transference of our attention. For a long time you have
had your attention on us. It was typical for everybody to

---

[1] Bubba is referring to the general Teaching, found in *The Knee of Listening* and *The Method of the Siddhas*, in which the individual is instructed to understand what arises, even if it is apparently extraordinary, rather than assume it as a goal or principle of sadhana. He has also written technical material relative to conscious conductivity of the life-force from the prior Light, but this material is only made available to devotees in the Community who have fulfilled the sadhana of the fundamental Teaching.

sit around and wait for the eye contact, in order to get zapped by it. But now I actually enjoy being able simply to have darshan, simply to look upon you, to look upon the Guru without any sense of being the object of attention. Now you are the object of attention and we are contemplating you.

BUBBA: The first phase of the Guru's work is an active one, in which he puts his attention on individuals. He does this in order to generate the Teaching, for if the Teaching is communicated, individuals will be able to live in true Satsang with the Guru as Siddhi. In the beginning, people demand to be made visible. The Guru's attention on them makes them appear visible to themselves. He does this so they will see the basic strategy of visibility and begin to understand. When they become capable of meditating on the Guru as Siddhi in God, he no longer needs to be active in that sense. Then he is merely Present as the Principle and Object of his devotee's meditation or life. And there is a perfect stage of that meditation and life, in which there is no subject or object.

There is a counterpart to all of this in sexuality. If you are "seen" during the play of sexuality, the energy is depressed. To see, to visualize, to see imagery within yourself or to see another person as a desirable or erotic object stimulates sexual energy or activity, but it doesn't fulfill it, since motion cannot become no-motion or sublimity, nor can it vanish the separate and separative principle which is its source. It doesn't amount to true union, but it stimulates energy, whereas to be seen suppresses the energy in self-consciousness. The true union, even in the play of sexuality, takes place when there is neither seeing nor being seen. When that whole subject-object theatre is gone, there is no intervention of the ego, nor of the mind, nor of the force of separative desires.

When an individual first approaches the Guru, his initial impulse is to be seen. He wants marvellous things to be done to him, he wants experiences, consolations, beliefs, and fixed ideas. Basically, all that just retards the process. But that is the nature of the student. He looks for contact with the "man," for helpful attention from the Community, and he wants answers to replace his mind of doubts and problems. But the strategy of all of that is to become visible. And he is not aware of the fact that the urge to be visible, to be seen, to have attention put on him, is actually the very thing that always retards the process of conscious and spiritual life in his case. When he begins to understand to the point where he relaxes that demand, meditation on the Guru becomes possible. Then he has become available to the Guru, and the Guru becomes the Supreme Object of his life. In that case, even his experiential life develops in appropriate ways. That is the level of the disciple.

In the perfect devotee, the demand to be visible, to enjoy realized self-meditation, is also undone. But he even transcends discipleship. In the devotee, the *strategy* of attention to the Guru is dissolved in the radical obviation of the separate self sense. In that case there is perfect *sacrifice* of attention, or attention as sacrifice, in which the "me" who is attentive is obviated in understanding. So in the true devotee there is no longer that subject-object theatre of experiential realization. But there is intuitive enjoyment of the God-Condition in the Form of the Guru and as his own Self-Nature. Then the Divine is his very Condition. In that case there is perfect union or non-separation between the devotee and the Guru.

I have said that I have begun to relax my secondary functions in the Ashram. I have relaxed the principle of my initiatory *activity*, in which I was required to put attention on people, and to generate the yogic and mystical aspects of the Siddhi. I no longer consider all of that to be my responsibility. And even the second aspect of that work, which is to live in the midst of the yielded attention of disciples, is being modified. I have decreased the amount of personal theatre that I generate or allow individuals to depend upon. I still live in the Ashram, I come and sit in Satsang, I talk, I see people. A certain dimension of the theatre of being present as an object for disciples must be maintained, at least for now. But, fundamentally, my work is now of that third or perfect kind. I am waiting for devotees. And when they come I live with them in Truth. In that case, there is no action, and there is not even any representation of myself as object.

To be object, the object of meditation for the disciple, there must be some secondary presence established that can be felt. There must be an aura, a pressure, some kind of force-manifestation. But, fundamentally, I have yielded that intention, and this body is the only manifestation of that I maintain as a regular source of that objective influence. But it is sufficient for the disciple. There is no longer any other action in this one to create that aura of yogic influence at the life-level, high or low. That Siddhi has been completely yielded into the Heart-Nature, the Condition of the Divine Person, prior to the body, the mind, and the worlds. So even though I am present and seem to be an object for disciples, even though I carry on a certain level of life-theatre, basically I am simply Present in that Condition prior to action. And that will naturally change the quality of experience that people have in the Community.

CRAIG: It seems that when I have been around you during the last few weeks, the experience has been that you just seem transparent. And when I am around you there is a reflection of that transparency back to myself. Then my own content becomes less and less real, more and more consciousness. There is a blending and a merging in which everything becomes fluid. In fact I don't feel that "pressure" now.

BUBBA: Under the literal pressure of the yogic aspect of

the Siddhi there is always something to be attained. There must always be some transformation, some movement, some experience, whatever. And at the times when it is all happening, when there is the most intensity, the most energy to that process, it seems very beautiful, absolute, and true. But most of the time, you are only struggling with it. It is a kind of enforced attention that, ultimately, is only another form of suffering. But in the midst of the life of understanding there is no such demand. In the Presence of the Divine Person there is nothing to be attained, there is no state to be attained.

And the Heart, the very Nature and Unqualified Presence that is the Divine Person, is the most absolute form of attraction. The usual man can't conceive of how that is so. He conceives of attraction as an "influence" generated through the manifest or material action of something or other. But the Heart is not an influence in any conventional sense, because it is not manifest in any conditional way. It is not Present in the form of energies or anything of the kind. So it is hard to imagine that it is the greatest force of attraction and even of absorption. But it is. And simply to live without strategic demands and expectations in the Company of the Guru, in the Company of the Divine Person, releases one of all of these conventional dramas, all limiting forces, all contracts, all forms of fixed and enforced attention. But the true enjoyment of that Company is not the secondary one of feeling the quality of release, of feeling relieved. These are only side effects. The fundamental enjoyment is that absolute Nature and prior Condition in which there is no longer any compulsion, any movement, any conventional birthing, surviving, dying, and all the rest. It is not just the negative realization that a burden has been taken away. It is positive or absolute enjoyment as the unqualified Self-Nature in its Divine Condition as the prior Light of all manifestation.

Also, as time goes on in that formless happiness, that

unreasonable meditation, you also realize that you are still alive. And you can still say "me" in the conventional sense without becoming confused by or in it. Therefore, the Heart-realization, the enjoyment of the Condition of the Divine Person, becomes grounds for wisdom. Then there is the enjoyment of principal insight into the nature of life and how it works, how to live, how to create. All of that comes quite naturally, without its being a great burden, a grave responsibility that involves conflict, dilemma, and striving. The enjoyment of spontaneous insight into the nature of all that arises is what I mean by the regenerated life of the Heart. The life of Amrita Nadi, or perfect intuition of the Divine Person, is one in which there is no loss of the Heart-realization while life is lived with intensity. And so the enjoyment of the Divine Person becomes the foundation of manifest life. And while dwelling in that absolute enjoyment there is continual penetration of the precise nature of all of this. The world begins to become obvious, directly obvious, without all the secondary psychisms and bullshit that fascinate the twinkie enthusiast.

CRAIG: Bubba, there is a point that often happens when I am about to go to sleep. It is not a witness point of view, but it is just being conscious of consciousness. It is a very strange dimension, where there is just the sense of not being identified with anything. There is still a focal point, but it is just consciousness of, I don't know how to describe it. It happens a lot. I will lie down, and it will just come over me. I will just be aware that I am aware, that there is just pure awareness.

BUBBA: When you say there is still a "focal point," what you are pointing to is the sensation of ego, of separate self, and that continues to be the form of consciousness even though, as in the case of such experiences, there is some intuitive blossom of the true Condition of that consciousness. The intuitive sense creeps through in those twilight passages between states of consciousness, but it is not the same as radical realization of the Heart. In the actual case of the realization of the Heart, there no longer is that leftover sensation of the ego. That point of view is absolutely gone. It is hard to imagine somebody existing or continuing to exist and communicate in conventional terms without that limiting sensation. But it is literally absent when there is the radical enjoyment of the Heart and the Condition of the Divine Person. There is no longer any point back to which the self-reference may be made. The self-reference is generated, but it is known only to be a convention, an artifice out front, not back, deep or within.

But this dissolution of self can't be done deliberately. It would involve too much fear. It would be terrifying beyond tolerance. The devotee does not wilfully release the sense or assumption of separated, separate, and separative self. It is undone by the Power or Siddhi of the Heart itself. That is the work of Satsang. It is a seduction in which that principle of self is made unnecessary in each case without passage through the great fear. But to do it yourself, to do deliberate sacrificial sadhana in order to get rid of the ego is just a lot of nonsense. Every individual would have to cop out at some point. Nobody would go beyond the point where there is nothing left but this sensation of the "me," without any content, without any theatre surrounding it, just that. Only Grace can take you out. It cannot be done deliberately. It depends on conscious enjoyment of the literal Presence of the Siddhi of the Heart, the Grace of the Divine Person. The Grace of Reality itself absorbs ego-consciousness and makes it identical to Absolute Consciousness. And it is all done in a very natural, easy transition. You couldn't do it yourself. You would refuse to do it as soon as you realized what was actually required.

BONNIE GODDARD: Christian people always say of

Jesus, "He died for us, He died on the cross for us." The Siddha goes through the death for the sake of his devotees, who then don't have to do the same. In fact, they can't do the same, but are instead absorbed through his path.

BUBBA: Yes. The Presence of the Divine makes possible a completely different kind of sadhana from that created by the usual man. The willful, self-obsessed person prefers the adventure of his search and attainment, his childish and adolescent wisdom. But that usual man will always miss the point. He cannot make the sacrifice. The ego cannot be sacrificed by the one who abandons it. It may only be absorbed, taken, assumed by the Divine Reality. So Satsang is the only Condition in which it can actually take place.

One who performs the true Guru-function of the Siddhas may at some point appear to go through some terrifying death experience, whose significance is ego death, because he is the irreducible instrument for bringing that Satsang into the world as a Grace. But it is not necessary for his devotees to go through that. If people in the Ashram seem at times to be going through a lot of this death concern, a lot of terror in the midst of sadhana, it is not because the Siddhi of the Heart is doing that. Such dramas are simply a manifestation of their resistance, their lingering commitment to the ego life and the adventure of their private search. They are still entertaining the possibility of that adventure in which they have experiences and overcome the world. The process in Satsang itself is very gentle. It is even enjoyable. The "event" is unnoticed.

Satsang is fundamentally a very simple, happy matter, in which concerns for attainments of any kind, including the concern for getting rid of the ego and its game, are unnecessary and inappropriate. If you persist in such concerns, of course you will suffer, like any other person concerned in the world. If you study the Teaching,

you will continually confront the demand that you understand this search of yours. If you understand, you will
always return to Satsang as a simplicity. Such Satsang is
natural, easy, functional dwelling in the Guru's Company,
and that becomes absorption of self. I do not mean
absorption in the yogic sense, in which the life-force is
absorbed and the mind only brought to a state of quiet
rather than radical knowledge of its Nature and Condition. But through the instants of this life of understanding,
this critical and radical process of intelligence awakened
into the Presence of the Divine Person, there is absorption
into the Condition of Consciousness itself. In such sadhana
the Siddhi of the Heart operates from "within," or from a
transcendent direction, and the life of understanding, this
intelligence in the midst of limiting conditions, operates at
the other or "outer" side of it. These two come together to
produce a very natural absorption into the condition of
Consciousness itself, rather than absorption of ego-consciousness in an experiential state that is distracting but not
in itself identical to radical Understanding. Such Satsang
involves ego death without the suffering of somebody's
dying. The transition from self to Self is not noticed. It is a
sublime transition in which there is no theatre at all.

"Ego death" is just the relaxation of the condition of
fixation, and enjoyment of that Condition which is always
already the case. You are not an ego now, and, truly, you
cannot become the Self of God. You are already that
Self-Nature. The Divine Person is always already your
Condition. It is only that there is a dramatization. There is
a repetitive, compulsive modification on which you are
always meditating, and by which you are always being
motivated in limitation. And you think all of that is what
you are. Therefore, you resist any encroachment upon it.
You avoid anything that threatens it. And the condition of
relationship is the principal threat conceived in that
dilemma, for it is the source and archetype of all lost

immunity. One who suffers such life-theatre and does the sadhana that is traditionally done to get rid of it would naturally go through terrifying experiences at times because, while enduring the threat to that, he is also assuming it. He is always putting out front the thing from which he is trying to get free. That is the dilemma, and that is the traditional double-bind. It is assumed that because you are temporarily living as the ego, you have got to do all kinds of things to destroy the ego. But that is not the position of one in the Satsang of the Heart, who lives in Communion with the Divine Person by Grace.

Such a one is not led to fix upon any propositions relative to his present condition of life. He is expected simply to view all that arises, to understand the ego as a condition and as a strategy of action rather than assume it as a principle. As a result, he becomes more and more absorbed in that which understanding itself is. He becomes thus absorbed, rather than in any of the states that are witnessed by consciousness, or in any of the modifications that are witnessed and understood. Such is the Power, the Consciousness, the unreasonable Happiness that is enjoyed in the case of understanding in the Company of the Divine Person. The Siddhi of the Guru intensifies that understanding to the point of perfect dissolution in God. And there is no sudden terrifying event. It must take place while alive.

Know this. My use of the yogic aspect of the Divine Siddhi was a way of turning to seekers in order to make the lesson of understanding.[2] It was a way of serving students, those who are moved to become visible and be seen. But now I only wait. The fundamental characteristic of the Maha-Siddhi, the Siddhi or Power of Grace of the Divine Person, is mere Presence. I have yielded to this economy of the Divine. Therefore, in the future, only those who have relaxed the demand for attention, whereby the search for visibility is served, only those who have already turned to me will know me as Siddha and Siddhi. I will make no effort to turn men to me by experiential means. But I will rely entirely on their maturity in understanding.

I am free to take on my fundamental work in this way only because this Community of Devotees exists. The Community now exists in the necessary and rudimentary form of a group of individuals who have seen and understood the demonstrated failure of the way of experience in their own case. Now this Community must represent the argument of the Teaching in the world. Now all of you must serve me by preparing those who respond to the Teaching. And you will do this by implementing the functional demand for true sadhana, the sadhana or real life of understanding, in which the search in dilemma is not exploited but understood. It is you who must prepare disciples and devotees for me in this manner.

---

[2]Bubba is referring to that specific and complex process which is described in *The Knee of Listening* and *The Method of the Siddhas*.

When those who enter this Community have relaxed the demand for attention and the search for visibility, when they have understood the strategic drama of their own actions, when enquiry in the form "Avoiding relationship?" is alive in them and Narcissus is constantly returned to his original Condition on the basis of that real intelligence, and when they have turned to me as Teacher, because of the Teaching, and Master, because of the Demand, then I will consider them disciples. Only such men know they are my own. Only such men can live in Satsang with me and know it. Only such men can enjoy life with me as Divine Communion. Only such men can know the Guru as Spiritual Master in Truth.

My disciples embrace the discipline of the Teaching most fully. And they know that I am the principal discipline. They find the Siddhi of the Divine Person Alive in my Company. For them, I am always Present and Active as the perfect communication of the Nature, Condition, Form, Source, and Process that is the World. The disciple lives a life of Revelation. But it is not in itself a life of experiential revelation. Experiences, high and low, may arise, but he is responsible only to understand in the midst of them. The Revelation in Truth given to the disciple is the awakened or realized intuitive Knowledge of the Divine Person.

When the disciple enjoys radical intuition of that very Nature, Condition, Form, Source, and Process that includes him and is his own, he meditates on the Guru as the Divine Person. Such a one is my devotee in Truth. My disciple is turned to me, but my devotee knows me in Truth. My devotee is always already merged in me, not merely by means of transcendental absorption in the functions of the life-force, but by virtue of understanding, the conscious process of radical intuition. To enjoy radical intuition is to know the Divine Person to be identical to the World. This intuitive comprehension alone is Knowledge, and one who thus knows the World is Master of the life-force. Thus, only my devotee in Truth can accept responsibility for life as the manifest Siddhi of the Divine Person.

Therefore, I do not invite individuals to come and live with me in order that they may receive or take something from me. I am the instrument of the Divine Demand. I am not here to fill every man, but to make a demand upon each one that he assume the prior Fullness and live in It. This assumption is possible only in the case of understanding. Therefore, I invite men to understand, and, only on that basis, to live in actual Divine Communion, and to do so in real sacrificial form, free of all demands, free of the search for consolation, attainment, dependence, independence, or any solution. That sacrifice is the Law. Thus, I invite individuals to come and live with me, in order that they may yield or give themselves, and all actions and things, even the world and all experiences or attainments, high or low, to me. Their yielding is not cash, not part of a deal. Divine Grace does not come as a result, for the Grace is always already given. Their true sacrifice is a *response* to Grace, a consciousness of Grace. Their sacrifice is continuous, and it is always done with the sense of *prior* fullness or fulfillment, because it is founded in understanding rather than the search in dilemma.

The Teaching and the Community are themselves the communication of Satsang, Divine Communion. What is apparently given or experienced in the midst of a life that responds to them is also a Grace, but it may not be earned, taken, or held. Therefore, what arises is never the point, but it is always only a paradox and a test, a form of the always prior Demand, which is itself the Divine Person, the Maha-Siddha, the Siddha-Guru. A sacrificial life, founded in humor, love, and understanding, is the sadhana made possible when Divine Communion is thus given as Grace, not promised as a reward or a future gift. And no other apparent reward or gift adds one iota to that Gift.

One who accepts the Guru's invitation is already eternally fulfilled. He asks for nothing but to live in that Divine Communion and yield all in the midst of it. And that Divine Communion is also yielded to him, in the forms of the Community, the Teaching, and the Demand or Presence which is the eternally Present Guru, the Divine Person. One who lives such Divine Communion as the Condition of life is a servant, a devotee, empty of demands and attainments. Such is forever the nature of his life of understanding.

The true devotee is constantly involved in perfect psycho-physical love of the Divine Person. This is the fulfillment of the sadhana or real life of understanding. *All* his thoughts are the attention of mind to the Divine Person. He need not consider only holy or cultic thoughts to be love of Him. *All* his speech is eloquent about the Divine Person. He need not consider only holy or cultic speech to be love of Him. *All* his actions are devotion to Him. He need not consider only holy or cultic actions to be love of Him. Then *all* that is received is received from Him, and by Him, in love. *All* that is yielded is yielded to Him, and by Him, in love.

Such a devotee is my own, and understanding, not the search by any means, is the Great Process wherein he is found in me. Therefore, I am devoted to this understanding in you. I will do nothing but serve this understanding in you. And by this same service you will gather all my own to me.

An Invitation From The Dawn Horse Communion

The published writings of Bubba Free John represent an invitation to all men to live in his Company and enjoy the perfect revelation of the life of Understanding. The Dawn Horse Communion is his principal instrument for implementing the sadhana or true activity that is the only appropriate foundation for life in Communion with the Divine Person, who is the Nature, Condition, Form, Source and Process of all beings, even the very World. If the humor of such an undertaking has been awakened in you through this literature, and if you feel prepared to sustain the happiness and the offenses of that sacrificial affair described by Bubba Free John, please accept his invitation. You may indicate your intention simply through a letter of inquiry regarding the initial services and opportunities provided by The Dawn Horse Communion.

The Dawn Horse Communion
Star Route 2
Middletown, California 95461

GLOSSARY

This glossary contains definitions of many of the technical and non-English language terms found in *Garbage and the Goddess*. A glossary which also includes other terms commonly used by Bubba Free John may be found in his book *The Method of the Siddhas*.

Ajna Chakra
The subtle yogic center between and behind the eyebrows, which governs the dynamic mind, will, vision and mental formation. The door of the functional God-Light.

Amrita Nadi
The "internal" or intuited structure of manifest existence, which is the very structure of Consciousness, of human existence, of conscious meditation. When meditation is the spontaneous intuition of Amrita Nadi ("the nerve in which the nectar of immortal bliss flows"), then all is known in Truth. Then God, Guru, the Self of all is known Perfectly. In one who lives the profound Knowledge that is the "Heart," the intuited Real Nature or Self, there is yet another spontaneous event: the regeneration of Amrita Nadi. Only one in whom this awakening is alive knows the true Nature and Form of the Heart as well as all of the processes of cosmic and personal life.

The ultimate Form or Structure of Conscious Existence, the Transcendent Form, intuited as the Divine Reality rising out of the Heart or very Self into the Bright

or Light of God. A transcendent structure or function in
Perfect Consciousness. The Great Form, the conscious,
moveless spire which extends from the Heart to the Light.
The Form of God, Guru, and Self which stands forever in
the Heart. The intuited Form of Reality. The Process or
Relationship between the Heart and the Light. It is your
own fundamental Form and Nature. The worlds are built
on that Form of which Amrita Nadi is the perfect knowledge.

Amrita Nadi is the realized intuition of the Divine
Person as the Nature, Condition, Form and Process that is
the Whole, manifest and unmanifest, the very World.

Ashram

An Ashram is a place where a Spiritual Master
gathers the community of his devotees and disciples in
order to live with them, instruct them, and communicate
the living force of his Presence.

Avatar

According to certain Hindu traditions, the Avatar is
the God-man, the exclusive incarnation of God, who
manifests on earth only at the beginning of every age. He is
considered to be the incarnation of Vishnu, the pre-
server-aspect of the Divine according to Hindu mythol-
ogy.

bhakti, bhakta

Bhakti is the yoga of devotion. In bhakti yoga, God is
sought by means of the intensification of pure ecstatic
love.

A bhakta is a devotee of God or Guru. Some individuals live primarily or characteristically in the qualities of
a bhakta, in the moods of loving service, which are
awakened when the vital and emotional being is turned
into the condition of Satsang.

bhava

Intense emotional feeling, fervent devotion to Guru or God. Guru-bhava is ecstatic absorption in and worship of the Guru as the Divine, often accompanied by extreme emotional states and fits of crying, longing, laughing, etc. It is characteristic of the awakening life of the true devotee.

bindu

A psycho-physical center or point that is the locus of specific energies and transmutations of consciousness. In this sense, all the chakras might be called bindus, as well as the causal center on the right side of the chest. Traditionally, the word refers to very subtle centers, or the experience of knowing them, usually in visual or super-visual terms. Thus, a vision of a single point or several points of light, sometimes colored, is usually referred to as bindu.

Brahman

The formless, absolute, omnipresent Divine Reality. A Hindu term for the Undifferentiated, all-pervasive, unqualified Nature or Being which is the ultimate Nature and Condition of the world.

causal being

The functional center or region of psycho-physical life which manifests as deep, dreamless sleep, awareness prior to cognition and action, and the separate self sense. It is the ultimate root of thought. Its epitome is in the heart, on the right side. When unconsciousness and the ego are undone in Truth, this region opens, revealing the true Heart.

chakra

Literally, a "wheel" or a "circle." The term refers to the internal centers, commonly symbolized as lotus flowers, through which the yoga-shakti flows, producing various phenomena in life, body and consciousness. The chakras are associated with but not identical to the various ganglia of the nervous system, of the spine and brain.

A subtle center through which the life-force moves. (See *kundalini* and *kundalini yoga*.)

conductivity

Refers to conscious participation in the Force aspect of the Divine Process. It involves intuiting the God-Light above the body, the mind, and the world, bringing it down, as life-force, into the psycho-physical dimension, and then releasing it back to the God-Light. This process is first spontaneously revealed to the disciple in the Company of the Siddha-Guru, and later is given to him as a conscious responsibility. (See *chakra, God-Light, kundalini* and *life-force*.)

contract

A conscious association with anyone, anything, or any condition, that is directed toward maintaining the illusion of separate existence. A person may have contracts with anything, from his breakfast to the Divine vision, but Bubba generally uses the term with reference to ordinary social agreements people make in order to guarantee personal security. (See *cult*.)

contraction

Resistance, a subtle sensation, structure and activity. The formation of awareness that *is* suffering. The symptoms and strategies of men, including the cramped sensation in the midst of the body. This primary activity, this contraction, is the root, support, and form of all the ordinary manifestations of suffering, all patterns of life that men acknowledge to be their suffering. This contraction, this "avoidance of relationship," is, fundamentally, the usual man's continuous, present activity.

cult

Any social arrangement that perpetuates and reinforces the form and activity of independent and exclusive existence among human beings. In this sense, a marriage can be just as much a cult as any other "secret" society. All cults are inward-directed, and express the structure and activity of Narcissus, even though that may not be readily apparent.

darshan

Literally, a seeing, a vision, a sight of. The term commonly refers to the blessings granted by Guru or God. The Guru gives "his" blessing by making his appearance, by allowing himself to be seen, meditated upon, or known. God gives "his" blessing in the same way, especially by appearing in the form of the Guru and his activities.

(the) Devi

The living Conscious Force or Divine Cosmic and Creative Energy. The living Power or Eternal Consort of Real-God. The Creative Force of manifest existence turned perfectly to the very Divine itself, and perfectly subservient to the Divine initiatory Power. The manifest function of the Divine in the worlds. The living God-Light. The World.

The worlds are the Divine, but only as the Devi, only in perfect conscious dependence on the Divine. The world or manifest existence is traditionally called *maya*, illusion, meaning something that is apparently separate from the Divine, that is not lived dependently in the Divine. So the world is "Shakti," the Goddess, which continually manifests all the opposites, all the pleasures, pains, and conditions of the usual life. Then the world appears to be independent, and all individual beings who make conventional assumptions within it are continually assuming that the various limited conditions in which they appear are real, separate from their selves, and independent of all other conditions, even the Divine. But when the individuals know themselves to be dependent on the Divine, non-separate from the Divine, when they consciously live that way from moment to moment, then the world becomes the Divine in the form of the Devi. It ceases to be *maya* or illusion and continually serves the Divine Reality. The Devi aspect of the World manifests the Divine Reality through the medium of dependence or perfect absorption in God-knowledge in the form of radical understanding.

The "female" aspect of the One Reality. In spiritual traditions the Devi is symbolically depicted as a woman. Bubba has said that the Community of Devotees is itself the Devi. That will become more obvious as individuals move into the perfect attention and dependence on the Divine that characterize the true Devotee. (See *Shakti*.)

devotee

(1) In a general sense, any member of the Guru's Ashram community; and (2), one in whom the meditation of understanding has been perfected, who remains perfectly conscious in the Divine at all times, and in whom the activities of enquiry, conductivity, and attention to the Divine as Amrita Nadi have become full. The primary orientation of the devotee is toward the Guru as the Divine Person and the World. In the true devotee all spiritual processes become responsibilities, and he engages in a creative life of service in the world. (The reader may gather from the context which meaning is implied at any point in the text.) (See *student, disciple*.)

(the) Dharma

When capitalized, Dharma means the Teaching, the way of Truth, including the living spiritual Power and the disciplines or conditions of spiritual life as well as the various instructions. When written in lower case, dharma refers to teachings which in some way reflect limited assumptions and are therefore in service to the Great Search.

disciple

One who has begun to resort to the Guru as Spiritual Master. Such a person has already become responsible for his life conditions and has begun consciously to enquire in the form: "Avoiding relationship?"

As a disciple, he receives instruction relative to the mature extensions of enquiry, which are re-cognition and radical intuition, and his spiritual life matures as the meditation of the devotee. The primary orientation of the disciple is toward the Guru as Siddhi. (See *student, devotee.*)

enquiry

The intentional activity by which consciousness reestablishes itself in its pure form, which is unqualified relationship, radical understanding, or Divine Communion. At any one moment, enquiry may take the form of a mental verbalization, "Avoiding relationship?" or it may simply be engaged as the silent presence of conscious understanding in relation to any area of life and consciousness. In either case, enquiry obviates the force of the particular activity of avoidance that one may be indulging at any moment. It does not assume that there is someone avoiding relationship ("Am *I* avoiding relationship?") nor does it deal analytically with the specific activity of avoidance ("*How* am I avoiding relationship?"), but it is simply the expression of the radical reassumption of the prior Condition of consciousness. As such, it is not a method for attaining understanding, but is itself a conscious extension of present understanding. Enquiry is truly realized only in the midst of the ongoing sadhana of the student of the Siddha-Guru, whose Teaching and Demands yield fundamental insight and release of attention to the Divine Person.

Force

Conscious Divine Power or Intensity. The Creative God-Light, intuited above the head, communicated as movement of energy or vital force through the descending and ascending circuit of conducted life. When printed in lower case, force simply refers to these movements of vital energy. (See *Shakti, God-Light, conductivity.*)

God-Light

The reflected and eternal Light of the Heart or Real-God. The Light of consciousness and of manifestation. The Light of the mind and of all things or forms. The unqualified Light that is intuited to be above the body, the mind, and the conditional world. The Prior Condition and Creative Source of the conditional worlds. Bubba uses the term "the Bright" when talking about the realized intuition of the man of understanding, and the term "God-Light" or simply "Light" when talking about the Divine Process in which the worlds are manifest, but it is the same Conscious and Divine Light in both cases.

gopi

An intimate female devotee and lover of the male, human form of the Eternal Guru. In ancient India, the gopis were cowherd girls who gave up their families and worldly lives to become the ecstatic consorts of Krishna, a Great Siddha.

Great Siddha

All Siddhas enjoy perfect Divine realization, and each functions as an unobstructed vehicle for the Divine Siddhi, but Bubba refers to some of them, such as Jesus, Gautama, and Krishna, as Great Siddhas, because of their historical importance and the significance of the dharmas they taught.

Guru

A term properly used to refer to one who functions as a genuine Spiritual Master. The "Siddha-Guru" is a perfect Master, a "Siddha" who functions as Guru for others, who is himself the very Truth that is awakened in the devotee. This Siddha-Guru is what Bubba generally means to indicate in his use of the simple term Guru.

The term Guru is a composite of two contrasting words meaning "darkness" and "light." Therefore, the Guru functions to release, turn, point or lead living beings from darkness (non-Truth) into light (very Truth).

Guru-bhava
See *bhava.*

Guru-Siddhi
See *Maha-Siddhi.*

(the) Heart

The "Heart" is another name for the realized Self, the intuition of Real-God, the unqualified ground and power of being and of all manifestation. The man of understanding is conscious as and from this "ground," the foundation position and capacity. The Heart is perfectly thought-free. The man of understanding is mindless, not because he suppresses thought, but his understanding of all that arises has become re-cognition or knowing again of thought itself, so that mind, or its principle, has fallen in the Heart. Even so, he continues, paradoxically, to function as an ordinary man.

The origin of the term comes from the experiential association of the awakening to the Self-Nature with the sense of the opening of the "causal" being or function in the right side of the chest, and the sense of the mind or process of thought falling into its root or origin in the trunk of the body.

Much of Bubba's writing is a progressive elaboration of this term. Therefore, consult *The Knee of Listening* and *The Method of the Siddhas* for a full understanding of its significance and function. (See *(the) Self*.)

jnana, jnani
Supreme knowledge, knowledge of Self, or perfect understanding.
Traditionally, a jnani is one who is perfect in Self-knowledge or jnana. By virtue of perfect understanding, the man of understanding exceeds the exclusive limitations of traditional jnana, but he also may be called a jnani, since Self-knowledge is the foundation of his existence.

karma
Action which entails consequences or re-actions. Thus, karma is destiny, tendency, the quality of existence and experience which is determined by prior actions or conditions. Latent tendencies, or patterns of action and reaction, condition and experience, that originate prior to and apart from the conscious mind.

kriyas
Spontaneous, self-purifying physical movements that arise when internal, spiritual force is activated in the yogi. These may be experienced as thrills in the spine, shaking of the spine, spontaneous compulsion to assume difficult yogic postures, etc. They may occur during meditation in the presence of the Guru and in the general course of internal intensification which occurs in the life of Satsang.

kundalini
The kundalini or kundalini shakti is the "serpent power" of esoteric spirituality. It is the very Creative Power of the universes, but it also lies dormant in man, coiled at the base of the spine. It may be awakened

spontaneously in the disciple, after which it ascends within him, producing all the various forms of yogic and mystical experience. Bubba indicates that the internal spiritual force is eternally awake, but man is not awake. Therefore, he recommends no efforts to awaken this force itself, but puts all attention to the awakening of the seeker to his prior, eternal and always present Nature and Condition. In the course of such sadhana, internal force may be awakened as a secondary event, but it is regarded and dealt with in quite a different manner than is recommended by the yogis.

kundalini yoga

A tradition of yogic technique in which practice is devoted to awakening the internal energy processes which bring about subtle experiences and blisses. But the true manifestation of shakti or internal spiritual force is spontaneous, a grace, awakened in the company of a Siddha-Guru, in the midst of the full and wholly conscious process of true and motiveless spiritual life.

life-force

When the God-Light manifests as the condition of man, it appears as the life-force, the subtle element of manifest existence mid-way between the gross bodily dimension and the conscious mental or super-mental conditions above it. Its functional appearance is first felt in the region of the throat. (See *conductivity.*)

Light

See *God-Light.*

loka

A world or realm of experience. The term usually refers to "places" visited by mystical or esoteric means.

Maha-Shakti

The Great Shakti, the Conscious Force of existence, which may be known independent of intuitive Knowledge of the Unqualified Divine Reality. (See *Shakti.*)

Maha-Siddha

The very Divine, the Lord Himself, the Divine Person. (See *Siddha.*)

Maha-Siddhi

The "Siddhi of the Real," the great, spontaneous Perfect Consciousness, Activity and Presence of the Siddha, or one whose Understanding is Perfect.

mantra

A word or sound-symbol repeated vocally or mentally, in order to induce meditative or mystical states, or to concentrate and purify the mind.

meditation

"The understanding of your activity is meditation. Consciousness itself is meditation. All the traditions agree that the best thing a man can do is spend his time in Satsang, in the company of the realized man, the Guru. That *is* meditation. That *is* the real condition. That *is* realization, that *is* perfect enjoyment."

This term is one of the most fundamental in all of Bubba's written work. It can be understood only by study of the basic texts as a whole. See "The Meditation of Understanding" section of *The Knee of Listening* for a discussion of understanding as the conscious meditation activity of the devotee. Also see the descriptions in *The Method of the Siddhas* where it is told how this process awakens in Satsang with the Siddha-Guru, who claims: "I am the meditation itself." He comes as the Teaching, the Object, and the Process of Meditation for his true devotees. (See *understanding.*)

Mother Shakti

The personification of The Divine Creative Power. (See *Shakti*.)

mudra

A yogic posture or bodily pose, especially of the hands, that signifies and symbolizes the movement and transmission of spiritual force. Like kriyas and other spiritual effects, mudras may arise spontaneously from time to time as signs of the purifying activity generated in Satsang.

nadi

A subtle or yogic nerve or channel of the life-force in the descending and ascending circuit of manifest human life. Bubba also speaks of Amrita Nadi, which is in itself neither yogic nor subtle, but is the most prior Form and Structure of Reality, Consciousness itself, the regenerated Life of the Heart and the God-Light. (See *Amrita Nadi*.)

Narcissus

In *The Knee of Listening* (page 26) Bubba describes Narcissus as follows:

He is the ancient one visible in the Greek "myth," who was the universally adored child of the gods, who rejected the loved-one and every form of love and relationship, who was finally condemned to the contemplation of his own image, until he suffered the fact of eternal separation and died in infinite solitude.

I began to see that same logic operative in all men and every living thing, even the very life of the cells and the energies that surround every living entity or process. It was the logic or process of separation itself, of enclosure and immunity. It

manifested as fear and identity, memory and experience. It informed every function of being,
every event. It created every mystery. It was the
structure of every imbecile link in the history of
our suffering.

navel

Bubba uses the word not merely with reference to the
navel itself, the specific physical and subtle center of
personal power, vitality, and vital force, but also with
reference to the whole great region of vital life. This
region includes all the soft organs of the body, from the
eyes to the anus, and is the center of the elaboration of
desire and the vital functions of money, food, and sex.

Parabhakti

Perfect Divine enjoyment. Absolute love and knowledge of the Divine, in which there is no cognized
separation between the devotee, Guru, God, or the world.
(See *bhakti.*)

pranayama

Regulated direction and arrest of the vital currents of
energy in the body by exercises of breathing. In Satsang, as
the Divine Process unfolds, the devotee may experience
automatic pranayama as a psycho-physical manifestation
of his awakening intuition of the God-Light and the
process of conductivity. (See *conductivity.*)

Prasad

The return of a gift to the Giver. Prasad is a term
equivalent to "grace." Food, drink, etc. which have been
offered to the Divine as God and Guru and afterwards
distributed among the devotees.

The Guru's gift of himself in the Form of Amrita
Nadi, the Form of Reality, Self, Guru, and God. Its forms

are Life, Light, and very Existence. The reception of the Guru's Prasad depends on the condition of the one who receives it. Those who truly live the condition of Satsang, who understand their own actions, and who turn to the Guru in Truth, with the sacrifice of all seeking, enjoy the Perfect Gift, the Grace of Prasad.

psycho-physical life

The usual man considers his life to be limited to the body and its experiences, while the traditional religious or spiritual man considers his mortality to involve only his body. Bubba teaches that both the psyche and the body disappear in the ultimate processes of death, and that only the prior Condition of Consciousness itself survives in the midst of change. Thus, he speaks of limited human existence as psycho-physical life, while he also speaks of non-mortal Existence as its true Nature and Condition.

radical intuition

The perfect and continuous understanding enjoyed by the Guru and his true Devotee. Radical intuition is the final stage of the intelligent process of understanding, whose previous stages are insight, enquiry, and re-cognition. It is unwavering attention to the Divine as unqualified Consciousness, prior to conventional self, mind, and desires. The one who enjoys radical intuition no longer conceives or assumes separation in any form, no matter what tendencies may arise to do so, but remains absorbed in the prior bliss of God-realization. (See *enquiry, re-cognition, understanding.*)

rajas, rajasic

The principle or power of action or motivation, one of the three qualities of which manifest existence is a complex variable. (See *sattwa, tamas.*)

Real-God
   The unqualified Ground of all being and manifestation. The pure, infinite, uncreated Consciousness that is
the Source, present Core, and ultimate Destiny of all
conditional and unconditional worlds, beings, etc. (See
Brahman, (the) Self.)

Realization
   In Bubba's Teaching, Realization is not a temporary
or partial Divine vision or revelation, but the perfect,
conscious life of the man of understanding and the true
devotee. It is continuous and unqualified existence in and
as Amrita Nadi. The perfected life of Satsang. (See *Amrita
Nadi.*)

re-cognition
   Consciously to know again. Re-cognition in itself is
the utter, radical reversal of all dilemma. It is sudden,
spontaneous, perfect, and it cannot in any way be indicated prior to its accomplishment. Most of our activities
are forms of cognition or simple knowing. The search, the
forms of motivated yoga, the remedial techniques people
acquire, are also forms of cognition. When the individual
understands or re-cognizes rather than simply cognizes his
own activity, the contraction and unconscious formulation
of consciousness or conscious life no longer occurs.
   The stage of understanding that follows or extends
from enquiry. In enquiry, actions are understood as forms
of contraction. In re-cognition, even the mind is known to
be contraction, or modification of always prior consciousness. (See *enquiry, radical intuition, understanding.*)

relationship
   No-contraction, the unqualified and conscious force
of existence realized and known in the form of manifest

life. The principal manifest condition of all beings and things and worlds.

sacrifice

Bubba uses the word to refer to change, the yielding of forms, the various "deaths" of which life consists, from waking up in the morning to the giving up of psycho-physical life. Sacrifice is the Law, the necessary principle of all manifest activity. The realization of action as sacrifice while alive with humor, love, and pleasure is the practical sign of understanding.

sadhana

Right or true action, action appropriate to real or spiritual life. It commonly or traditionally refers to spiritual practices directed toward the goal of spiritual and religious attainment. Bubba uses the term without the implication of a goal. He intends it to mean appropriate action, or action which is generated where Truth is already the case, not where it is sought.

sahasrar

The "thousand-petalled lotus," the highest chakra or region of conscious awareness described in the esoteric textbooks of the kundalini shakti yoga. It is generally associated with the crown of the head, the upper brain and the higher mind. The yogi looks to merge the internal shakti or life-force with this region. He directs the internal forces to this place, and enjoys trance-blisses as well as cosmic visions. Bubba does not regard it as a terminal or goal but as the highest functional region of the subtle or supra-causal conscious force, a window to the God-Light above.

samadhi

Spiritual Consciousness. The term *samadhi* is also

traditionally used to refer to trance states, spontaneous ecstasies without bodily cognition. Or it may refer to extremely subtle or sophisticated realizations of the nature of ordinary conscious states. Also yogic or psycho-physical trance. Meditative enjoyment. There are many kinds of samadhi, most of them, the traditional kinds of samadhi, are the samadhis of the life-force, vital and subtle. Therefore, they are temporary, they are symptomatic, they are experiences that occur when there is a peculiar activity in relation to one's living circuitry. When certain forms of concentration are coupled with certain movements within, we have these samadhis of the life-force. But the highest and only true or perfect samadhi is Truth itself, the very Self or Reality, the Heart, Knowledge of the Divine Person.

Satsang

Satsang literally means true or right relationship. It is commonly or traditionally used to refer to the practice of spending time in the company of holy or wise persons. One can also enjoy Satsang with a holy place, a venerated image, the burial shrine of a saint, or with the Deity. Bubba uses the term in its fullest sense, to signify the very relationship between a genuine Siddha-Guru (and thus the Divine Person, the Maha-Siddha) and his devotee. That relationship is seen to be an all-inclusive Condition, effective at every level of life and consciousness. Divine Communion. The Company of the Divine Person.

(the) Self

The Self is the true, perfect and unqualified Being that is the fundamental Nature and Consciousness of every apparent and self-limited individual. When the Self is realized, it is found to be no different and non-separate from very Reality, Guru and God.

The Self (or Heart) is not a static condition, not the

"thing" of Being, but the very Condition, the Process of Eternal Transformation, in which there is no dilemma, and which, paradoxically, is eternally One and Unqualified. In its regenerated or radical and inclusive form, rather than its revolutionary, traditional, and exclusive form, it is not different from Amrita Nadi, or knowledge of the Divine Person.

Shakti

The living Conscious Force or Divine Cosmic and Creative Energy. Spiritual Force. The very creative power and motion of the cosmos. In *Garbage and the Goddess*, Bubba generally distinguishes this term from the "Devi." The Shakti, in that case, is the Goddess of *maya*, or the illusion of separate existence. She is the world lived as separate and independent from the Divine Consciousness. Shakti is a "whore" who seduces living beings into the assumption that they are limited to the conditions, qualities, and destinies that arise in life from moment to moment. These include everything from the grossest physical circumstances to the Divine Vision itself. When the world is lived continuously in conscious dependence on the Divine, it has become the Devi, that same Conscious Force known in perfect subservience to Real-God and the God-Light.

The complement of Siva. The "female" aspect of the One Reality. When written in lower case (shakti), the term refers to that same Power in the form of various energies and activities, high or low, within the individual. (See *(the) Devi, kundalini, Siva, Siva-Shakti.*)

Siddha

A "Completed One," one who comes in the Forms and Activities of God. A man (or woman) of radical understanding. One who lives consciously as the Heart. One who functions as the Heart for living beings. A

perfectly fulfilled or accomplished one. The term is used
to refer to the Great Souls or Master-Teachers who live
perfectly in God while they are also active in the paradoxical and spontaneous functions of the Divine in the
created worlds. It is a Sanskrit term meaning fulfilled,
perfect. A Siddha is a God-realized being alive in the
world for the sake of mankind and all living beings. The
Siddhas communicate the living Force of Reality. They
live it to living beings. They simply live the natural state of
enjoyment with other beings.

Siddhi

The spontaneous and Perfect Consciousness, Presence and Power of the very Divine, which is communicated to living beings through the unobstructed agency of
the Siddha-Guru, or one whose Understanding is perfect.
When written in lower case (siddhi), the term refers to a
form of yogic accomplishment, an extraordinary or subtle
functional ability. (See *Maha-Siddhi*.)

Siva

The Perfect, Formless, most prior, unspeakable Divine Being. The very force of prior and unmoved consciousness. The "male" aspect of the One Reality. (See
Shakti, Siva-Shakti.)

Siva-lingam

An oblong stone worshipped in a vertical position in
the Hindu and tantric cults as an expression of the Power
of the absolute, unmanifest Divine.

Siva-Shakti

The perfect union of Siva-Shakti is fundamental and
unqualified Intensity, the very Self. All relationships, all
forms of exchange, are ritual enactments of the One
Intensity that is Siva-Shakti.

student

One who is first approaching the Guru and beginning the way of understanding. He gratefully turns to the Guru as Teacher, studies the Teaching, responsibly adheres to the life conditions required by the Guru, and observes the discipline of relationship, or life as service. He begins to observe his own activities in relation to the Guru's Presence and demands. The student stage matures as enquiry in the form: "Avoiding relationship?" The primary orientation of the student is toward the Guru as Teacher and as the Teaching. (See *disciple, devotee.*)

subtle being

The functional center or region of conditional life which manifests as dreams, visions, thought, and psychic being as well as the subtle, ascending process of internal energy. Its epitome is the region of the ajna chakra and also that of the throat chakra. (The sahasrar may be said to be the highest subtle center, but since it is open to the transcendent God-Light, more subtle than subtlety, it has been called the supra-causal center, or the center of the cosmic, pre-cosmic and transcendent Light of Truth.) (See *causal being, navel, sahasrar, vital being.*)

tamas, tamasic

Tamas is the principle, power, or quality of inertia. (See *rajas, sattwa.*)

tapas

Austerity. The "fire" of sadhana or spiritual discipline. The tapas that one undergoes in the life of understanding is not a motivated asceticism, but the discipline of doing what is appropriate from the point of view of Truth, no matter what tendencies or impulses arise.

understanding

When a man begins to re-cognize, consciously to

know again his subtle motivation, this is what Bubba calls "understanding." When a man begins to see again the subtle forms of his own action, which *are* his suffering, that re-cognition is understanding. When this becomes absolute, perfect, when there is utterly, absolutely no dilemma, no form in consciousness interpreting the nature of existence to the individual, when there is no contraction, no fundamental suffering, no thing prior to consciousness, this is what Bubba calls "radical" understanding. It is only enjoyment.

This is, of course, another of the most fundamental terms in Bubba's literature. Its significance and function may be grasped only by a study of *The Knee of Listening*, *The Method of the Siddhas*, and *Garbage and the Goddess* as a whole, under the conditions of actual sadhana in Satsang.

Upanishads

The Upanishads are the chief philosophical documents of India. They give more abstract philosophical expression to the range of mystical knowledge which is expressed in ritual and symbolic form in the even more ancient Vedas. Although they contain a range of apparently contradictory viewpoints, non-dualist, theist, etc., the central teaching of the Upanishads is that of Vedanta: the individual self or being and the Supreme Self or Being (Brahman) are One.

Vedanta

The later philosophical traditions of Hinduism. Literally, "the end *(anta)* of the Vedas." The interpreted teachings of the Upanishads, whose central truth can be stated, "The individual self or being and the Supreme Self or Being (Brahman) are One." The term is commonly used to refer to one of the principal schools of Vedanta, founded by Sri Shankara about 800 A.D. (Advaita Vedanta). But all